THE **ROARING RED FRONT**

STEWART McGILL & VINCENT RAISON

THE ROARING RED FRONT

THE WORLD'S TOP LEFT-WING FOOTBALL CLUBS

FOREWORD BY
PROFESSOR TONY COLLINS

First published by Pitch Publishing, 2022

Pitch Publishing
9 Donnington Park,
85 Birdham Road,
Chichester,
West Sussex,
PO20 7AJ
www.pitchpublishing.co.uk
info@pitchpublishing.co.uk

A CIP catalogue record is available for this book
from the British Library.

ISBN 978 1 80150 144 6

Typesetting and origination by Pitch Publishing
Printed and bound in Great Britain by TJ Books, Padstow

Contents

Stewart: To my wife, still no clue why she puts up with me.

Vincent: To Richard Earle, the only teacher who didn't think I was an idiot.

About the Authors

Stewart McGill

Football fan, martial arts instructor, political activist, traveller, writer and podcaster, Stewart is the author of several football articles for the *Morning Star* and is a commentator on political economy issues. He has also produced several podcasts on the links between sport, politics and the working-class movement.

Vincent Raison

Co-author of *Today South London, Tomorrow South London* (Unbound, 2018) and *Shirk, Rest and Play* (Unbound, 2022), . Vincent has been a freelance writer for 25 years, writing for *The Guardian*, *The Independent*, Huffington Post, Channel 4, Sky and ITV, among others. He also features monthly on the Deserter Pubcast on the merits of beer, crisps and the avoidance of work.

Foreword

by Professor Tony Collins

THIS IS a book about going to football matches, watching football, and talking to football fans. It takes us around the world, visits many different stadia, and introduces us to supporters from different clubs and cultures. It takes us deep into the nuances and complexities of why football means so much to so many men and women across the globe.

But *The Roaring Red Front* is also far more than this. It tells the story of football supporters and clubs who take a stand against oppression and exploitation, and have unashamedly aligned themselves with left-wing movements and campaigns. Through the observations of Stewart and Vincent, conversations with fans, and explorations of the history of each club, the book takes us into football's alternate world.

It's a world where the corporate culture of modern football is challenged, where the sport has a responsibility for its communities, and where the quest for equality for all is at the heart of the game. This is a story about the game you won't find in the mainstream media, and no one has told it with so much passion and insight as the authors of *The Roaring Red Front*.

It's no accident the book ends involving a team from Glasgow. Ever since it caught the imagination of Glasgow's shipyard and factory workers in the 1870s, football has been at the heart of the city's popular culture.

Glasgow was one of the world's industrial powerhouses. By World War I it was a centre of industrial militancy – nicknamed the

'Petrograd of Britain' by some – and the world capital of football, boasting three stadia which could hold over 100,000 spectators. Tens of thousands of supporters gathered every Saturday afternoon to watch the city's professional teams, and thousands more played the game. By one estimate, there was a football club for every 160 young men in the region by 1900.

Nor was it just men. Thousands of women watched the game too. From 1917 many working-class women started playing the game in local factory teams, and Glasgow would remain a centre of the women's game for decades. The city embodied the link between football and radical opposition to the status quo.

One of its most prominent militant trade union leaders during the war was Willie Gallacher. In 1920 he played in goal for an international side in a hastily organised match against a Russian team in Moscow. The Russians dominated the match, so much so that according to some reports the game was abandoned at half-time.

Gallacher wasn't the only British player in the international side. Alongside him were Sheffield's J.T. Murphy, Hull's Dick Beech, Edinburgh's Dave Ramsey, and Essex-born Jack Tanner. None of them were renowned footballers. In fact, they were known across Britain for being revolutionary trade unionists – and they were in Moscow to take part in the Second Congress of the recently formed Communist International.

The International had been created by the Bolshevik Party in 1919 to build revolutionary parties around the world that would emulate the success of the October Revolution. Hundreds of delegates from all over the globe made their way to Moscow to discuss revolutionary strategy. Yet in their rare moments of relaxation, football was the automatic game of choice.

This was because the sport had emerged from the butchery of World War I as an international language of the working class. Partly this was due to its popularity among soldiers of all sides but, more importantly, the game had become a symbol of international solidarity. During Christmas of 1914, troops on both sides of the fratricidal conflict had defied their officers, declared an informal truce, and played football between the trenches. This was, remarked Lenin at the time, an example of fraternisation that could lead to the end of the war and of capitalism itself.

Despite the fact its rules had been codified by the British upper classes, its famous clubs led by local businessmen, and its committees stuffed with venal bureaucrats, on Saturday afternoons the overwhelming majority of its players and spectators came from the industrial working class. As Marx himself had noted, 'for the worker, life for him begins where [work] activity ceases, at the table, at the tavern seat, in bed'. And from the late 1870s, hundreds of thousands of people who worked in textile mills, shipyards, and coal mines had added football to that list.

So, for working-class men and women, football was always more than a game. It was a communal gathering, a place to express local and class pride, and a 90-minute space in the week that was truly theirs, beyond the reach of the boss, the bureaucrat, and the moralist.

This was true wherever the game was played. Many of the clubs featured in Stewart and Vincent's wonderful book acquired their radical reputations following World War I. Others became anti-establishment clubs during further waves of radicalism towards the end of the 20th century. Regardless of who 'owned' the club or the intentions of its officials, the character of these teams was primarily defined by their supporters.

And that perhaps is the point of *The Roaring Red Front*. Football is what you make of it. There was never a lost golden age when it was 'the people's game'; the sport was never owned by or belonged to ordinary people. It was only through struggles by supporters to create an identity for their teams that these clubs became seen as beacons of opposition to the establishment. In that way, by highlighting the importance of collective activity to social change, football does indeed offer lessons for life.

As this book makes clear, one of those lessons is intrinsic to the everyday experience of being a football supporter: at its best, the game demonstrates the importance, and joy, of collective action, international friendship and human solidarity. And in doing this, as Willie Gallacher and his comrades understood in Moscow in 1920, football also offers the promise of a better world.

Introduction

'An astonishing void: official history ignores soccer. Contemporary history texts fail to mention it, even in passing, in countries where soccer has been and continues to be a primordial symbol of collective identity. I play therefore I am: a style of play is a way of being that reveals the unique profile of each community and affirms its right to be different. Tell me how you play and I'll tell you who you are.'

Eduardo Galeano, *Football in Sun and Shadow*

'A crowd exists so long as it has an unattained goal.'

Elias Canetti, *Crowds and Power*

'It is true that football is the most important of life's unimportant things.'

Arrigo Sacchi

WE'RE BOTH huge football fans and ardent lefties; though like most football fans, and certainly most lefties, we by no means agree on everything. As leftist football fans, we made the pilgrimage to Hamburg in December 2017 to see FC St Pauli, in many ways the 'guv'nor' of the left-wing clubs. We met our great friend Sonny there, had a fantastic time and came back a little smitten with the club, the St Pauli neighbourhood, and the idea of a book about the

13

top leftist/anti-fascist football clubs across the planet. They say you should try to write the book that you want to read, and this is most definitely an example.

Life is very much a game of chance. We were in the St Pauli gift shop before the game against Duisberg in December 2017 when one of us, McGill, realised he had to leave. St Pauli have been mediocre in the second rank of German football for most of their history but they know how to market a *Kult* and their merchandising of the brand is impressive, particularly so for a bunch of lefties. To avoid spending too much money he left the shop and stuck on the Celtic/ St Pauli scarf that he had just bought; partly through necessity, Hamburg in December makes you understand why Scottish people describe a particularly cold day as 'Baltic'.

As he was waiting outside a smiling face approached and said in perfect English, 'Hi, I was at Celtic last week, I saw you guys play Motherwell.' This was the start of our beautiful friendship with Sonny that took us to the mighty Shebeen pub in the backstreets of St Pauli, to the brutal Hamburg derby in 2019, to meetings in 2021 with St Pauli legend and security chief Sven Brux and the chairman, Oke Göttlich; and a very odd, late-night lesson in a boxing gym in the red-light district.

During the travels for the book, we had a few chance meetings that took us deeper into the clubs we were visiting and left us with hangovers that no human should have to feel. In many ways, the most notable was Vince Raison's with one of the Oi! bands, Lumpen, in a craft beer bar called the Bulldog Ale House in Cosenza, Calabria. The words 'Oi' and 'Bulldog' may connote fascism to many of you but as we discovered in a few places, that which is evoked by a word, cultural reference or icon can vary considerably across different cultures. And everything is different in Calabria, very different.

After our first St Pauli trip we chatted to a few people representing different clubs across Europe. Seeing club stickers and scarves from literally across the globe in the Jolly Roger pub in St Pauli, we began to think about writing something on the international phenomenon of leftist/anti-fascist clubs globally and the skein of relationships amongst them. After a visit to Rayo Vallecano in Madrid a year later, in which we had a good crack with a very friendly bunch of Celta Vigo fans flying the Pan-Celtic flag who were looking forward to a visit to Derry to check out the left-wing political scene, we thought even more that there could be an interesting set of stories here.

During the first Covid-19 lockdown we wrote a series of articles for the *Morning Star* newspaper about leftist clubs that attracted a lot of interest. This project eventually evolved into *The Roaring Red Front*. We have covered: big clubs with international followings such as Liverpool, Boca Juniors and St Pauli; local clubs with a universal appeal like Rayo and their *hermanos de la izquierda* Cádiz; clubs that effortlessly exude cool like Bohemians of Prague and Red Star from Paris, Jules Rimet's team; some small outfits that make a big noise like Dulwich Hamlet; two teams committed to helping refugees and other vulnerable people, Napoli United and United Glasgow – we were able to arrange a solidarity match between these two, the 'No Mean City' derby; Palestino of Santiago, the team for the large Palestinian population of Chile that never forgets where it came from; and the pride of the Midwest, the motorised passion that is Detroit City. And more.

We met some great, interesting, warm people and had some very good times. It wasn't all fun, travelling during the time of Covid posed many challenges and on a few occasions we wished we were doing this in our early 30s rather than our 60s, but we won't complain any more than that. The book is no succession of hagiographies. It is an evaluation and not just a celebration. There can be an entitled, aggressive sanctimony to the ultra movement, irrespective of which political foot they kick with: Vince being surrounded by angry St Pauli fans for daring to take a photograph outside the stadium that showed their faces; Cosenza fans making violent threats to their players at the end of the game through a megaphone – though we did meet the fan who made the most threats the day after and he was suitably embarrassed about it; and of course we encountered some wholly unnecessary sectarian in-fighting within the left, but that's unlikely to shock anyone.

We didn't want to write just a regular history of the clubs laced with a few experiences of meeting a colourful bunch of fans, though you will find plenty of both in here. We wanted to explore the following themes, *inter alia*, and to provide a history of the neighbourhoods and barrios concerned to help fill the 'astonishing void' described by the great Eduardo Galeano above.

- The role of the football club affiliation in determining and shaping a leftist identity and mindset amongst their supporters.

- The role of an aestheticised tribalism in politics in general and how these football clubs fit into that paradigm.

- How the clubs matter in relation to the wider global political issues, and particularly can they be part of an effort to 'sex-up' left-wing politics and increase their guttural, emotional appeal in an attempt to take on a political right that has recently been much more successful than the left in reaching out to the tribal heart that beats loudly in global political partisanship?

Can the clubs be part of an attempt to make internationalist and inclusive principles more attractive as a counterpoint to the seductive slogans and symbols of the growing nationalist and nativist movements across the western world?

In short, do these clubs actually matter? Of course they do, and not just because they bring pleasure and pain to millions across the globe. Sacchi was right – of all the things that don't really matter, football matters the most.

Stewart McGill and Vincent Raison

Cádiz

Founded:	1910
Stadium:	Estadio Nuevo Mirandilla
Capacity:	20,724
Nicknames:	*Las Piratas, El Submarino Amarillo*
Ultras:	*Las Brigadas Amarillas*

– VINCENT RAISON –

THE FIRST thing I learned about Cádiz was that it was not pronounced Cádiz, with the emphasis on the *-diz*, but Cádiz, with the emphasis on the first syllable, like Cardiff, but quicker. Much quicker. Because speech is so fast in Cádiz, there isn't time to say all the letters. Consonants and vowels are discarded with such regularity that you half-expect to find them piling up around the city's palm trees and pretty squares.

But speech is about the only thing in Cádiz that is too fast. The pace of life in this southwestern corner of Andalusia is noticeably relaxed after the pointless rush of London. The people are warm and welcoming; the lunches long and languorous.

We arrived in the Old City by train from Seville, its ancient walls announcing a place of great antiquity. Indeed, it was founded by the Phoenicians around 1100 BC, long before the rest of Spain. They called it '*Gadir*'. A singular place, not isolated, but standing alone.

'Cádiz represents a city, a province, and a way of living life, very different from what is lived in the rest of the Spanish state,' said Jose, a lively member of the *Brigadas Amarillas*, Cádiz's ultras, a man steeped in the character of Cádiz. 'We are the oldest [city in Spain], and that has carved a deep feeling of belonging.'

Despite its natural gifts, Cádiz province is the poorest in Andalusia and one of the more impoverished in Western Europe. Sun and sea can mask a great deal, but in recent years, the city's population has declined somewhat. Among the causes of this is the city's peculiar geography: it lies on a narrow strip of land hemmed in by the sea so there is limited new land to be developed. And because Cádiz is built on a sandspit, sinking foundations deep enough to support high-rise developments is too expensive to be viable.

All this explains why Cádiz's skyline hasn't actually changed that much since mediaeval times, why it's such an old city in terms of demographics. There's a slight feeling of sadness at forgotten glories you get when walking around the town during the day. But not around the stadium on matchdays; that's a joyous celebration of *Cádismo* and an affirmation of all the good things that football can bring to a people: a focus for a party, a vehicle for creativity and community vigour.

Our contact in Cádiz, Samuel, had arranged a stadium tour for us with some more of the *Brigadas Amarillas*. They were proud to show us the Nuevo Mirandilla Stadium, home of Cádiz CF. Constructed in 1955, it has twice been completely rebuilt. Originally it was known as Estadio de Ramón de Carranza, but was renamed after a public vote. De Carranza was a Francoist mayor of Cádiz linked with the *coup d'état* of 1936, which led to Franco's fascists forcibly taking over from the democratically elected leftist government. Franco would rule Spain until his death in 1975. Most people over 60 in Spain remember life under fascism, a rare and unwelcome living European memory. Thousands of Franco's political opponents were killed during the White Terror and political repression continued to target liberals, socialists, communists, Jews, Romanis, atheists, feminists, trade unionists and gays throughout his reign. So fuck that guy.

Watching Dino Zoff and Paolo Rossi lift the World Cup in Spain in 1982 for Italy, I was oblivious to the fact that the country was only a few years from fascist rule. It would have been unimaginable to hold such a global tournament under Franco.

Cádiz chooses not to honour those dark days under the General. While there is nothing uniform or unanimous about the politics of the population, both the city and the province have impeccable leftist credentials. The mayor, José Mariá González Santos, known simply as Kichi, is a member of the Izquierda Anticapitalista party (Anti-Capitalist Left).

'Cádiz resists,' he said on being voted in for a second term in 2019.

The city is remarkable in that it holds a 55 per cent stake in its energy supplier, Eléctrica de Cádiz, supplying most of Cádiz with renewable energy. €500,000 of its profits go to the city's disadvantaged to prevent 'energy poverty'. This is a stark contrast to many energy companies, whose profits go to shareholders and who will simply cut the supply of those unable to pay, before taking legal action against them. It is no small thing, and reflects an essential difference between right and left; capitalism and socialism. One punishes those who are struggling financially, and one assists them. One blames the poor for their poverty, the other tries to alleviate it. It's a simplistic view, yes, but hard to dispute.

Kichi managed to garner support not just from traditional left-wing supporters but even from across the political spectrum, partly because he is a *gaditano* (a Cádiz native, the word recalling Phoenician roots), doing his best for his hometown. In a city with a village feel, he is the boy next door, all grown up and now at the head of the *gaditano* family. You won't be surprised to hear that he supports his local team as well.

Kichi's partner, Teresa Rodriguez, is also a prominent politician. In the 2015 and 2018 Andalusian parliamentary elections, she was the presidential candidate for Podemos, the left-wing populist party. Podemos emerged from the *Indignados* movement, the outraged anti-austerity campaign that also inspired the Occupy movement and was itself inspired by Latin America's 'turn to the left' at the beginning of the 21st century. Eyebrows were raised that Rodriguez made no secret of her affection for the *Brigaradas*

Amarillas (I would call them the Yellow Brigade, but it sounds much better in Spanish). The reason this was considered contentious for someone running for high office is that the *Amarillas* have enjoyed a few rucks over the years, including pitched battles with *Biris Norte*, Sevilla's ultra group and Andalusian rivals.

Jose would dispute that there is any real beef with Sevilla these days though. 'On a historical level, there has always been a rivalry with Sevilla FC, and to a lesser extent, against Betis. Fortunately, there is no rivalry today that makes us hostile towards any normal supporter of any team. Our greatest rivalry would be against any team with right-wing fans.'

But, unthinkably, the right are on the rise throughout Spain, including Andalusia, through the right-wing ultranationalist Vox. Vox have been accused of being anti-feminist, Islamaphobic, anti-immigrant and homophobic. They are currently Spain's third-largest party.

Cádiz's leftism is not merely restricted to the city. The Socialist Workers' Party is the biggest party in the province of Cádiz and the region of Andalusia, even with Podemos taking a significant portion of the left vote. The political slant of Cádiz's fans is not an anomaly. They do represent the city and province of Cádiz.

'*Brigadas* anti-fascism is part of our DNA,' explained Jose. 'Our history is marked by the fight against fascism, both at the ultra level, as well as at the social level in our city in the last 39 years. It is our way of life.'

Thanks to Spain's unique history, anti-fascism has real meaning among the ultra groups of the country. Most violence that erupts here has little to do with football and everything to do with politics. It is quite unlike the UK, where clubs tend to be apolitical. Spanish ultras may trace their roots to English hooliganism – an empty, loud expression of tribalism combined with lager – but not their political convictions.

Entering the stadium – past the emblem of the *Brigadas Amarillas*, with its central image of Che Guevara, past the club emblem, and past, what's this? A painting of Andy Capp? It was a surprise to us, being old enough to remember the violent misogyny of the *Daily Mirror* comic strip, but Andy Capp has become a global left-wing football icon. He represents the working-class roots of the beautiful game, in contrast to the capitalist machine it has become in which players can be traded for more than £200m and season tickets can exceed £2,000.

We walked up the steps to take in the yellow and blue seats around the pitch. I presumed the yellow represented the sun and the miles of impeccable sandy beaches of Cádiz; blue for sea and sky but I was wrong. The colours come from the club's historical connection to an old Cádiz football team, Mirandilla FC and the La Salle religious order it sprang from. From certain vantage points you can see the water of the Bay of Cádiz, making it one of the best stadium views imaginable.

It was good of the guys to show us round and answer questions like, 'So, who is your biggest rival, Sevilla or Betis?'

'Xerez!' They chorused, echoing humanity's strange compulsion to be irked by their nearest neighbour, a reaction repeated throughout the world, even one they rarely play, though other *Amarillas* would later tell us they have no problem with Xerez whatsoever.

In the UK, the rivalries of Sunderland and Newcastle, or Portsmouth and Southampton, for instance, are ignited by the irrational belief that the people just a few miles away are fundamentally *other*: different, or even inferior. Here in Cádiz, many see anti-fascists everywhere as brothers and sisters and only fascists worthy of contempt, whoever they support and wherever they come from.

El Mágico

Just past the image of Hartlepool's 'finest', Andy Capp, we came to a stencil of Mágico González, Cádiz's legendary forward who lit up the 1980s and early 1990s here, whose sublime skills are still remembered in awed reverence.

'He is one of the best players I have ever seen in my life, there is no doubt about it,' said Diego Maradona. El Mágico – the magical one – was called 'The best footballer you've never heard of', by *World Soccer* magazine, as his extraordinary abilities were not reflected by his fame outside of Spain and his native El Salvador. There are those who played with him who thought him even better than Maradona, who admitted trying to copy González in training, without success.

Mágico was first introduced to Spain in that 1982 World Cup, impressing in an El Salvador side that did well to qualify. Clubs lined up to sign him, like Paris Saint-Germain, Atletico Madrid and Sampdoria, but he chose Cádiz, where he could continue doing the things he loved best: scoring goals, nightclubbing, drinking, smoking and sleeping.

Doubtless, he could have had a more lucrative and silverware-laden career, but as he himself explained,'I don't treat football as a job, I just play for fun.' Yes, Messi and Ronaldo have achieved great things, but how good would they have been on 20 Marlboro a day and a bellyful of booze?

With his touch, his vision, his audacity, he was a consummate crowd-pleaser. Why slot the ball into the net when you can lob the keeper and leave the fans awestruck, struggling to take in what they had just witnessed? Why be efficient when you can bring joy? Why simply contribute when you can dazzle?

'Mágico González did not want to win everything, because he understood life as we in Cádiz understand it,' Jose told us. 'He played for fun, to be able to live, and to be able to enjoy himself. He was a poor person with an innate talent in his feet, and who, for example, missed a gala at which he was being honoured with an award because he was playing soccer with children in a courtyard. He is a god here in Cádiz. Those who are too young to have seen him play live know all his goals from videos. Everyone here has experienced El Mágico.'

In his first season with Cádiz, he scored 14 goals and helped them gain promotion to La Liga. In 1984 he was invited to join Barcelona on a tour of the USA. Some say he chose to return to Cádiz because he missed it, others that Barça were put off by his indiscipline and passed on the tantalising opportunity to have Maradona and González in the same team.

In Los Angeles, Mágico refused to leave his hotel room when a fire alarm went off (set off as a prank by Maradona) as he was entertaining a lady friend at the time, which didn't impress Barça officials, already wondering whether their star player really needed a notorious playmate to escort him to Barcelona's nightclubs.

Returning to Napoli from the 1986 World Cup, a triumphant Maradona heard the fans singing 'Maradona is better than Pele,' and declared that González was better than himself *and* Pele. 'These fans are great but what they don't know is that there is a player even better than Pele and I,' he told a journalist. 'He is Jorge González, El Mágico, and he still plays in Cádiz – he's phenomenal.'

Because of Mágico's genius, he was indulged by the Cádiz coach, David Vidal. His late nights sometimes meant missed training and he would refuse to do fitness training, or any training that didn't involve a ball. Cádiz were lucky to have him, and he was lucky to have Cádiz.

Brigadas Amarillas

The day after our stadium tour we met with Samuel and his partner, Rocío, their friend Natalia and Jose, at Peña Flamenca Juanita Villar, a delightful tapas bar they favoured in the La Viña district of Cádiz, near the city beach and away from the tourists, an area Rocío called 'Cádiz-Cádiz' – proper Cádiz, to differentiate it from the periphery. The football stadium is on the outskirts and Rocío took some pleasure in telling us that she puts her data roaming on when she goes to that part of town.

The story of Cadiz's ultras began back in the 1980s when some young anti-fascists formed a group to express their support for the club and oppose racism and supporters of fascism. They started making their presence felt, travelling to away games in large numbers, noisily supporting their team and putting on pyro displays.

Pyrotechnics are not a part of UK football culture but they are an important expression of visual support on the Continent. Ultra groups fill the air with smoke from their flares, some coordinated to make a more powerful sight. Fans use all they have to support the team: singing, chanting, waving flags and, yes, setting fire to stuff. Pyros are still something of a mystery to the Premier League spectator, but in many European countries they signify that extreme ultra support, helping to create a fevered atmosphere to inspire their team.

The *Brigadas Amarillas* soon became notorious not just for their away support but also for their political demonstrations at home, where they protested against mass unemployment in their province. Counter-demonstrations meant fights, arrests, fines and greater notoriety, but also stunted the growth of the group.

In *Political Ideology and Activism in Football Fan Culture in Spain: A View From the Far Left* by Ramon Spaaij and Carles Viñas there are some telling insights from Cádiz fans. In the study, some of the *Vieja Guardia* (Old Guard) of the *Brigadas* are described as being too committed to violence. Some have gone on to change their perspective, including Pedro, a fan then in his late 30s, who told the study:

'We have a long history of violent clashes with fascist groups. We used a lot of violence against that other [fascist] violence but our violence was understood differently by the media and the state.

'But I also have to admit my own mistakes, and one of them has been to defend our beliefs through violence, putting other possible forms of struggle aside ... some people have been using violence for the sake of violence. Our philosophy has changed a bit though. I am now much more involved in grassroots activities like education and raising awareness.'

Even successive relegations in the 1990s didn't douse the passion of supporters. People don't back teams like Cádiz for the glory of trophies. They do so because they believe in something and believe the team reflects the things they hold dear.

It was also in the 1990s that they forged a friendship with Spain's other notable anti-fascist ultras, the *Bukaneros* of Rayo Vallecano, from the barrio of Vallecas in Madrid, whom we will meet in the next chapter. It started with letters (remember them?), stickers, fanzines and visits and now, nearly 30 years later, a strong brotherhood that has grown between them.

'We continue to have an excellent relationship with the ultras of Rayo', says Jose.

So strong is the bond, they have a saying: '*Sangre Gaditana en vena Vallecana.*' – Cádiz blood in Vallecas veins.

'Time, travel, and new technologies mean that today we can say we also feel at home in places as far away as Bilbao and Tenerife. in general, we have good vibes with almost all the anti-fascist fans in the Spanish state.'

It's heartening to see left-wing fans united, celebrating what they have in common, loudly proclaiming their anti-fascism and forming a network of commitment to social justice, especially given the often-fractured nature of leftist support.

The *Amarillas* were generous with their time and more than happy to share their knowledge and passion. Our eyebrows were raised when they arranged to meet in the square a full four hours before their kick-off against Barcelona, but we were keen to get the full Cádiz experience. We're used to having a couple of pints before a game, but this was something else.

Gradually the square began to fill with yellow shirts, some downing beer, but also, surprisingly, plenty drinking gin and tonic or martinis. A picture of a supposed Barcelona ultra went round. Would they be showing up and causing trouble?

'Ultra? It's just a fat guy in shorts,' said Rocío, dismissively.

Jose had already explained that Cádiz fans tended to be welcoming, but they were not afraid of sticking up for themselves. 'That is something we are especially proud of. And although Cádiz is not an Andalusian or pro-independence bastion, as such, it is a place that is kind to other fans with anti-fascist and pro-independence tendencies.'

The 'fat guy in shorts' was nowhere to be seen though, so the fans were free to stand down. And as the drinks and the sun went down, the singing began, growing ever louder, enveloping more fans until the square was alight with songs and flares. It was a privilege to be there, as the excitement at the prospect of watching their heroes do battle with the Catalans.

Despite taking on one of the giants of European football, the Cádiz fans were optimistic. They had beaten Barcelona for the first time two seasons ago and Barça were not the team they once were. They had been bitten by their own dog because money does not make a loyal pet. Disastrous financial and football decisions, coupled with loss of revenue due to the pandemic meant that an unrecognisable Barcelona team, shorn of its stars, would face Cádiz that evening at the Nuevo Mirandilla.

* * *

Matchday: Cádiz v Barcelona, September 2021
Stewart McGill

Such was the party before the game, loud, raucous, but wholly good-natured without even a whispered suggestion of aggro, that I wasn't sure I wanted to go into the stadium. However, people had been kind enough to make the effort to secure my possibility of entry and, of course, the artistic needs of *The Roaring Red Front* were calling loudly. The things we do for our readers, eh?

The lack of any tension at the party contrasted greatly with similar affairs before big matches in the UK, evidence of a different relationship with alcohol and a different attitude to having a good time. I was thinking about this as I queued to get into the stadium on a warm late September evening. I realised that even a grumpy old lefty like me could be mellow in a city like this: you're never more than 500 yards away from a beach, the food is terrific, the beer is as cold as the people are warm and there are very few Tories about.

My seat was very high up in a very steep stadium with narrow stairs. Not for the first time I was glad that I could hold my beer and offered myself a little pat on the back. The self-congratulation was only marginally challenged when I had a couple of vaguely embarrassing stumbles. When you get to a certain age you don't actively 'fall', you 'have falls'; things happen to you. However, I did fully realise then that I was no longer the kid who could run around terraces with five-inch heels on my platform soles and 32-inch flares. I regretted that it wasn't 1975 any more, something that happens a lot.

I've watched Cádiz a lot on television so it was a little magical to actually be in the stadium. It's compactly pretty with calming yellow and blue tones and, as Vince writes above, some of the best views you will see from any football ground. I felt a bit bad about Vince not being able to get into the ground but I knew he'd be looked after in a local bar watching the game with a couple of beers. He'd also be spared having to negotiate those steep steps going down on the way out of the stadium after the match, something to which I was not looking forward.

The atmosphere was terrific, partisan but good-natured with no rancour. Maybe it would have been a little different if the Barcelona crew had shown up, the fat man in the shorts with some friends, but this crowd was 100 per cent *gaditano*. As I was chatting to Jose from the *Brigadas Amarillas* earlier, the yobbo gene was activated by alcohol and I expressed a wish that the *Boixos Noi*, Barcelona's right-wing fan group, would make an appearance: Jose very determinedly concurred with this, I don't think too many in the *Brigadas* are shy about any physical aspects of the struggle.

There was a bit of a show from the stadium lights before the game and the announcer tried a little too hard to whip up the crowd. I don't really like all these imported American attempts at razzmatazz. The *gaditanos* around me, regular, no-bullshit working-class guys who came for the game, also looked mightily unimpressed. In their statement of 9 January excoriating the club's owners the *Brigadas* stated, 'We do not understand what that speaker is doing, cheering in such a ridiculous, artificial and childish way, as if it were an NBA franchise.' They also used the phrase *'tan poco propia,'* roughly translating as 'so little like us,' 'this is not what we are.' This tells you something about the aversion to modern/business football felt by the *Brigadas*. Often the people who run football don't really understand those who watch it and patronise them as plebs who just like a bit of a circus. The ludicrous opening ceremony of Euro '96 with the knights in armour is the most egregious example but there are plenty of others.

The football itself was competent, but it was one of those games that we used to refer to as a game of Don Howe's Face, both had nil-nil written all over it. Cádiz played well enough against a Barcelona side who clearly did not want to play for their manager and the problems they experienced later in the season were no surprise after watching this game. In the words of the great Jimmy Sirrel, the legendary Notts County manager for much of the 1970s and 1980s, 'If ye dinnae score, ye dinnae win.' Possibly the most profound words ever spoken about a game that many over-complicate.

You know the game's getting a bit dull when you spend an unreasonable proportion of the first half wondering how to best translate and scan the rather distasteful 1970s chant 'You couldn't score in a brothel' into Spanish. '*No podrías anotar en un burdel*' was my best effort; not great regarding the rhythm but a little better than most of the goal attempts on the field. To be fair, things improved decidedly in the second half: Negredo forced a great save from Barcelona's Ter Stegen in the first minute of the half. Memphis Depay missed one that I could have put away even wearing my platform soles, but then forced a great save from Ledesma in the Cádiz goal. Salvi was put through beautifully by Espino, my favourite Cádiz player by some distance, but again Ter Stegen did the job with a fine save. In the fourth minute of stoppage time Piqué went on a charge redolent of past Barça glories and put through Depay for a clear chance; he missed in a way redolent of Geoff Thomas for England against France in 1992. Poor Memphis really did have a bad day at the *burdel*.

As the action ground down to the Don Howe Face, the focus, passion, and hatred centred on Ronald Koeman. He's put on a few pounds since his playing days but the hair is still nicely blond. His black t-shirt and trousers were just a little too tight and he looked like a slightly lumpy fusion of pantomime villain and dame. The *gaditanos* clearly hated him, but probably not as much as his team did. His sending-off in injury time provoked the most excitement of the evening.

'All I said to the fourth official was that there were two balls on the pitch. They send you off for nothing in this country. I asked the referee in a calm manner, but let's leave it as it's not my problem,' said Twankey/Captain Hook after the match. The sending-off did seem a little excessive. Maybe the referee didn't like him either. Barcelona sacked him a month later after a 1-0 defeat at Rayo Vallecano. 2021/22 wasn't a great season for *Los Hermanos de la Izquierda* but they did at least make a contribution to this story.

The sobering impact of the game meant that I was able to negotiate the stairs without too much embarrassment and I will always remember with fondness my time at the Nuevo Mirandilla and the people we met in Cádiz. Sometimes the game doesn't matter that much, though I looked forward to a better match-up at the weekend in Madrid when I was due to see Rayo Vallecano v Cádiz in Vallecas. I wasn't disappointed.

* * *

Recent Seasons

Cádiz may not have a Mágico, but they have a strong team spirit and are afraid of no one. Until being relieved of his duties in January 2022, coach Álvaro Cervera was the closest they came to a hero figure in recent times. When he took over the helm, Cádiz were in the third tier of Spanish football. Two promotions later and they were taking on Barcelona on an equal footing. One of his quotes '*La lucha no se negocia*' – the fight is not negotiable – has been taken on as a motto of the club and is stitched into each Cádiz football shirt. 'He understood the idiosyncrasies of Cádiz, adapting perfectly to our way of life, customs, and our feeling for this city and club,' said Jose.

Founded in 1910, its early history includes a merger with Mirandilla FC, friendlies and regional competitions before emerging in the *Segunda División* after the Civil War. It wasn't until 1977 that they tasted top-flight football, and only from 1985 to 1993 did they hang around longer than a season until now.

Cervera took over in April 2016 with Cádiz's place in the Segunda B playoffs in danger. An inauspicious start saw them take just one point in his first four matches in charge, the last of the regular season, but it was enough to scrape into the post-season contest. But they found their feet in the playoffs, beating Racing Ferrol, Racing Santander and Hércules to secure promotion to the second tier after a six-year exile.

A stirring first full season under Cervera saw Cádiz reach the playoffs in fifth place, before going out to Tenerife. The next two seasons saw them just miss out before finally going up in second place in 2019/20. It would be their first season in La Liga since their solitary year's stay 15 years earlier.

In October, they achieved the impossible: deservedly beating Zinedine Zidane's Real Madrid in the Bernabéu to go third in La Liga, with a goal from Anthony 'Choco' Lozano. In December, they beat Barça. They went on to finish 12th – their highest-ever position – full of confidence that their stay in the top flight could be a long one.

However, the 2021/22 season would prove to be a difficult one. The team would fight for their place in a hugely competitive league – after all, the fight is not negotiable – and they have some very good players, such as McGill's favourite, Uruguayan left-back Alfonso Espino, veteran striker Álvaro Negredo and Choco, their talented Honduran striker. But a habit of conceding late goals heaped pressure on the coach, who saw points slip from their grasp thanks to defensive frailties. Wins at Vigo and Bilbao and an excellent point against Real Madrid at the Bernabéu couldn't hide the fact they went into 2022 without a home win. And so, following an uncharacteristically timid defeat in Pamplona, coach Cervera was sacked and replaced by Sergio González – his brief: to keep Cádiz up. He immediately oversaw an improvement in form, finally getting some home wins, against their brothers from Vallecas and also a very good Villareal side, before an astonishing victory over Barcelona at the Camp Nou. However, by the final game of the season, Cádiz still found themselves in the bottom three, playing away at Alavés and needing to better the results of Granada or Mallorca to stay up. In the second half, Mallorca took the lead at Osasuna, and Granada got a penalty. Amid unbearable tension, Granada missed their penalty and Cádiz substitute Choco Lozano scored minutes later, allowing them to leapfrog Granada and prompting tears among Cádiz's faithful. With five minutes left, Alavés were awarded a penalty before VAR helped the referee rule it out. When the final whistle went, Cádiz were safe by one point. Cadistas exploded in relief and joy as fans partied long and hard into the night.

But for the *Brigadas Amarillas*, the perilous position at the wrong end of La Liga was not their only concern. They have seen the *Segunda División* before – and worse. What animates them is the direction the ownership of the club wants to take them in. Because Cádiz CF is always about more than just football.

La Lucha

In November 2021, 25,000 metal workers went on strike in Cádiz after failing to reach a collective bargaining agreement. Blockades restricted access to Cádiz's industrial zone, turning the strike into a wider crisis. Cadistas would naturally oppose any attempt by management to use high unemployment and rising prices to persuade the workforce to accept a disadvantageous deal. The owners of Cádiz CF however decided to parade the players for a team photo in the shipyard, asking for 'common sense' to prevail. This was interpreted as using the football team to support the management in their battle with the workers, against the very nature of the club, city and province.

In addition, the president of the club, Manual Vicaíno, has voiced ambitions to move the club to a new stadium outside the city of Cádiz, disregarding more than a century of history and disrespecting those fans who have shown constant devotion to the club. This is a club with a heart; not a franchise that goes where the money flows.

There had been a suspicion that their president didn't have the club's interests at heart and didn't understand Cadismo. That sense was confirmed by the repugnant sight of the former Sevilla president, José María del Nido, in the bars of the Mirandilla. A man with known connections to fascism, Nido was sentenced to seven years in prison for corruption and embezzlement. *Brigadas Amarillas* were horrified at his presence.

'The natural connection between the team and the city has been broken. We are concerned that all the feelings that make us who we are will be commodified to a point as false as it is obscene,' they said in a stern statement that followed the tweeted picture in the shipyard.

'Cádiz CF does not understand itself without the people of Cádiz, because the people of Cádiz do not understand their day to day life without Cádiz CF. We want our sons and daughters to feel the passion and pride of belonging to a humble club so they can feel special in a world dominated by so-called big clubs that resemble multinationals. We do not want to look anything like them, with their globalising and impersonal concept.

'The sports corporation may be owned by majority shareholders in a commercial register, but it belongs to the municipality and its entire province. No one, absolutely no one, is going to put their financial interests or their business or personal goals first without encountering Cadista fans, brigades, and many of their tough fighters defending the values that have always illuminated the club: humility and the banner of Cadismo.

'We are what we defend. We are simply not going to allow it. You will have us to deal with.

'*Salud, Cadismo y Libertad!*'

As Samuel would tell us, 'There are many people within the *Brigadas Amarillas* who have been pressing for a long time for the group to be tougher with Vizcaíno and now the conditions are there to go against him. In recent years, it has been difficult because at the end of the day we left Second B and in two years we went up to the First Division after almost 20 years.'

Now the president no longer hides his contempt for workers' rights, his connection to fascist crooks and his ambition to tear the heart of the club out to see if he can turn it into gold outside the city. And now he will have a fight on his hands. Because *la lucha no se negocia.*

The Englishman of Cádiz

While the stadium was indeed renamed the Nuevo Mirandilla, there was talk that it could have been named after the former Liverpool, Brighton and Manchester City striker Michael Robinson. Thanks to his exemplary work as pundit and presenter, the much-loved ex-Republic of Ireland international had become something of an institution in Spain since moving there in 1987 to play in Pamplona for Osasuna.

After joining a consortium that rescued Cádiz CF from financial ruin, he became director of football. 'Getting involved with Cádiz was the best thing I've ever done. It was maybe the craziest but definitely the most gratifying,' he told *The Guardian*'s Sid Lowe. 'I meet so many ex-players who are affluent and don't like football but I love football. And Cádiz is football.'

Cádiz was Robinson's favourite city and he had a somewhat hopeful theory that he was descended from there as a result of the Spanish Armada washing up near Cork. Sadly, he passed away in 2020, shortly before Cádiz's return to La Liga.

'I believe that the word does not exist that explains what it means to be Cadista,' he said, but he understood it better than most. He believed in the beauty and emotion of football and felt at home in this strip of land slipping off the end of Spain into an Atlantic idyll. Laid back, fun-seeking, humanitarian – none of these come close to explaining what it means to be a Cadista. Better writers than us will try and fail to capture its essence. Those that know, know, but struggle to articulate it.

Robinson often pondered what made the place and its football club special though and few have come as close as him to defining them.

'Cádiz is a good socialist place. Warm, relaxed, friendly. It has the most humble, open people. It's spontaneous and natural and they love football. There's an entire society behind the club – a city and a region. There's only 120,000 people in the city yet we've filled our ground for 47 consecutive months – with special people.'

He described the experience of going to see Cádiz as poetry. He loved this place, its people and its football club and it's easy to see why.

Rayo Vallecano

Founded:	1924
Stadium:	Campo de Fútbol de Vallecas
Capacity:	14,708
Nicknames:	*Los Franjirrojos*
Ultras:	*Los Bukaneros*

– STEWART McGILL –

RAYO VALLECANO first registered with me as a club of interest as a result of my wearing a St Pauli shirt in Crete. This is an intriguing little planet, more connected than we realise. I heard an excited cry of 'St Pauli! St Pauli!' behind me. A young guy working in a camera shop had seen the shirt and ran out very excited wanting to talk.

We drank coffee in the co-op cafe he has established with a group of other local left-wingers. He also played in their football team and was as big a fan of Rayo Vallecano as he was St Pauli. He didn't like Livorno though, whom we cover in a later chapter, as they were 'a little too Marxist-Leninist' for him. I knew about Rayo but was surprised that they had any international following. They're not St Pauli – but then again 'who is?' as David Coleman would ask – but they're one of the most interesting clubs that we cover in this book, with a committed and active fanbase. And they have a great kit. Maybe it's wrong, but looks do matter.

Vallecas

Rayo were founded in Vallecas in 1924. Rayo means lightning or thunderbolt. In the early 1950s Rayo adopted the diagonal red stripe across their white shirts in admiration of the Argentine side River Plate. River visited Madrid in 1953, the teams exchanged gifts and have been friends ever since. River have the reputation of being the right-wing team in Buenos Aires but this is clearly not an issue for either set of supporters.

Vallecas is a tough, friendly and diverse neighbourhood in the south-east of Madrid, about 30 minutes' walk from Atocha station in the city centre. Think of it as a bit like south-east London's Elephant and Castle but with better wine and less traffic. It also has far fewer high-quality Colombian restaurants than the Elephant, but so does anywhere else, including Bogota.

The barrio has a long-standing leftist reputation: during the Civil War it was an important and strategic Republican stronghold battered by Franco. Vallecas grew considerably during the Franco years and took in many migrants from provincial Spain. As these were often people that had suffered from the vicissitudes of capitalism and the cruelty of fascism, the migration served to intensify the barrio's leftist sentiments.

Vallecas is more than a neighbourhood. It actually spans two of the 21 districts (Puente de Vallecas and Villa de Vallecas) that make up Madrid. Around 306,000 people live there. It's more like a mini-city within Madrid and is home to nearly ten per cent of the city's population. The first large wave of immigration in the 1960s from other Spanish provinces was followed by that from other countries (mainly Moroccans, Romanians and Ecuadorians in recent years). In March 2018, of the 179,406 unemployed people registered in Madrid, 27,051 were from Vallecas. Nine per cent of those were under 30 years old – the highest percentage in Madrid.

Despite its problems, Vallecas is a very pleasant place to visit with a great variety of restaurants, as you would expect. It's clearly not a wealthy barrio but I have never felt any sense of threat there. If you go to see Rayo then stay in Vallecas for a taste, and smell, of the 'real' Madrid. Though many *cuidadanos* of Vallecas will tell you that Madrid is something that happens somewhere to their north-west, a close but actually very distant neighbour.

The Football

Rayo are a classic yo-yo club that oscillates between the top and the second flights of Spanish football. It makes following them interesting as most seasons seem to be either a fight for promotion or against relegation. 2020/21 in the second division looked to be an exception as Rayo spent a large part of the season in mid-table mediocrity with little hope of promotion but a fine late run meant that they scraped into the play-offs in sixth place. Despite losing the first leg of the final 2-1 at home to Girona, Rayo won the second leg in Girona 2-0 on a very emotional night and returned to La Liga. After a promising start to the 2021/2022 season with new signing Radamel Falcao – an ageing but legendary Colombian striker – scoring freely, there was even some talk amongst Rayo fans of European football in 2022/23. A mid-season slump put an end to that *sueño*; however, after a brief flirtation with the potential of relegation Rayo fought their way to mid-table respectability by the end of the season.

Rayo did enjoy a legendary season in the UEFA Cup in 2000/01. They had finished ninth in La Liga the season before, their highest-ever placing, and got into Europe via their high position in the Fair Play League. They beat Constel·lació Esportiva of Andorra 16-0 on aggregate in the qualifying round but that didn't really raise too many hopes. After a couple of victories against Scandinavian opposition, things began to look more interesting. Subsequent victories against Lokomotiv Moscow and Bordeaux took the Stripe to the quarter-finals against the Basque side Alavés and people began to dream. There was a major European quarter-final to be played in the tiny Campo de Futból de Vallecas, one end of which is a wall. Alavés won 4-2 on aggregate and lost in the final to Liverpool, thereby depriving Rayo of the right to say they went out to the winners.

I must confess that of all the teams we cover in this volume Rayo, along with Palestino, are my favourites, so every time I think about that European run it's a little *agridulce*, as I will probably never see Rayo play in Europe. UEFA no longer offer places in competitions to teams that do well in fair-play leagues, and the current Rayo side is pretty combative, so that route would probably be closed anyway.

Players

Famous former Rayo players include Diego Costa, the aggressive Brazilian who played successfully for Chelsea in between suspensions, and Laurie Cunningham, formerly of Leyton Orient, West Bromwich and Real Madrid. Rayo was Laurie's last club before his tragically early death in a car crash.

Wilfred Agbonavbare, Rayo's Nigerian goalkeeper between 1990 and 1996, is the club's most popular recent player. He died from cancer at 48 in 2015. There is a mural dedicated to Willy on the stadium's outer wall. Its inscription reads, *'Por tu defensa de la franja, y tu lucha contra el racism. El Rayismo nunca te olvidare.'* It translates to, 'For your defence of the Stripe and your struggle against racism, Rayismo will never forget you.' 'Rayismo' represents the fans and spirit of Rayo Vallecano.

Agbonavbare had an amazing game at the end of the 1992/93 season against Real Madrid. He saved a penalty from Michel, later to become a Rayo legend as manager, and managed a number of incredible saves to earn a point at the Santiago Bernabéu. He was also magnificent in the 2-0 victory earlier in the season against Real.

These incredible performances evoked the worst aspects of humanity among an element of Real's fans who shouted racist insults at him during the match, including *'Negro, cabrón, recoge el algodón'* – 'Black, bastard, pick the cotton' – along with Ku Klux Klan chants.

One middle-aged Madrid fan even exclaimed, 'The fucking black guy of Rayo is to blame,' on live television, much to the amusement of the teenage fans surrounding him. One younger fan said, 'We are going to beat up the black son of a bitch of Vallecas on Sunday. At least I am.'

When asked after the match about the racist abuse he suffered, Agbonavbare responded, 'It's normal, I'm black, and having made as many saves as I did today, I expected them to shout at me. But I'm a footballer and it's nothing. I'm only concentrated on the match.'

The emerging *Bukaneros* were not so sanguine as Willy and emerged with a plan to fight racism and the fascism that feeds upon it on the terraces. The *Bukaneros* are by far the biggest Rayo fan grouping at present, but they took a while getting there, and it was not a smooth path to the top spot.

The *Bukaneros*

At the end of the 1991/92 season, a group of seven young men agreed to organise themselves into an anti-fascist focus at the Vallecas Stadium the following season. They called themselves the *Bukaneros*, after the *Batalla Naval*, celebrated every year by the people of Vallecas in memory of the events of a very hot day in July 1981 in which Vallecanos, desperate for cold water, opened up the fire hydrants and began the campaign to have the area declared a seaport, despite being 300km (185 miles) from the nearest beach. Vallecas is different. It becomes clear after a while why you see the alternative spelling 'Vallekas' so often.

At the time, the dominant group on the terraces with about 100 members were the apolitical *Brigadas Franjirrojas*, the 'Red Stripe Brigades' – it always sounds better in Spanish. They had taken over from the '*Komando Vallekas*', a name that sounds over-dramatic in any language. The *Bukaneros* co-existed with the *Franjirrojas* for a couple of years and the group grew slowly to 15 members over that time and made a few away journeys, including to Cádiz where the enduring friendship with the *Brigadas Amarillas* was formed. The *Bukaneros* were always very clear that they stood for three things with passion: Rayo, the working class and anti-fascism. This was always going to put them into some conflict with the *Franjirrojas*, and this became more pronounced as that group began to be directed by some of the Vallecas section of the *Ultra Sur*, the hardcore rightist and Franco-loving section of Real Madrid's support.

In 1995/96 some of the newly formed Madrid Section of the *Brigadas Amarillas*, founded by *gaditanos* who had moved to Madrid for work, joined the *Bukaneros* and the group grew from 15 to 40 members. This is when the conflict with the *Franjirrosas* started to get a little more aggressive and after two years that latter group was no longer a factor on the Rayo terraces. In the unforgiving words of the *Bukaneros* website, the hostilities bore fruit *'al terminar por completo con aquel cáncer de la afición rayista'* – 'by completely ending that cancer of the Rayo support'.

The *Bukaneros* website then goes on to report that:

> 'New material was released (like that first shirt with the skull smoking a firecracker), there were more trips always accompanied by the *Petas* [see below], and for the first time Rayo beat a frightening Real Madrid at the Bernabéu with a 2-1 victory in front of 500 travelling Vallekanos.
>
> 'In the 96/97 season, everything went right for the group: some *tifos* were made with rolls of toilet paper (the largest number were against Hércules and against Atletico Madrid), we had four flags, several banners, a couple of drums and finally we increased in numbers to about 60 people. There were some incidents with rival groups with a longer history and the name *Bukaneros* was already beginning to be known nationally. That season the fanzine ran regularly, not missing any of the 19 home league games with a print run of 100 free copies.'

The *Peña de las Petas* were one of the main Rayo fan groups of the 1980s and so called because of their fondness for marijuana and hashish (a *peta* is a reefer). The *Bukaneros* were basically an offshoot of the *Petas* led by younger members wanting to become more active and independent. Despite that, the *Bukaneros* have only veneration for the memory of the 'mythical and unforgettable *Petas*'.

The website shows that the *Bukaneros* are not shy about violence nor quietly boasting about their competence at it. This is important to remember, a left-wing firm is still a firm and has a reputation to uphold, members of the pacifist left should probably stand elsewhere in the stadium.

The history section of the website also mentions *tifos* in nearly every paragraph. *Tifos* are large-scale visual displays of any choreographed flag, sign or banner in the stands of a stadium. They have their roots in Italian football (*Tifoso* = supporter) and emerged in the 1960s and 1970s in tandem with the rise of the ultras culture. Some of the displays are now quite stunning and indicate that ultras, not just those in Rayo, like to be seen as well as heard. There can be a certain level of elevated self-importance and self-dramatisation in ultra culture that we will investigate more in the St Pauli and Cosenza chapters, and it is understandable why some see *tifos*, and pyro, as symptomatic of a need to become the spectacle rather than just observe, an assertion that the ultras matter and their importance should not be neglected. There is something to this, and in the plainer language of the terraces and the *curva*, some ultras across the range of political persuasion are up their own arse. However, it's probably kinder and more accurate to see the *tifos* as a product of a more benign conceit, that described by Jacob Bronowski in *The Ascent of Man*:

> 'The most powerful drive in the ascent of man is his pleasure in his own skill. He loves to do what he does well, and having done it well, he loves to do it better.'

Rayo *tifos* are no longer made from toilet paper.

I can't say the same in, all honesty, for pyro; it's coloured smoke and anyone can let off a canister.

In 1997 the first '*Día contra el Racismo en los Estadios de fútbol*', now a regular event, was held. The *Bukaneros* worked with the Madrid organisation SOS Racismo and the club to turn the match against Osasuna into an event against racism. A huge banner was displayed in the stands with the following legend, 'Against racism, live football in colour', and 100 immigrants from Senegal, Morocco and some Latin American countries were invited by the club, which also reduced ticket prices by 500 pesetas for the day. For younger readers, the peseta was the currency used in Spain before the euro.

In 1997/98 the death of the *Brigadas* was confirmed and the *Bukaneros*' reign fully commenced. *'No pocos grupos se atreven a venir a Vallekas, pero los que vienen no salen excesivamente bien parados.'* 'More than a few groups dared to come to Vallekas, but it didn't turn out well for them,' according to the *Bukaneros* website. A firm is a firm.

The *Bukaneros* have been the top firm in Rayo since that time and have become one of the most widely known and respected across the country. Their position was consolidated during the reign of the Ruiz-Mateos family. Businessman José María Ruiz-Mateos was Rayo's largest shareholder between 1991 and 2011. A 'colourful' character who spent some time in prison for fraud and currency offences, he became very popular with the support, as did his wife, Teresa Rivero, who became the club's president in 1994. He ingratiated himself with the *Bukaneros* by paying for their travel expenses during a spell in the second division and employed a formal coordinator between Teresa and the *Bukaneros* who travelled with the group for away games.

By 2002 the club had 11,000 season-ticket holders and in 2004 the ground was renamed the Teresa Rivero stadium. It didn't end well. The financial problems of the Ruiz-Mateos family translated into issues for the club and the fans had to make donations and buy shirts to help pay the players and other club workers. The fans ripped Teresa Rivero's letters from the stadium and the *Bukaneros* responded, inevitably, with a tifo imitating the poster of the movie *The Godfather* with the words *'La Familia'* next to a portrait of José María Ruiz-Mateos.

In 2011 Raúl Martin Presa took over as president and relations between the club and the *Bukaneros* have steadily declined to a serious level of toxicity that has come to dominate discourse about Rayo. More about the *Bukaneros* and Presa below. Next, we will talk about the much more edifying subject of watching Rayo play in Vallecas, though the second of the match reports will partly explain just why so many fans, not just the *Bukaneros*, hate Presa as much as they love the team.

Matchdays: Rayo v Celta Vigo, January 2019

We went to see Rayo play Celta Vigo in January 2019, when Rayo were in La Liga Primera. After a trip to see Picasso's *Guernica* and the amazing Goya rooms in El Prado Museo we took off down to the south-east to see a different but no less important side of Madrid culture to fill the Galeano Void.

We had a few beers and wines in Vallecas first. Madrid is much colder in January than you think, so we needed it. Vallecas certainly isn't Knightsbridge but it's not really Elephant and Castle either: I've lived in south-east London for over 30 years and can say definitely that Vallecas has an ostensibly much 'kinder and gentler' culture; even on matchday there was no menace in the air at all. And the wine was much better and a lot cheaper. We went early to the Mesón Moreno, the most popular bar with Rayo supporters. In this part of Madrid they still give you tapas with every drink. The food and the wine were pretty good, the atmosphere loud but mellow and the temptation to stay and just watch the game on the bar's television grew. To help fight this we took off for a walk around the neighbourhood, much of which has been recently redeveloped to the detriment of character. More of the old Vallecas was standing when Almodóvar shot the movie *Volver* there with Penélope Cruz in 2005, and after having seen that I must confess to being a little disappointed at the look of the place.

We realised that we had time for another glass of wine before the game began so we found a small backstreet Colombian bar with décor and lighting like a bad discotheque in 1975. The wine was not so good but *la dueña* looked like a prettier version of Halle Berry, so all thoughts of the old Vallecas and Penélope Cruz slipped quickly from my head. Let's hope that Penélope Cruz does not read this, her disappointment will be bitter.

I left that bar and *la dueña* slightly reluctantly but was glad I did. The atmosphere inside the stadium was impassioned but with none of the aggressive hatred or racist garbage that can make watching British football so dispiriting. This was partly due to the good relationship between Rayo and Celta's left-leaning fans.

We were in the section below the Celta supporters, and at half-time a group of their boys were leaning over the front row exchanging high-fives with the Rayo fans and flying the Pan-Celtic flag. We stopped for a chat: they were a thoroughly pleasant bunch of young men, who spoke good English and were looking forward to visiting Derry later on that year, a good port of call for leftist 'Pan-Celticists'.

Vigo is in Galicia and the people there see themselves as Celts, hence the name Celta Vigo. However, these guys looked 100 per cent Spanish and nothing like those of us from the pasty fringes of northern Europe. Somewhere along the way their Celtic ancestors made some good choices. Though Galicia is one of the wettest parts of Europe, so maybe not.

The game was terrific and, despite having only 39 per cent of the possession, Rayo won 4-2 with a hat-trick from Raúl de Tomás, then on loan from Real Madrid. He left for Benfica in July of that year and is now with Espanyol; he was their top scorer with 23 goals in 2020/21 as the side won promotion and he achieved his first cap for Spain in November 2021. The Stripe could really do with him now as they struggle to escape from Jimmy Sirrel's profundity, 'If ye dinnae score, ye dinnae win.'

We were lucky: great games and Rayo victories were not common in the 2018/19 season and the club fell back to the second flight. We had a few drinks after the game – you can probably detect a pattern here – and I was delighted that a couple of Rayo fans complimented my James Connolly t-shirt. This is a barrio that knows proper left-wing politics.

Rayo v Cádiz, September 2021

This was the Sunday after the Cádiz v Barcelona game, the big leftist derby I was booked to see in Cádiz before the pandemic ended those plans. I arrived in Madrid on a grey Friday afternoon and took the 30-minute walk down to Vallecas with a real sense of nostalgia. This was a little odd as it had only just been two and a half years since I first made that trip, but the pandemic had turned everything previous to it into a slightly romanticised Before Times. Times in which we were mostly happy and you didn't mind if complete strangers hugged you at football matches after a goal.

It was really good to be back in Vallecas and in a very nice apartment literally two minutes' walk from the stadium. The lady from the agency who let me in was Colombian and, of course, knew Elephant and Castle well after having lived in London for a couple of years. She recommended a couple of good restaurants; I went to the nearest, which was Arabic with no alcohol but some excellent food. I didn't recognise it at the time but that nice gentle no-booze night helped prepare me for the trials that followed.

The Queue

I'd heard in Cádiz that it could be problematic getting a ticket for Rayo these days if you weren't a season-ticket holder, and that prices and ticketing in general had been a source of tension between the president and the fans for a while. This was no shock; most things did seem to be an issue between Presa and the fans. The shock was about to happen. It was lengthy, very painful for a middle-aged man and turned me into an angry Rayo fan bereft of any pretensions of authorial objectivity.

Any remaining tickets for the match were to go on sale at 10am on Saturday. I normally turn up way too early for things, one of the many reasons why I am much better suited to travelling alone. For some reason this morning – maybe I'd carried the gentle languor of al-Andalus with me on the train from Cádiz – I decided to unbutton and had a slow breakfast at one of the many tiny cafes in Vallecas. The food was tasty and incredibly cheap, but when you live in London pretty much everywhere seems overly reasonable in price. In good spirits, I got to the ticket office just before 10am and saw an enormous queue. I cursed the loosening of the buttons.

I followed the queue around the curve of the stadium. It was peopled mostly by young men bronzed after the Spanish summer; had Nigel Farage been here he would probably have taken a picture and used it as one of his hideous anti-immigration images. The thought of the fate of Farage in Vallecas cheered me momentarily but faded as the enormity of the queue unfolded, and I'm using enormity in the correct sense here. I thought, 'To hell with this,' decided I could cover matchday just through being in Vallecas and checking out a couple of bars. So I went for my second *jamon y café* of the morning.

Knocking back the second coffee I was struck with massive guilt: I couldn't let people down; I had to see this game and I had to try to understand the experience of being a Rayo fan. I joined the queue at 10.30am. By 12.30pm there had been limited movement and I was beginning to flag. There were a few other foreigners in the queue, British, French and German, all of whom drifted away by 1pm with the realisation that this was going to be a long one. This gave me a little boost – 'This is going to be one *extrañero* that doesn't quit.' Philip Roth's line about 'the ecstasy of sanctimony' is one of the most profound in human history, though no rival to the wisdom of Jimmy Sirral.

By 1.30pm I was beginning to feel down again and hunger and other bodily needs were calling, but I realised that I had to stay, otherwise the last three hours would have been a total waste. This realisation helped me feel better until about 1.50pm when I was sure I heard a young Spanish boy telling his dad, '*Si, estan cerrando*,' – 'Yes, they are closing.' I assumed I'd misheard, my rusty Spanish impaired by too much time in the sun. But no, at 2pm there was a general disappointed-more-than-angry-sigh and around half the queue sat down and began to devour their packed lunches. I checked with the guy in front of me who confirmed with a resigned but still overly happy smile that the ticket office would close between 2pm and 4pm. '*Siesta,*' he said. Despite having thousands of people queuing outside, the club takes a *siesta*.

I sat down for the two hours and was glad that I never go anywhere without water and a very powerful mobile phone recharger. This was obviously not unexpected, most people in the queue had brought food. Some slipped home to get a bite and asked others to save their places.

The queue was resigned and quiet, I thought back to the self-righteous anger of queues I'd been in with Arsenal and Millwall fans; the quality of the packed lunch food was not the only huge contrast at work here. This queue was generally quiet and a little subdued, *madrileños* are lovely people when you get to know them, but a little reserved, a bit similar to Londoners. In Andalusia the line would have been buzzing with animated conversation. In Napoli there would have been loud denunciations of the criminals in suits. In Buenos Aires people would have become great mates by now, exchanging baby photos and inviting family members to come along to meet their new friends in the queue.

By 5.30pm I'd struck up some conversation with the young guys around me, a delightful bunch of young men in their early 20s who clearly loved the club but hated the management. Some said that this would be their last time losing their Saturday to buy tickets for this club that clearly despised them. I suspected that they had all said that before.

We got into the ground at 6pm. It's now 'we' and not 'I'. We were all angry Rayo fans. I had bonded with these guys despite them being 40 years younger than me and from a different culture. Football can be a great social glue as well as a source of tribal animosity, and the idea that people of a different culture can't get along is just drivel. I'd rather share a day in a queue with these guys than the likes of Farage. By 6.15pm I could see that there were only two people selling the tickets, one of whom looked like he remembered the 'days when it was all fields around here' and with the best will in the world was a little slow. After some advice from my new friends on the best position I emerged at 6.30pm after eight hours queueing with a ticket for Rayo v Cádiz and a huge hunger allayed by euphoria.

Being a football fan is mostly a succession of disappointments punctuated by moments of unalloyed fleeting joy. This was one of those latter moments and it lasted longer than usual. The three-minute walk from the stadium down the hill to one of the few traditional Spanish restaurants left in Vallecas was one of the best moments I have enjoyed on any of my travels. Even my arthritic right knee felt good and I glided painlessly down the road.

The restaurant wasn't quite ready to open when I got there but the staff seemed to sense my disappointment and sat me down in the corner with some beer and *tapas* until they were able to serve. I don't remember what I eventually had but I've enjoyed very few meals as much as that one.

The Match

On the Sunday of the game I met up with the great Frankie Taylor, a lefty Facebook friend from Ireland who has lived in Madrid for many years and is a big Rayo fan. There's always a risk meeting social media friends in the real world but I'm delighted to report that I got on with Frankie quickly and easily. I've done this a few times now when travelling and I've been lucky. I had a bit more luck later that day.

Vallecas was jumpin' and sunny. Cádiz and Rayo fans were mixing very cheerily in the very busy bars in the main street so we went to a square around the corner where I met Frankie's other expatriate mates, all very sound people. We stood outside a bustling bar but bought very cheap tins of beer from the local supermarket. The crack was good and I didn't even complain that much when the pyro began. Probably some residual euphoria was working here. About 20 minutes before the game I announced that I had to leave for the stadium amidst some surprise that I actually had a ticket, many people having given up on ever seeing one of those again.

Raúl Martin Presa did his best to thwart me again at the stadium. He did it to everyone but I was taking it personally.

There were two gates open for the whole crowd to get in, and I was confronted again with the enormity of the queue. As I walked angrily to the end of the line, I heard an unexpected cry of 'Stewart!' in a Spanish accent. It was my new buddies from yesterday, a stroke of luck made even greater by the fact that they were not too far from the front of the queue. They kindly asked me to join them and I very gratefully accepted.

Despite the great work of the patron saint of travelling football fans I still got in 15 minutes late, missed the first Rayo goal and discovered that my seat number didn't actually exist. The old man yesterday had maybe sensed my ageist impatience and effectively put me on the stairwell. When I asked the people in the area around me where I could sit, I was told with some bemusement, 'Wherever you can.' The seat numbers don't mean a whole lot in Vallekas.

This was a good competitive game. Leftist fraternity didn't affect anyone on the pitch nor in the stands, to be honest. There was no animosity or aggro but both sets of fans, although quite happily sitting together, were very keen on their side winning and were vocal in their criticisms of the opposition's attempt to thwart them. Elias Canetti writes about the impact of the stadium, the arena, in his *Crowds and Power* and I began to understand him here. The focus and the rules of the stadium have also had an influence on the growing enmity between Liverpool and Everton fans, formerly allies as we'll see in the Liverpool chapter later on.

Cádiz equalised after 25 minutes and the game became even more competitive. Falcao scored for Rayo just before half-time and though Cádiz kept pressing Rayo just looked that little bit too good – no big tactical differences, Rayo just had better players. One of those better players, Isi Palazon, scored a fine deciding goal just before the end of normal time by cutting in from the right and putting a great left-foot shot in the top corner, strangely reminding me of a goal I saw Charlton's Derek Hales score against Fulham in 1976, a reference that will please my Charlton-supporting co-writer.

The game ended with a convincing 3-1 victory to Rayo and much rejoicing from the crowd of 5,903. Yes, all that drama in getting in a crowd of less than 6,000. Attendances were still restricted due to Covid at the time, but Rayo are still getting crowds under 10,000.

Ponce, the Cádiz captain, made a point of applauding the Rayo fans at the end and was received warmly, but this was the only time in the stadium that you felt that you were watching a match between brothers, the *sangre gaditana en vena vallecana* derby. I went back to find Frankie and his friends drinking in the Mesón Moreno on Vallecas' main drag. It had been a quite different story in the bars around the ground, apparently, with lots of lefty bonhomie and sympathy for the defeated *gaditanas*. One of Frankie's Irish mates had even given his last bit of hashish to a disappointed Cádiz fan as a show of solidarity. I left early and headed back to my now favourite Spanish restaurant in Vallecas. Frankie and his mates were great and I look forward to seeing them again in Vallecas, but hell they were drunk and it's no fun when you're the only sober one.

¡Presa Vete Ya!

¡Presa vete ya! roughly translates as 'Presa, get out now!' and was the most commonly heard and most passionately sung chant in Vallecas that afternoon. The anger was understandable: that the fans were prepared to stand in line for eight hours and longer for a ticket demonstrates their love of the team, that they are forced to do so unveils the contempt in which they are held by the club's management. After I bought my ticket on Saturday there was still a huge queue behind me. The ticket office closed at 8pm and the police were called in case there were problems with the thousands of people who had waited in line for a day but couldn't get a ticket. An absolute disgrace.

The story of Rayo right now is dominated by the tensions between Presa and the fanbase, particularly the *Bukaneros*. The following episodes give an insight into why team captain Oscar Trejo reportedly said, 'If I were a fan, I would shout and swear because it's the only way to open eyes and heat ears – this is a place where it's problem after problem.' The much-respected Argentinian captain also said in an interview in October 2021 shortly after the Cádiz game, 'The fans do not deserve the treatment they are getting.'

The Zozulya Affair

In January 2017, the club signed Ukrainian forward Roman Zozulya on loan from Real Betis.

Zozulya was alleged to have hard-right sympathies which stood in direct opposition to the Vallecano support. The signing sparked outrage. On his first day of training at his new club, fans turned up with a banner reading, '*Vallekas no es lugar para Nazis*' – 'Vallekas is not the place for Nazis.'

The club subsequently cancelled his contract and Zozulya returned to Betis. Zozulya rejected the allegations against him and still does; he was supported by many at the time, including ESPN, which ran an aggressive defence of him.

However, the *Bukaneros* did a proper investigative job on Zozulya and published the evidence in an online document that included: his support for the Neo-Nazi Azov Battalion, a Ukrainian National Guard regiment; him holding up the badge of the Dnipro White Boys, a right-wing football firm; pictures of him posing next to a scarf of Stefan Bandera, a Ukrainian nationalist who collaborated with the Nazis, helping to kill over one million Ukrainian Jews, and, of course, the notorious photo of him posing in front of a basketball scoreboard reading 14-88. Eighty-eight represents Heil Hitler, H being the eighth letter of the alphabet, and the 14 represents the 14 words beloved of white nationalists from the slogan, 'We must secure the existence of our people and a future for white children.' In the photo he is also wearing a basketball shirt with the number 18 on the front, the first letter of the alphabet is A, the eighth is H. An unsavoury picture should be emerging now.

Zozulya signed for Albacete shortly afterwards and returned to Vallecas for a game against Rayo in December 2019. Unsurprisingly, the Rayo fans issued abuse at Zozulya continually and referred to him as a 'Fucking Nazi'. What was surprising was that the game was called off at half-time because of this chanting. Calling a Nazi a Nazi gets a game called off in Europe, but not the incessant racist abuse at black players? Another topic, another book.

'With the support of Rayo Vallecano, Albacete and La Liga the referee has suspended the game in Vallecas,' Albacete said in a short statement. 'This decision was taken with one objective, which is to safeguard the values of our competition and the sport which we all love.'

Presa condemned the chants directed at Zozulya and said, 'Tonight is a very sad night for Rayo and for sport. We want to categorically condemn the insults that a section of the fans directed towards an opposition player. Football should be about unity not separation. I spoke to Zozulya and gave him a hug because he is a human being and he deserves respect.'

Nazis deserve respect? Many would take exception to that, not just the *Bukaneros*.

Ukraine's President Zelensky also supported Zozulya throughout, describing him as 'not only a cool football player but a true patriot'.

Zozulya: The Postscript

Presa invited two members of Vox, the racist right-wing party that has unfortunately achieved some traction in Spain in recent years, to watch Rayo v Albacete on 26 April 2021. This match was probably chosen carefully in order to maximise antagonism. Presa actually posed for a photo with the Vox representatives in which one held a Rayo shirt and the other a scarf. He said, 'I thought it was good because Rayo is a team open to everyone and Vallecas is a neighbourhood that welcomes all people, educated and peaceful.' Vox do not welcome all people and this was a straightforward provocation by Presa.

Particularly so after Vox had just three weeks earlier opened their regional election campaign with a rally in the Plaza del Nica in Vallecas, known locally as Red Square. This was a direct act of provocation that did, of course, end in violence as the *Bukaneros* and others from the barrio came out to let people know that fascists were not welcome.

The day after the Albacete game, 50 *Bukaneros* turned up in Hazmat gear to symbolically cleanse the stadium after it had been soiled by the visit.

The Boycott

The *Bukaneros* boycotted the first eight games of the 2019/20 season due to excessive price increases for season tickets. On several occasions, players and the coach Paco Jémez had called for their return, sometimes expressing their understanding of the reasons for their anger against Presa. Eight games is a respectable hold-out but such is the call of the stadium and the addiction to the game, fan boycotts are seldom effective.

Shirtless in Vallekas

The appointment of the odious Carlos Santiso as women's coach, see below, further soured relations between the club and the supporters. Not only the *Bukaneros* were angry.

To avoid the inevitable demonstrations at the 2 February Copa del Rey quarter-final game against Mallorca at Vallecas, Presa prohibited entry to all those carrying anything identified with the *Bukaneros* . As the game started, one of the biggest for Rayo since the UEFA cup run, the *Bukaneros* were not there. Security staff were stopping anyone entering with any flags, scarves or shirts that referenced them. After about 25 minutes, the *Bukaneros'* end began to fill, looking a little like a Newcastle United end as many fans entered the ground shirtless in order to see their team. February nights in Madrid are not warm so fair play to the guys.

'*Bukaneros si, Presa no*' was a common cry across the stadium that night. As Robbie Dunne, author of the excellent *Working-Class Heroes: The Story of Rayo Vallecano, Madrid's Forgotten Team*, says, 'It's easy to romanticise Rayo and Vallecas, to assume they are a homogeneous whole fighting the good fight. The truth is there are fans in the stands on a Saturday who couldn't care less about the politics. There are fans who might have even welcomed the leader of Vox into the stadium,' but that night the stadium was behind the *Bukaneros*. The Rayo Vallecano Peñas Association, an umbrella organisation of Rayo groupings was forceful in its statement:

'At the time we opposed the signing of a Nazi, today we do so in the face of a degenerate chauvinist. Neither the ideas of one nor the actions of the other represent the values of the Stripe in any way, so we hope that he will be dismissed and not further tarnish the name of our club'.

Solidarity can arise partly through a shared suffering, for the club's biggest game for 20 years the Rayo management released no ticket information until two days prior to the match. Tickets were still only available if you bought them in person at the stadium and the queues began at 5am on the first day of their availability.

Rayo won and went through to the semi-finals of the competition, a great achievement for what remains a small neighbourhood club despite its growing international reputation. But all was overshadowed by the poisonous relationship between the club's management and its support.

* * *

Rayo Vallecano Femenino
Vincent Raison

On 6 November 2021, the ref's whistle blew to signify the start of the *Primera División* match between Real Madrid Femenino and Rayo Vallecano Femenino at the Alfredo Di Stéfano Stadium. Rayo kicked off, passing the ball backwards to the edge of the centre circle. Then an extraordinary thing happened. All of Rayo's players stood still in silent, stationary protest at the working conditions they have endured at the hands of the club's management. All 11 Real Madrid players did the same in support. After 30 strange seconds, the game continued and the fans applauded.

We have already seen how the club's contempt for their own fans beggars belief, but their treatment of the women's team is even more shocking.

This was not the first attempt to highlight Rayo Femenino's plight either. In August, they held a press conference along with AFE – the Association of Spanish Footballers – to bring to the public's attention a number of issues that needed to be addressed: the players had not been registered with social security, which is a legal requirement; they had no access to the club's medical services, gym, physiotherapists, or equipment; they were not allowed to use the club car park like the men; they had insufficient Covid testing and they were unable to secure a meeting with the club's president to resolve the situation.

Óscar Trejo and Mario Suárez from the men's team expressed their support and said they and the rest of the players would have attended the press conference if they hadn't been training.

Days after the Real game, the club was reported to the government after their defender Camila Sáez suffered a clash of heads in a match against Athletic Bilbao and the club had no doctor to treat her. Bilbao's medic had to treat both players before Sáez's injury forced her off. It suggests a dangerous level of cost-cutting by the club and reflects Raúl Martin Presa's intention to close the women's section ever since his arrival in 2011. Fans protested his decision sufficiently to reverse it at the time, but the annual erosion of support from the club continues to endanger the women's team's existence.

Not surprisingly, the demoralised team suffered on the pitch. Bottom of the table, they were relegated in the 2021/22 season. Yet when Presa took over, he inherited the best women's team in Spanish football.

Rayo Vallecano Femenino began when the club absorbed a local women's club, CD El Buen Retiro, in 2000. Three years later, they won promotion to the top flight where they remained until 2022's relegation ever since. In 2008, they won the Copa de la Reina and narrowly missed out on a league and cup double, coming second to Levante on goal difference. The following year they ran away with the Superliga Femenino, losing just one of their 30 matches to win the title and qualify for the Champions League.

Despite opposition to the move, the league changed its format to three regional divisions that culminated in a play-off final. In the next two years, Rayo beat Espanyol in both those two-legged finals to complete three consecutive titles. The winning goal in that 2011 showpiece was scored by a brilliant 20-year-old, Jennifer Hermoso, who ended up scoring 50 goals in 90 games for Rayo. Now with Barcelona, Jenni is the record goalscorer for both Spain and Barça.

But then Presa took over the champions and it's been downhill ever since. It used to be hard to tell whether the club's administration is actively malicious towards the women's team and the fans, or simply incompetent, but if you read on, I will spell it out. What is clear is that their very successful women's team is being constantly disrespected by the club. Despite this, the players exhibit a deep feeling for Vallecas and whatever their trials on the pitch this season, their biggest problem is the club itself, which Rayistas believe contradicts the social values of Rayo Vallecano.

To add unbelievable insult to injury, the club hired a new coach for Rayo Femenino who had lost his previous job at the club after a leaked recording revealed him telling staff that raping a girl together would be the best way to build team spirit.

Carlos Santiso said, 'We need to grab a girl, but overage so we don't get ourselves into trouble, and to *cargarnosla* – [there is no direct translation but broadly means to "screw her"] there all together. That's what really brings a staff, a team together. Look at the Arandina lot.'

Three players from third division Arandina CF were jailed for 38 years each for the gang-rape of a 15-year-old girl in 2017.

It is hard to imagine a candidate less suited to coaching Rayo Vallecano Femenino. It would appear to be a deliberate attempt to insult women, Rayo fans and players alike. To ruin female football in Vallecas. Raúl Martín Presa, you don't deserve Rayo Vallecano and the club and its supporters deserve better than you.

* * *

Final Thoughts

I love Rayo as a team and Vallecas as an area. When I return to Madrid I won't think of staying anywhere else. However, I don't think I have too many illusions about the *Bukaneros*. Like any ultra groups of any political persuasion they contain people that like and pursue violence for its own sake, there are tendencies to elevate their own importance, and some of them would probably think that they should be running the club rather than the people that own it, irrespective of who those owners are.

That being said, they are on the side of decency and inclusivity and I'm glad that there are people like them around, particularly given the existence of groups like Vox and the EDL. Whilst I suspect that the *Bukaneros* would find a reason to pick a fight with anyone in charge of Rayo – they are classic malcontents and perform a valuable role as such – the vehemence of their opposition to Presa and his management is wholly understandable. And yes, they could probably do a better job than him. Like all Rayo fans, I look forward to the party when he finally leaves. Let's hope he's not in charge of the ticketing.

The *Bukaneros* hate '*fútbol de negocios*', business football, nearly as much as they do Nazis. The thing is, as Robbie Dunne says, Presa can't even get the business side of it right. In fact, he's terrible at it. The infrastructure is grim, there is no clear branding or merchandising strategy, relations with the fans are abysmal and there is no attempt to leverage and enhance the club's growing international reputation through an English Twitter account, for example.

St Pauli is a club whose example could show the way to Rayo, though there would doubtless be serious execrations about '*fútbol de negocios*' from the *Bukaneros* if that were the path to be followed.

St Pauli

Founded:	1910
Stadium:	Millerntor-Stadion
Capacity:	29,546
Nicknames:	*Freibeuter der Liga* (League Buccaneers or Pirates)
Ultras:	*Ultra Sankt Pauli* and many others

– STEWART McGILL –

FC ST Pauli has become the top left-wing club, a powerful symbol of anti-fascism, anti-sexism, resistance to racism, grassroots left-wing politics, and extending a hand to refugees rather than demonising them. As politics has grown more contentious and issues of identity, race, immigration and inequality have forced more divisions across Western societies and the far-right have grown to cast a longer and darker shadow, support for St Pauli has grown exponentially in Germany and internationally. Whether you like them or not, and plenty don't, St Pauli matter.

I first read about St Pauli in the late 1980s in *When Saturday Comes* (WSC), the UK football magazine. The article spoke about the club's growing 'bohemian', punk and anti-establishment fanbase reflecting the changing nature of the St Pauli neighbourhood. The crowds were small then, getting a ticket as a visiting fan did not require serious money, friends on the inside, or securing a publishing deal to write about the world's top left-wing football clubs.

WSC did mention that the football was not very good but the politics were cool, something that has been almost obligatory in any article about St Pauli since the club gained international recognition. However, in season 2021/22 St Pauli had a very good team, were challenging for promotion throughout the season and just missed by a few points. This is to be welcomed, as the club president Oke Göttlich told my colleague Vince Raison (see below), he wants the club to be successful, he wants to show that the model can work. As St Pauli has become a global brand and a very successful purveyor of merchandise there have, of course, been cries of 'betrayal' and accusations of souls being lost. All of which is understandable and may express a kind of truth, but St Pauli are qualitatively different from the vast majority of European clubs including those that we cover in this volume, maybe with the exception of Red Star. The fact that the management of both clubs talked to Vince indicates the difference. By no means everything is perfect and by no means is every St Pauli fan a secular leftist saint: plenty suffer the ultra trait of taking themselves way too seriously, but you'd need a determinedly righteous heart not to fall a little bit in love with the team and its city.

St Pauli: The Neighbourhood

Like its football team, the area punches well above its weight in terms of reputation. The population was estimated at just over 22,000 in 2019, of whom 26 per cent are classed as 'non-German'. The median age is 42, younger than that of Germany as a whole, 46 years, but still indicative of the fact that Germany is an ageing country. St Pauli is a bohemian inner-city barrio with a high immigration percentage but its median age is still higher than that of the UK's 40.5 years and America's 38 years. For some perspective, Nigeria's median age is 18 and Ghana's is 21. Demographics are ignored when people talk about the future, as is football when historians talk about the past.

St Pauli's population has been in a steady decline for some years, unlike that of Hamburg, the city's population dipped to 1.7 million in 2000 but has risen to around 1.8 million today, primarily because of the growth of technology-related employment.

In the 2020 Hamburg state elections, St Pauli voted 36 per cent Green and 30 per cent for Die Linke, The Left, the most left-wing party of the six represented in the Bundestag. Die Linke only polled 4.9 per cent in the 2021 election; its support in St Pauli is unusually high. Hamburg as a whole is a town that prides itself on being a little different. Many people told us of the city's self-image as a liberal, tolerant oasis contrasting with much of Germany, seeing itself as more akin to a place like London than some of Germany's less inclusive cities. The Christian Democrats received 3 per cent in St Pauli and the Neo Nazi AFD 2.4 per cent. Unfortunately every village has more than one.

St Pauli is of course famous for The Beatles, the Reeperbahn and prostitution, of which much more later.

St Pauli: The Football

The club began its existence in 1899 as a loose, informal group of football enthusiasts in the St Pauli area. Officially founded in 1910, they didn't play as a separate St Pauli football team until 1924 and played with no real distinction in various low-level leagues until the end of World War II.

Since the war, the club has also had a pretty undistinguished footballing history, spent mostly in the German second tier. The limited highlights included a win against Bayern Munich, the then reigning world club champions, in the 2001/02 season, plus a few wins against the hated local rivals Hamburger SV, historically by far the biggest club in the city. Despite the win against Bayern in 2002, the club was relegated that season and the year afterwards they fell to the third flight of German football.

St Pauli were in real financial trouble and had to raise funds with some urgency. They printed t-shirts with the club's crest surrounded by the word *Retter* (Saviour) that sold 140,000 in six weeks and organised a lucrative benefit game against Bayern Munich. Fair play to Bayern for taking part, particularly after the win in 2002 led to the printing of the very popular *Weltpokalsiegerbesieger* ('World Club Champion Beaters') t-shirts just to rub it in. The City of Hamburg also bought the club's Centre for Young Excellence training facility for €720,000.

A good run to the semi-finals of the German Cup in the 2005/06 season helped consolidate the club's improving financial position. They were knocked out in the semi-finals by a Bayern Munich team not playing for charity.

Why such a concerted effort to rescue a not very successful club from a small neighbourhood? By this time St Pauli had become a *Kult*. In the 1980s more and more alternative people, left-wingers and squatters moved to the St Pauli area, often people that had lost their jobs working in the harbour. They started going to football and they decided to act inside the stadium as they did outside, which meant not accepting any racism or right-wing hooliganism. This was the start of the transformation of St Pauli FC and the development of the current vibe.

During the 1980s and 1990s, right-wing hooliganism linked to neo-Nazism was threatening football right across Europe, but St Pauli fans took a stance that has developed into part of the club's *raison d'être* and ethos: they became the first team in Germany to officially ban right-wing nationalist activities and displays within the ground.

During those decades support grew considerably. Many of the new fans came from Hamburger SV, shocking for those of us born into a football culture that views changing your club as not just taboo but beyond any pale marking out the limits of acceptable human behaviour. Particularly if it's to your city rivals. Personally, I know more than a few left-wing Rangers fans that hate the sectarianism and right-wing politics that afflict some of the support but there is no way they would defect and start cheering for Celtic: the call of the tribe is too strong.

But in the 1980s, as right-wing extremists began to take over football terraces across Germany, including at the Volksparkstadion, the stadium of Hamburger SV, many fans began to turn their backs and look for an alternative. They found it at the Millerntor.

'They say that you can never change your football club, but in Hamburg in the 1980s that was different,' explains Jorg Marwedel, a Hamburg-born author and journalist with Germany's *Suddeutsche*

Zeitung. 'I grew up an SV supporter, but the whole situation with the neo-Nazis became too much for me, and I wasn't the only one.'

Currently there are no openly right-wing or fascist groups to be found on the terraces at the Millerntor, in stark contrast to other German clubs who have suffered real problems with neo-Nazis, including SV Hamburger.

Matchdays
St Pauli v Duisburg, December 2017

Vince and I first visited St Pauli in December 2017 to see them play against Duisburg. Duisburg is a tough industrial place in the Ruhr and surprisingly also a port city, the world's largest inland port with 21 docks and 40km of wharf.

I was hanging outside while Vince succumbed to the seductive merchandising skills of the world's biggest left-wing club. A guy coming out of the shop noticed my Celtic shirt and scarf and came over for a chat. This was Sonny, whom we mentioned in the introduction. Sonny has now become a much-valued friend and was very important to how this project developed. Much of what follows could not have been written without him.

After several beers and Mexicanas – tequila and tomato juice hotly spiced to take on the Baltic cold – Sonny took us into the stadium and gave us a wee tour before we took our places standing in the St Pauli south curve, or *Südtribüne*.

The crack was 90 (the best crack), like British football in the 1970s but better: all the great feeling of being at one with a unified collective, expressed through the singing, the chanting, the synchronised jumping up and down with arms interlocked; all that without the underlying threat of violence, the racist garbage, the songs mocking fans from the north for being unemployed, the homophobia and all the other nonsense that keeps people away from mainstream British football.

If you're a leftist football fan then there is an element of nirvana about St Pauli, particularly on your first visit after a few Mexicanas, most of which you haven't had to pay for.

The game itself was a 2-2 draw, pretty dire stuff, but St Pauli certainly felt then that it wasn't about the football; it was all about the party, and the celebration of an inclusive anti-racist, anti-fascist and anti-authoritarian counterculture.

St Pauli v Hamburger SV, March 2019

This was the first Hamburg derby for many years. Sonny did a great job getting tickets for us but on the eve of the game my son was taken ill, so I could not attend. Vince went by himself and didn't have the best of football times, to be honest.

On the way to the game, he had a disquieting run-in with some St Pauli supporters. He took a picture of the ground and some of the people going to the match and was surrounded by an angry bunch of St Pauli fans demanding aggressively that he delete the photos. He was with Sonny who calmed the situation down and Vince did delete the photos, but the reaction of the fans seemed absurd, paranoid, and self-dramatising. Sonny explained later that this excessive caution derived from a series of problems with a police force that was seen as hostile to St Pauli and they may even have thought that Vince was an undercover cop. The reaction still seemed excessive and posing as a Charlton fan in his early 60s would be seen by many as an over-elaborate cover for Vince, but Sonny's explanation helped put the incident in some context.

St Pauli lost the game 4-0. The pyro merchants put on a half-time display at both ends: the *Südtribüne*'s was so big it held up the start of the second half. The good thing about the day was the extraordinary turnout of international St Pauli fans, people were there from Glasgow, Belfast, Mexico, Madrid, Marseilles, Livorno, the Netherlands, the United States, Turkey and elsewhere.

St Pauli v Hansa Rostock, September 2021

By the time of this match we had signed the book deal and watching this grudge game was a formal part of the research. Sonny was on the case and made sure that this was a very organised visit with appointments planned from pretty much the moment we got off the plane. We do not perpetuate facile national stereotypes, but this level of detailed and efficient planning was unique on our travels.

The *Fanladen*

First we met Julian from the *Fanladen*, not long after we landed in Hamburg. *Fanladen* literally means 'fan shop', but it's about so much more than that. Its purpose and its self-image are nicely encapsulated on its website:

> 'More than 30 years ago active FC St. Pauli supporters founded and organised the Fan-Project St. Pauli which is situated in the *Fanladen* St. Pauli at the *Heiligengeistfeld/* middle of *Gegengerade*-Stand of the Millerntor-Stadium. The *Fanladen* team is responsible for taking care of the fan scene and the Fanladen is the key coordination center and one of the central meeting points for the fans as well as the home of many fan-organisations (e.g. board of registered supporters clubs, anti-repression group) and fanzines. It offers special assistance to local and international supporters and visitors that want to get in touch and visit an FC St Pauli match.
>
> 'The *Fanladen* works independently and is not owned by or part of the club, which means that the *Fanladen* can represent the fans without being under pressure of commercial or political needs of the club. Despite being independent, the representatives and employees of the *Fanladen* are members of different committees and panels of the club in order to take care of the fans' interests. This close cooperation between the independent *Fanladen* and the club is one of the key structures making FC St. Pauli different from other clubs.'

The *Fanladen* may literally mean 'fan shop', but it's much more than that; it's an important part of the club and its self-image. Its representatives see it as a breeding ground for a new fan culture in Germany and a means of giving a voice to regular fans – the 'ragtag' as the English translation of the site calls them.

We enjoyed a long chat with Julian, a very committed guy who sees himself primarily as a social worker. People get emotional about football, so I'm not surprised that Julian sees himself as such.

There are always going to be tensions between the people who run any club and the supporters and the *Fanladen* provides a focus for communication among the major players. The fans may not agree with everything but decisions are not just delivered with lofty fiat by remote directors from their tax havens as is all too often the case in the UK. To a certain extent German ownership rules for football clubs militate against this, but the St Pauli *Fanladen*, its importance to the structure of the club and its ethos, represent a serious point of departure for how football clubs can be run. To make it possible, the will has to be there at the top of the club and as Julian reminded us, several St Pauli board members came from the fan scene that blossomed from the 1980s onwards. Those board members have not forgotten where they came from and that's one of the many things that makes St Pauli very different.

The Museum

Next, we were given a tour of the very impressive club museum that provides a nice balance of coverage of the football and the politics. 'A club like no other deserves a museum like no other' is the museum's motto. The Scotsman's Prayer contains the line 'Lord, give us a good conceit of ourselves' and in this respect some could say that any similar St Pauli prayers have been truly answered. However, St Pauli do have a lot to be proud of and the museum and its motto reflect that pride.

Our guide Sönke Goldbeck took us expertly through the museum with the usual perfect English. The story of both the club and the economic and social conflicts in the area are told vividly through photos and exhibits. The importance of the squatters' movement is emphasised, in particular the battles around the Hafenstraße occupation, a long-running conflict that expressed and perpetuated St Pauli's reputation as a centre for left-wing social movements and opposition to gentrification. Aside from any accusations relating to the Scotsman's Prayer, this is truly a football museum like no other for a club that is like no other.

Sven Brux

We then met the redoubtable Sven Brux. Sven was actually born in Cologne, where he was beaten up for being a punk. Like many, he found an oasis of tolerance in the St Pauli neighbourhood after having been sent there to do his national service in 1985. He got involved with the club, became a major figure in the fanzine and has worked for St Pauli since 1989, he is now head of security. There was a group training in Mixed Martial Arts (MMA) next door to us which brought a wry smile to Sven's face. Like everyone else at the club, Sven is very proud of the phenomenon that St Pauli has become but, a little like many of us who have been around for a while, he exudes a sense of restrained nostalgia for how things were and an amused detachment at how things have evolved.

He said that the nature of fans has changed considerably since the 1980s and even into the 1990s. The fans were more working-class in those days, many of whom laboured on the harbour in contrast to the 'fucking students' that dominate the stadium today. He said it with a smile on his face that connoted irony and even affection for the 'fucking students', but we knew what he meant. It's a generalisation but with an element of truth, there is a definite middle-class feel about the St Pauli fanbase, which you certainly don't get in Cádiz or Vallecas. There is nothing wrong with being middle-class, not at all, but I think Sven and I share a certain longing for the day when the terraces were a very working-class affair with any evidence of bourgeois manners or received pronunciation treated with suspicion.

We would also agree that by no means was everything better back in the day. He said that there was no Nazism in the fanbase of those days, but a level of racism derived from working-class attitudes was not unusual.

(Recent research in the UK has actually shown that working-class people are actually less bigoted than middle-income earners. The same is probably true in Germany as well so it's interesting how the narrative of the bigoted working-class has become so pervasive, even among the political left: the answer is probably to be found in Gramsci's theory of bourgeois hegemony somewhere.)

There were fan groupings that did not want to change, such as St Pauli United who actually worked with SV hooligans to attack a St Pauli bar after a match. Groups like these were forced out as the ethos of the club evolved, reflecting changes in the neighbourhood and the migration of fans from SV to escape the growing Nazi problem there.

The New Kids St Pauli fan group was also forced out in recent years, not because of any right-wing tendencies, but because they were too violent. Sven is proud of the fact that no St Pauli fan has a nationwide ban; though not everyone is a Sankt, as we will see later. He is also very proud of the fact that he knew the people who now run the club as kids on the fan scene back in the 1980s and 1990s and that they have kept their values. Sven likes that St Pauli is not a club for glory hunters and that does not wish to compromise its values through changing the name of the stadium to that of a sponsor, for example; he also points out the fact there is very little advertising at the Millerntor. You get the feeling that the compromises that Sven despises will never take place as long as he is there: he's a link with the past, a talisman, a symbol and a man with a bit of an edge. One Hamburger SV manager said that St Pauli would never enjoy any success as long as Sven is there: we can only hope those words come back one day to haunt Hamburg's 'other team'.

Sven also spoke with pride about the work that the club does in the community and its strong, progressive voice in local politics. They will never forget how the neighbourhood saved the club in 2003 and will always try to put something back into the locale.

St Pauli are also at the forefront of the movement to welcome refugees in Germany. They are associated with a refugee team in the city, FC Lampedusa St Pauli, named after the Italian island on which the EU fund a detention centre from which around 300 West African refugees arrived in Hamburg in 2012. To further their protest at the immediate attempts of the local government to deport them the refugees turned to St Pauli with a simple message: 'Help us set up a team to provide a safe environment and raise awareness for the refugees of Hamburg.' The club was more than happy to oblige. St Pauli also regularly give away tickets to refugee clubs and local youth movements.

We talked a little about the relationship with Celtic, something that Sven was crucial in establishing. He told us a couple of tales and about the refusal of some Celtic fans visiting Hamburg to heed his warnings about the nature of the various clip joints that pockmark the city.

The Celtic and St Pauli relationship goes back to 1991, when Sven and other St Pauli fans did a tour across Europe and wrote of their experiences in the St Pauli fanzine. 'It started with a first visit in 1991 to Glasgow as part of our tour of going to different fanzine editors in Britain. We wrote an article about the trip and our experiences and after it was published more and more St Pauli fans got interested in Celtic FC and its supporters. Fan groups started going to Scotland and vice versa to Germany and European matches.'

The relationship grew and blossomed when Celtic played Hamburger SV in the Europa League in 2009. SV have long had a relationship with the other club in Glasgow that has had a strong catalytic impact on the Celtic and St Pauli romance, though the romance is going through a bit of a rocky patch at the moment.

Celtic's Green Brigades are resolutely pro-Palestinian and like to fly their flag. St Pauli fans are wary of nationalism and the display of any national emblem inside the ground is banned. Some mutual understanding is required to resolve this dispute: I write as a pro-Palestinian activist but can understand why

Germans do not want to appear to be too vehemently anti-Israel. Sonny is pro-Israel, I'm not, but he remains a good man and I respect his views and value his friendship. This kind of nuance and compromise is inimical to the ultra mindset so the dispute is unlikely to fade away.

We begin to talk about the game against Hansa Rostock. Sonny mentioned the unique St Pauli tradition of playing the song of every visiting club to St Pauli. 'Not against fucking Hansa,' replied Sven with no little lack of compromise in his voice. St Pauli and Hansa have history. The game the following day was going to be interesting.

The Match

Hansa won the last-ever season of the DDR championship in 1990/91 and along with Dynamo Dresden were admitted to the Bundesliga. Both the team and the city have suffered since: the high standard of the football compared to the DDR saw the team fall quickly down the divisions; economically Hansa's port had a privileged position in the DDR and did rather well, in the new federal republic it faced stiff competition from other ports and the city has struggled ever since with unemployment and economic precarity.

Some people in Rostock began to look for a scapegoat. It was against this background that the notorious riots of August 1992 took place, in which right-wingers attacked a number of centres housing immigrants from Vietnam and Romania, and a xenophobic culture developed among some Rostock people. Hansa's story makes for a depressing microcosm of what has happened across much of the old DDR since unification.

St Pauli's first match against Hansa took place around this time. Hansa's fans did not take to the left-wing internationalist ethos of St Pauli, already established by that time, and there were several violent incidents. Things have not improved over the decades and it is clear that this is a huge game for St Pauli fans, the hatred of Hansa being even greater than that for SV.

Just in the interests of balance, the Rostock Landkreis Rostock II constituency was held by the Social Democratic Party (SPD) from its creation in 1990 until 2009. In 2009, it was won by Steffen Bockhahn of Die Linke, the left-wing party. The Christian Democrats took it in 2013 but the SPD got it back in the 2021 election. Not everyone in Rostock is a fascist.

Nobody from Rostock was due to be at the game. The fan groups had initiated a boycott in protest at the city of Hamburg's strict laws about the need for a 'green pass', proof of Covid vaccination, before anyone could get into anywhere, including football stadiums. The police still turned out in massive force and formed grim-faced phalanxes all over the neighbourhood.

We kicked off by visiting the Shebeen. People were demonstrably nervous about the game, not so much about the potential of violence, but about the result. Vince and I left for the game a little earlier than we would usually do. Sven had very kindly given us press passes, so, although the Shebeen's Mexicanas are one of the best things in human history, the siren-like allure of free drinks dragged us away. The press and VIP area was good and for the first time in my football-watching career I prepared for the game with a few Proseccos. However, we have men-of-the-people credentials to maintain, so we headed down to the *Südtribüne* about 30 minutes before kick-off, but had the Prosecco been a little bit better, who knows?

We joined Sonny near the Ramba Zamba group at their place in the centre of the *Tribüne* near the fence. Sonny gave us the usual warnings about pyro, not taking photos or films. He introduced me to an Irish guy, Kevin, who had a tattoo of the St Pauli skyline covering most of his large forearm. Kevin came on a trip to St Pauli about 20 years earlier, liked the vibe, got a job in a bar, decided to stay for a while, settled down and started a family. Kevin seemed as unimpressed as I was with the statutory pyro display before the match. After this bonding I spent a fair bit of the next couple of hours chatting to him; we discovered in the middle of the second half that both our fathers had been asked to join the Provisional

IRA by the same man. This is a strange and small little planet. Both turned the Provos down. I'm not sure about Kevin's, but my father moved away from the North of Ireland for a little while to avoid any 'misunderstandings'.

The game itself was an easy victory for St Pauli. They were two up after 18 minutes, the second goal being scored by the brilliant Daniel-Kofi Kyereh, the Ghanian international and easily the best player on the pitch. The goals were treated with absolute delight accompanied with much hugging amongst strangers. In the time of Covid when we had grown used to keeping even close friends at a distance, this was warmly redolent of the Before Times.

Kevin was still not going to relax, like me he was tormented by the slightly odd football cliché about a 2-0 lead being the most dangerous score. On the hour St Pauli went 3-0 up and after the obligatory round of hugs Kevin turned to me and said, 'St Pauli 3, Fascists 0.' He was a much less tense individual now.

St Pauli scored one more against a really bad Hansa Rostock outfit, you could almost feel sorry for the small number of Hansa fans that had made it into the ground. But not quite.

At the end of the game the TV company made the odd decision of interviewing some of the defeated Hansa players just by the *Südtribüne*. Inevitably this was accompanied by a lot of boos and chants in English of 'Who the fuck is Hansa Rostock? Hey! Hey!' and thrown paper cups. My mate Kevin, who was not impressed by this at all, exclaimed that they shouldn't be doing this and walked off home angrily. I think Kevin felt that St Pauli fans should be better than this, but football often fails to bring out the best in people, particularly when leavened by real political hatred.

The St Pauli fans sang in their strange mix of English, German and other languages all the way through the game and much organised and choreographed fun was had by all. Towards the end of the first half I took my phone out with the intent of sneaking a wee photo of the pitch through the railings. Some guy behind me wearing a porkpie hat tapped me on the shoulder and told me to watch the game rather than look at my phone. I took the photo.

Surely the anti-authoritarian ethos of St Pauli would demand that I did. Later in the second half the girl behind me, who was very small and couldn't really have seen much of the match, reminded me of my duty to raise both my arms when I was a little slow to do so as part of a group chant. Serious and demanding business this ultra stuff.

We went for a beer and a few Mexicanas afterwards in the Shebeen. Despite the great win there was a sizable group of young men standing around quietly looking ready for a row. Most had small red scarves on, indicating their militancy and willingness to fight for the club. Outside the Shebeen I had a good chat with one of the red scarves who was actually pretty jovial, again with humblingly great English and was very interested in the book. I liked the guy, though was a little disappointed later when he invited me to 'join the party', that is take some cocaine in a quiet place with his mate. Given the trail of dead bodies and misery inflicted by the cocaine trade across the countries associated with its production and distribution, I am not tolerant of its usage. I remember thinking, 'This isn't very left-wing,' echoing the words of a guy from Barcelona we had met the previous night who joined us on an unexpected tour of the deeply unpleasant red-light district.

Hamburg Vice

The night before the match, and after our meeting with Sven, we had a great meal in a famous Hamburg restaurant, The Old Commercial Room, with Sonny and his mate Bastian. We then took off to a very interesting bar with a mixture of young and old people dancing together to traditional-sounding German music. Here we met the guy from Barcelona, a friend of Bastian's.

In the interests of showing us the fullness of Hamburg's culture, we were taken down to the Reeperbahn via a street prohibited to women and men under 18, Herbertstraße. A 6ft-high metal gate at the entrance of the street declares, 'Entry for men under 18 and women prohibited.' The street was lined with girls in lingerie in shop windows, banging on the inside of the windows aggressively, looking for business.

We then went to the *Zur Ritze* bar, which loosely translates as 'To the Crack', with naked spread female legs drawn either side of the door. I assume that you're getting the subtle picture. This is a famous bar that also has a boxing gym downstairs. Bastian is a tour guide and bartender in Hamburg and knows the people who run the place, so we were able to go downstairs and check out a gym that has produced some quality fighters. Bastian then gave us an impromptu tour-guide session, telling us about the history of the pimp wars in the city and the role of the gym in those wars. He's a good guide so he told the story well, but not quite well enough to veil its wholly sordid subject matter. It was during this time that the Barcelona guy, probably sensing my discomfort, said to me in whispered bemusement, 'This isn't very left-wing, is it?' He was right.

I understand that Hamburg is a big port city and that prostitution is part of the history and culture. But it's a hideous business run by a really grim bunch of people who exploit the poverty, vulnerability and often the drug habits of the women involved, many of whom come from poor backgrounds in eastern Europe. I don't think I'm going out on too much of a leftist limb by saying that pimps are dreadful people. St Pauli's sex industry seems to have become a legitimised part of the city's tourist trade and the area did have the feel of a knocking-shop theme park, sanitised enough to give an air of respectability but still selling the basic goods to keep the punters coming.

By no means everyone in Hamburg is relaxed about the industry. On International Women's Day in 2019, Hellen Langhorst and her colleagues in FEMEN Germany, a women's rights group, painted slogans saying 'women are not goods' and broke the gate. 'The gate marks gender apartheid. The violence in prostitution came from the pimps and not from other women. In the end, it's protecting just the men, to use the women for prostitution without any witnesses,' she said. Tour guides tell visitors that the sex workers don't want women

73

around as they see them as potential 'competitors'. Langhorst does not accept that argument and it does sound like total garbage.

The dismantling of the gate by the activists went viral on social media that year. But the local government repaired it the same day.

St Pauli's compromise with Susis Show Bar reached in 2011 is also discomfiting. The bar installed a large mirror and a pole in their box at the Millerntor for their strippers to dance for guests invited to watch games. This caused a protest and club bosses acted: the women were only allowed to dance after the game was over.

'We had a discussion with the owner of the box and made it clear there cannot be dances during the matches,' then St. Pauli president Stefan Orth told *Bild* newspaper. 'There can be performances after the matches, there can be dances, but they must not end up nude. If they dance just once naked, they will be out of here!'

To be honest, it's hardly a telling blow for emancipation. There is something deeply distasteful about women being reduced to decoration for men's titillation, particularly wealthy businessmen in football boxes, and it would be nice to think that St Pauli will one day completely disown this business. Whether Hamburg as a city is prepared to do something about the prostitution business that stains its liberal reputation remains to be seen; maybe it is a long tradition but so was slavery for centuries and that has ended across most of the planet. It will probably take a revolution in the collective head as well as the streets to end the sort of thing we saw at Herbertstraße, and I acknowledge that prostitution will probably continue to exist in some form or other, but its dark side should never be ignored nor should anything about it be sanitised. As I write this in a Santiago that is still celebrating the success of the revolution that began in 2019, I think about the full meaning of a graffito that you often see on the walls in the city centre here: *'La revolución será feminista o no será'.*

Conclusions

FC St Pauli and its fans are not perfect. The club has issues that reflect some classic left-wing tensions between purist failure and success through compromise, between maintaining principles and keeping the finances in a shape offering the chance of something more than just survival; and the neighbourhood and Hamburg as a whole may need some work on the attitude to women and the ugliness of prostitution. But there is so much to love and admire about this organisation and its home city.

This includes the fact that St Pauli are run by people who emerged from the fan scene who have kept their values and deliberately limited the level of compromise. They listen to the fans and people like the *Sozialromantiker* movement, who in 2010 created the alternative Jolly Rouge skull and crossbones on a red background as a symbol of their objections to what they saw as the growing commercialisation of the club. These were some of the most voluble voices against the Susis Bar box in the Millerntor. The Jolly Rouge skull-and-crossbones flag features in the museum – no black-washing of history here.

Sure, some of the ultras take themselves too seriously and seem to view their performance as something as important as that of the team's, if not more so. This is not unique to St Pauli ultras and can be a source of annoyance to other fans. The German weekly *Die Zeit* ran an article in 2019 proclaiming that St Pauli had a fan problem after trouble at the derby at the Millerntor and some of the comments in the article were illuminating, one reader typified the attitudes of many fans:

'The ultras are annoying. Most fans want to see good games: masking up, fights, annoying pyro and the oh-so-great-choreos really interest no one except the ultras. Everyone wants to be a star these days. Shame about the beautiful sport.'

I can understand that, but the ultras do create a great atmosphere and are overwhelmingly on the side of *Die Engel*.

There has been a lot written about St Pauli in recent years and much of it forms a Great St Pauli Celebration. Dissenting voices such as those commenting in *Die Zeit* have seldom been reported and the fans are presented as a slightly heroised monolith. While I might not agree with everything that was said in those comments, I think it's important that such views are given some airtime and that the club should listen to those people as well as the louder elements of the ultra movement. The word 'hubris' was mentioned in one of the comments. Hubris is often the factor that provokes tragedy in Greek theatre. It would be a hell of a tragedy if the St Pauli project were to be undermined and devalued by the behaviour of a minority of hubristic fans who see themselves as the real spectacle.

Having said all that, there are many things to celebrate and the St Pauli phenomenon is astonishing. As Sven Brux says, 'We're just a club without one single sports success in our history and a tiny ground in a red-light district. It's amazing this has happened.' It's partly because the club fills a need.

St Pauli stands as an unequivocal force for good and gives leftist and anti-fascist fans the world over a beacon of hope that another form of football is possible. The club does many good works and has a brand highly associated with 'cool' which helps perpetuate the values of decency that it represents. And while the desire of the *Sozialromantiker* element to hold on to the purity of principle is commendable and understandable, so is the desire of the club president to achieve success to demonstrate that this model can work: that is what could help spread the model and begin to undermine the bases of modern, business football.

And it's not all about the politics. One of my favourite vignettes uncovered when researching this chapter was this:

> 'As reports go, someone from the *Südtribüne* once raised his fist, picked up the megaphone and chanted, "Never again fascism. Never again war." To which someone else replied, "Never again third division."'

Football matters.

* * *

Oke Göttlich Profile

– Vincent Raison –

I don't know what I expected of Oke Göttlich, the president of the most famous second division club in the world. After all, he was the head of not just a successful football club that sells out its stadium every match, but also a global operation that encompasses over 500 official fan clubs and many more besides. By any measure, FC St Pauli is huge and this is the man overseeing it all.

I suppose I didn't expect someone so young and so open. Someone who became disarmingly frank when I asked about his first involvement with the club.

'Like many St Pauli fans, it was coming to watch matches with friends, drinking alcohol and puking in the North Stand.'

Oke was born in Hamburg and spent his early years there, coming to his first matches at the Millerntor as a teenager. He studied sports science, became a sports journalist and a music entrepreneur before being elected St Pauli club president in 2014.

'I'm always working in what I love: football and music, which fits well with St Pauli,' he told me.

The structure of German football is very different from the UK's. You can't just buy a club because you are wealthy (though Red Bull Leipzig are testing this theory). Control of football clubs is in the hands of its members who must own 50 per cent of shares, plus one share to ensure clubs cannot be controlled by external investors. There are exceptions, such as Bayer Leverkusen (owned by Bayer) and Wolfsburg (owned by Volkswagen) whose ownership predates the Bundesliga. Fifty-plus-one is a vital regulation, though. It means no one can buy the league, as Manchester City have been accused of in England, and Chelsea before them. Competition should not be adulterated by money.

'As Christian Streich, the Freiburg coach, said, "Clubs should be owned by people who love the club, not single investors." That is why we fight for this fifty-plus-one rule wherever we can. This is really important. That people who are dedicated to the club are the ones making decisions about money and strategy. If you just see it as an organisation in which money is coming in and you want to get a return on an investment, you don't care if it fails or not. It's old school, but we only spend money we have.

'People like [those on] our board, who are all unpaid volunteers, but experts in certain fields like finance and sustainability, or law, have a huge dedication to our club. But the highest rank at St Pauli is a member.'

I asked him how other clubs responded to St Pauli and its ethos. After all, it is noticeably different from its peers.

'No, other clubs are different,' he laughed. 'We are cool.

'We are fine with each other. I get along with my other colleagues. I have even been voted on to the board of the German Football League by the 36 other clubs of the first and second Bundesliga. People see our voice as something that needs to be heard sometimes; a different opinion.'

If St Pauli attracts any criticism – other than from the far-right – it's that they have become *too* commercial, with an overwhelming merchandise operation that includes an online store in North America. Some locals have moved on from St Pauli to local fourth-tier club, Altona 93, who share a bond with Dulwich Hamlet, who in turn have attracted disillusioned fans of Premier League clubs. Oke isn't afraid to take criticism on board though.

'There will always be somebody who says, "We are less commercial than St Pauli and we're the real non-commercial club," and I'm loving that. The more radical non-commercial clubs we have, the better, because then we have a better game.

'I think it's really important to have these discussions. Sometimes we are the bad guys, always having to present new options to be able to compete in professional football. And our members help us navigate through these options. Sometimes we get it right, sometimes we don't – and then we have a discussion. I see criticism not as criticism but as feedback.'

But while St Pauli merchandise is no cheaper than anybody else's, considerable effort has gone into making their gear fairtrade and sustainable, with a sustainability working group drawing up a code of practice for their partners and suppliers.

It could be said, though, that it is the clubs who embrace the cult of money, who are happy to let it run riot through the sport, who are the ones dominating the game. It has even been observed throughout our travels for this book that success on the field is not so important for left-wing clubs. Integrity and inclusivity rate higher. But Oke has no hesitation in voicing his ambitions for St Pauli.

'It's not like we are saying, because we are playing professional football we need this money. It's: how can we get this money to make our sport better and get promoted and win the Champions League. Because I'm telling you we want to win the Champions League, because then we are reaching the most people with our values. This is the big goal we all should have.

'I don't believe we would lose our values if we are successful. The more successful we are, the bigger platform we have to spread our values. Winning is not something bad. I want the left to know that. We [on the left] sometimes have problems with winning. Like we are overcoming other people. I mean, this is the nature of sport, so either we like sport or not. If you believe sport is something that is good for the health, good for society, but is also a competition, where we have rivalries, then we must not be afraid of winning.'

So where does Oke Göttlcih see FC St Pauli in five years' time?

'We have lots of tasks on the infrastructural side but we also have to fight for our youth academy. We have to grow and make it better. It's very important.

'I'd like to see St Pauli as successful as possible and really be able to spread our values.

'I would like to see St Pauli in five years' time being one of the most sustainable clubs in Germany, and to stay in the first division for more than three years. But we will still spread our values no matter what league we are in. In five years, we want to be a challenger in German football, on and off the pitch, in many different aspects: sustainability, social responsibility, fan culture.

We can't win everything. But we want to be able to say at least we tried to do something we stand for.'

The president does seem to personify what St Pauli is about. But he also represents what it could be about. Not just the 'left side' but a bridge to improving debate and soothing divisiveness.

'One of our slogans is, "A different football is possible." If we want to fight for these things we have to go into areas where we are potentially not welcomed.

'With the hype around social media we have lost our potential for discussion; to talk with people who have different opinions but are still able to have a beer together and maybe find a compromise, or find the right path or maybe agree to disagree. This is where we have to be cautious to ensure we are not losing our ability to debate.'

'I think St Pauli is a great football club for debate and stands for being a platform for debate, trying to change things, not only to be against things but asking, "How can we work out a different direction?"'

Oke Göttlich: ultimately just another member of a football club, but also an inspirational force at the head of an inspirational football club.

Bohemians 1905

Founded: 1905
Stadium: Stadion Ďolíček
Capacity: 6,300
Nicknames: *Klokani* (The Kangaroos)
Ultras: Barflies United, Rude Boy Bohemians,
           Sektor 1905

– VINCENT RAISON –

YOU MIGHT imagine that the boisterous fans of Bohemians Praha 1905 – downing copious amounts of delicious Czech beer, filling the air with weed smoke and waving flares and toy kangaroos – haven't a care in the world. But not long ago they almost didn't have a club to support. And it's only their extraordinary devotion, along with the help of the wider football family, that saved the Czech Republic's left-wing outliers from extinction.

In 2005, their centenary year, FC Bohemians Praha could have disappeared from the football map altogether. Insolvent, relegated to the third tier and facing an opportunist rival using their name, colours and badge, the future looked bleak. But the fans dug into their own pockets, and with help from St Pauli fans in Hamburg and Bohemian FC fans in Dublin, they paid off debts and formed a phoenix club, Bohemians Praha 1905. After many legal struggles, they won the sole right to call themselves Bohemians in the Czech Republic and have battled their way back to the top flight of Czech football. People power saved the former champions of Czechoslovakia, and now the Bohemians Supporters Trust owns more than ten per cent of the club, giving the fans a say in the club's oversight.

They might be only the third biggest club in Prague after Sparta and Slavia, but Bohemians' Ďolíček Stadium (The Dimple) has become something of a pilgrimage for groundhoppers due to its unique atmosphere. The chants and flags and benevolent ambience are a stark contrast to the bile coming from right-wing fans that oppose them. Czechia does not have a particularly right-wing population, but the extremists that do exist are often drawn to football, making Bohemians an attraction for any football fan offended by racist ideology.

The fans here are not interested in rucking though. They just want to have a good time – all the time – with ska, punk, reggae, weed, beer and friendship.

Along with songs like 'Kouříme trávu' ('We smoke grass'), sung to the tune of 'Roll Out The Barrel', you might see fans waving toy kangaroos, the club's symbol and mascot. Back in 1927, when the club was known as Bohemians AFK Vršovice (Vršovice being the Prague suburb that houses the Ďolíček Stadium), they went on a tour of Australia, playing some 19 matches. They were given two live kangaroos in honour of their visit, which they in turn donated to Prague Zoo. Ever since, the marsupial has appeared on the club badge and their nickname has been *Klokani* (kangaroos).

On the pitch, the club has also distinguished itself. They won the Czechoslovak First League in 1982/83 and qualified for Europe nine times in the 1970s and 1980s. But if their badge and mascot display a certain whimsical charm – a club that doesn't take itself too seriously – their most famous player eclipsed the marsupial on the field of play. Antonin Panenka was a gifted midfielder, with a fine range of passing who spent most of his career at Bohemians. In 1976, he represented Czechoslovakia at the European Championships in Yugoslavia. His country reached the final against West Germany in Belgrade's Red Star Stadium. Tied at 2-2 after extra time, the game went to penalties. At 4-3, Uli Hoeneß missed for the Germans. Panenka stepped forward, with the weight of a nation on his shoulders. A successful kick would see them crowned champions of Europe. As West Germany's keeper,

Sepp Maier, dived left, Panenka delicately chipped the ball straight into the middle of the goal. His incredible calm under pressure saw him dubbed a poet by one journalist. Pelé said he was either a genius or a madman. Whatever, the Bohemian was a European champion.

Many have adopted the Panenka penalty since, from Zidane to Messi, but there is only one original. And today, Bohemians' most famous player is the president of the club.

While the years between 1973 and 1995 were the most successful era for the club, its golden year was undoubtedly the 1982/83 season. The previous year had seen them win the Czech Cup against Dukla Prague but lose the Czechoslovak Cup final to Slovan Bratislava. But their third-place finish in the league saw them qualify for the UEFA Cup for the fourth year running.

There was great optimism at the start of the season. If you've never won a championship, it's hard to imagine doing so, but there was no doubt that this year they were going to be contenders. Under the guidance of their legendary manager Tomáš Pospíchal, they were a match for any team in the country. Not only that, they played stylish, attractive football. Since Pospíchal's arrival in 1977, they had improved every year and had established themselves at the top level of the Czechoslovak game. The feeling was that it was now or never to finally bring home the title.

They started the season with one defeat in the first 18 matches, including wins over Slavia, Dukla and Ostrava. They also knocked Saint Etienne out of the UEFA Cup in front of a packed Ďolíček, with fans perched precariously on nearby roofs to get a glimpse of the *Klokani* against glamorous opponents. Though shorn of Michel Platini, Saint Etienne were a technically superior side that still boasted Patrick Battiston and Dutch legend Johnny Rep in the side. In beating them 4-0 in front of a delirious crowd, Bohemians announced they could compete with not just Czechoslovakia's elite but Europe's.

After defeating Dundee United in the quarters, top scorer Pavel Chaloupka netting the only goal of the two legs on a pudding of a pitch in Prague, their European campaign came to an end in the semi-final against Anderlecht in front of 45,000 fans at the Heysel Stadium. Their league form was undisturbed though as they wrapped up the title with a game to spare, having led the division virtually all season. Finally, they were champions and would compete in the European Cup the next season.

* * *

Naturally, Bohemians have links with other left-wing clubs. A fan group called Barflies United describe themselves as 'Rude Boys Bohemians & St. Pauli Skinheads who love Bohemians 1905, FC St. Pauli, beer and fun and hate nazi scum!' You'll often see St Pauli and Bohemians flags side by side at games.

The Barflies also hosted a Love Football Hate Racism football tournament in 2016 with 25 teams competing at Prague's Great Strahov Stadium, a giant facility with a 250,000 capacity, along with anti-racist fans from across Europe. During the pandemic they have been active in collecting medical supplies and provisions for the elderly and their carers, expressing their humanitarian beliefs through action, not just chants.

The club also maintains its friendship with Bohemian FC in Dublin, whose 2020 away kit was produced in conjunction with Amnesty International and was emblazoned with the legend 'Refugees Welcome'. Plus they have a relationship with AS Trenčín in Slovakia, whose ultras represent one of the few left-wing groups in Slovakian football.

Bohemians' biggest rivals are probably Slavia Prague, whose ground is just 1km away from The Dimple, but it is a football rivalry that doesn't spill over into violence. They both want to win the Vršovice derby, but they don't particularly want to fight each other. For one thing, they share an intense dislike for Sparta Prague, the most successful club in Czech football but one associated with right-wing sympathies and a history of anti-Semitic fans.

Apart from Sparta, Bohemians are also opposed to clubs like Baník Ostrava who have fans who revel in offensive right-wing chants and anti-Muslim banners. While Bohemians prefer spliffing to scrapping, their fans will not ignore racist behaviour.

After the glory days of the 1970s and 1980s and the dark days of 2005, the club has revived. They have been in the Czech First League since 2013 and in the 2019/20 season finished eighth, qualifying for the championship round – the postseason competition for final places.

It would be wonderful if these unbelievable fans were rewarded by the club making their mark on Czech and even European football again but they will be there supporting them whatever happens.

Matchday: Bohemians 3 SK Dynamo 1, November 2021

Stadion Ďolíček is in Prague 10, the Vršovice area of the capital, just south-east of the city centre. As previously mentioned, the club was originally called AFK Vršovice before the first of 15 name changes saw it arrive at Bohemians Praha 1905 in the year of its rebirth, 2013. It's an unprepossessing stadium, but like many places in Prague, charm is more important than luxury. And like Rayo Vallecano's Vallecas Stadium, and Red Star's Bauer Stadium, it currently only has three stands, the area behind one of the goals off limits for fans.

A green kangaroo on a stone emblem high above the turnstiles announces your arrival at the Ďolíček. Peering through the gates, a classic old football terrace conjures up days of yore, watching football as a wide-eyed child, straining for a view from the concrete steps with a father, tobacco smoke and eternal optimism for company.

The main stand basks in all-seater comfort along the length of the pitch, while a thin band of uncovered seats on the opposite side of the pitch houses the fans of the opponents for our visit, SK Dynamo České Budějovice – from the city that is home to the Budweiser Budvar Brewery. Only 20 or so hardy souls made the journey from South Bohemia to cheer on the Purpurová, but hats off to them.

We stood in Sektor B, behind the goal. There are seats to one side of the terrace, which people are free to sit in if they want to, but there is no extra charge to do so. A platform at the bottom of the terrace hosts a drum and a guy with a megaphone to lead the support, a similar but more modest approach to St Pauli's. Behind us stands a bar, serving great Czech beer, mulled wine and food. I was surprised to note on our tickets that on the list of forbidden items to bring into the Ďolíček, weed and alcohol featured first, well ahead of guns and knives. Why anyone would want to smuggle in alcohol is beyond me, given the easy availability of cheap beer in the stands, but guns and knives are the last things on the mind of this mob. As the crowd slowly gathered it became clear that this was among the best-natured crowds I'd ever had the pleasure of watching a game with.

It was November, but not too early to see our first Father Christmas of the season, resplendent in a green and white Santa suit, next to a little helper with his green Mohican. McGill and I had become used to being the oldest people in a crowd by now and it mattered not a bit as the beers went down, huge banners were passed over our heads, songs were sung and flares were lit. Many football drummers struggle to keep a rhythm but the *Klokani* drummer was clearly pretty good, driving the crowd on while the song leader got everyone going. Not that they were in any way reluctant.

The match itself failed to ignite at first, reflecting the mid-table form of two sides who had struggled to put any sort of run together.

'I can't see either of them scoring today,' said McGill. 'Another beer?'

Fate welcomes temptation, so as soon as my pal had turned his back on the game to head up the terrace to the bar, Dynamo failed to clear a corner and Ibrahim Keita struck the ball left-footed into the net to put Bohemians 1-0 up and send the crowd wild.

'Ibra! Ibra!' sang the crowd. It sounded like he was something of a hero, even though this was only his second goal of the season, but then anyone who scores a goal is a hero of the moment.

The team in green increased their lead on 35 minutes through Petr Hronek to give the fans a rare sense of ease at the break.

The crowd was small, just 3,500 or so, but they made a racket and had a laugh for the whole match; drinking, smoking weed and singing in a 90-minute party, with a pause for half-time. Unlike St Pauli, all the songs were in the native tongue, but it wasn't hard to get the gist of some of them. We're all familiar with the opposing keeper facing a rising 'Ooooh' as he goes to take a goal kick, usually followed by a chant reflecting his competence. The Bohemians chant ended with what sounded like 'Eeyore, eeyore!' which I thought was self-explanatory, but I asked someone to translate the rest of the song.

'They are saying he is a hole,' she said.

'He is a hole?'

'He is a hole.'

OK. It turns out what I heard was 'Díro! Díro!', which does indeed translate to 'hole'.

Bohemians started the second half well but Dynamo managed to pull one back without seriously threatening Bohemians' control of the game. *Klokani* then had a goal disallowed for offside thanks to VAR. It seemed strange to have this kind of technology in such surroundings, in front of a crowd below the average of a fourth-tier match in the UK, but it was a reminder that this was top flight football, regardless of the modest attendance.

Sektor B sang even louder, with celebratory call and response songs with the main stand. The sound echoed not just in the ground but off the buildings that overlooked The Dimple, giving the impression of much larger numbers, as if the apartments were joining in.

Few left the ground when the final whistle blew as the players gathered to face Sektor B, savour the moment and join in with the applause. They had done the fans proud and it was clear these guys meant something to them, as substitute goalkeeper Patrik Le Giang told us:

'What do the Bohemians fans mean to me? A lot! Every game I play for Bohemians I play also for them because they are fantastic. After my professional career, I will tell everyone that I was a goalkeeper of this club. I'm so proud of that.'

Patrik's time after Bohemians came much sooner than expected, as, after 50 games for the club, the January transfer window would see him move back to Slovakia to play for FK Pohronie.

As the crowd dispersed to continue their enjoyment of Czechia's gift to the world, Pilsner, we met a multinational group of friends – a Brit, a Czech, a Spaniard and two Americans – who lived in Prague and had come to think of Bohemians as their team.

'I did go to Slavia once, but as soon as I came to the Ďolíček, I knew this was where I belonged,' said Josh. We spent the rest of the evening in their company, drinking in one of Prague's countless fine bars. Though we're fairly ancient, being adopted by 20-somethings and being taken to the places they love in this wonderful city felt pretty special.

Czechia Context ·

As far as I can tell, the Czechs have never invaded anyone, but have endured occupation by both the Nazis and the Soviets in the 20th century, which achieved nothing more than a pressing need to be independent from bastards.

While the Czech Republic was only formed as an independent nation in 1993 with the peaceful division of Czechoslovakia, its history is as ancient as any in Central Europe. The country is inextricably linked with the various forms of Bohemia, now a region that makes up the largest and most populous part of Czechia, but previously it has been a duchy, a principality and a kingdom. Czechoslovakia itself was formed from the embers of World War I and the collapse of the Habsburg Empire, when it declared itself independent from Austria-Hungary. Its independence only lasted until 1938, when Hitler annexed the Sudetenland, the borderlands populated with Sudeten Germans, after Great Britain, France and Italy (but not Czechoslovakia) granted him permission to do so in the 'peace in our time' Munich Agreement. It was intended to sate Hitler and avert war.

However, with Czechoslovakia's borders breached, it was not long before the Nazis took over the rest of the country and the rest of the world found out how just how insane Hitler and his followers were.

The Czechoslovak resistance succeeded in assassinating the acting governor, Reinhard Heydrich, a brutal piece of shit even by Nazi standards, who was an architect of the Holocaust. In response, the Nazis executed every male over 15 in the village of Lidice, near Prague, and killed many women and children in their concentration camps before levelling the village with fire and explosives, all because they mistakenly suspected it was a hotbed of partisans. It's a chilling reminder of why life must never be breathed into fascism again. It's not just inhuman, it's anti-human.

Towards the end of the War in Europe, anti-Nazi feeling was so high that Czech citizens spontaneously attacked the occupiers to try to liberate Prague from German rule in what became known as the Prague Uprising. After four days of intense fighting, the Soviet Red Army arrived to overrun what was left of the German forces. Bolstered by the uprising and a liberating army from the USSR, the Czechoslovak Communist Party (CCP) became the largest party in a coalition government in the free election of 1946. It would be the last free election for 40 years as, with Soviet backing, the CCP assumed total command in the *coup d'état* of 1948.

The attendant economic reforms and restrictions to free expression and movement saw the spirit of Czechoslovak independence rise again by 1968, culminating in the Prague Spring, a period of protest and liberalisation. Freedom of the press, speech and travel was restored along with civil rights in what first secretary Alexander Dubček dubbed 'socialism with a human face', before it was summarily crushed by hundreds of thousands of Warsaw Pact troops when Soviet tanks rolled into Prague once more.

In 1989, a student march to commemorate the 50th anniversary of a student protest against Nazi occupation turned into a demonstration against a regime that had delivered 20 years of political repression, authoritarianism and economic stagnation. The police waded in, kicking off a chain of events that led to the end of one-party rule and brought about the Velvet Revolution, which saw the playwright and dissident Václav Havel become president of the new democracy.

This remarkable and volatile history of an ostensibly peaceful nation leaves it with a particular relationship to extremism. It's hard to tell who is responsible for the neo-Nazi 'Good Night Left Side' graffiti at Slavia Prague's ground, but it is clearly visible on their premises. And yet Slavia have been subjected to considerable anti-Semitic abuse from Sparta's right-wing fans over the years – unforgivable in a city that saw thousands of Jews transported to their deaths in Nazi concentration camps. The abuse is down to a section of Sparta fans and their mistaken belief that Sparta was founded by Jews. In fact there was a club founded by Jews in Prague. DFC Prag was one of the best in Europe at the beginning of the 20th century before the German occupation of Prague saw them banned and subsequently dissolved.

As Josh told us, 'With Sparta and Slavia there are definite aspects of the fanbase that is right-wing. The treatment of Kamara from Rangers really highlighted that. Even chatting to fans of the teams, that animosity always comes out.'

Slavia's Ondrej Kudela was banned for 10 matches for racially abusing Glen Kamara in a Europa League match against Rangers in 2021. Yes, 2021. Six months later, Rangers returned to Prague, to Sparta's Letná stadium where Kamara was constantly jeered by home fans. The stadium only had 10,000 spectators, all from local schools, along with their 'responsible' adult, after Sparta employed a loophole to their stadium ban for previous racist chanting and monkey taunts in a Champions League match against Monaco. In a society that did not experience multiculturalism until relatively recently, there have been incidents of racist abuse going back to 1995. They occurred at Sparta but would be unthinkable at Bohemians.

'It's just my impression, but Bohemians is the closest club I've found which is apolitical. But in Prague that kind of makes you left-wing,' said Josh. 'From the chants and from the people you see at the ground, I think it's an outsider club, those who never found a kinship with Sparta or Slavia. It makes it perfect for those who fall through the cracks of football culture and make it a breeding ground for more left-wing ideology. The fact that so many different people are passionate about the club lends itself to a more inclusive environment, which in turn brings out that left-wing nature.'

Sparta are indeed trying to rid themselves of their racist and anti-Semitic element, but it is not a new battle, nor one from which they have emerged victorious.

Klokani

It might seem strange that a 1927 tour of Australia was so significant for a neighbourhood Prague club, but when they returned to compete in the Czechoslovak First League the next season, they had a new name and a new identity. English-speakers struggle to say Vršovice (versh-o-vic-se), so the team obliged by renaming themselves after their home, with a word recognisable the world over: Bohemians. Essentially it means Czechs, rather than louche, artistic adventurers, yet an unconventional spirit seems to be a part of the club.

In Oz, they played three goal-rich 'Test Matches' against the Australian national team, along with 16 other matches against regional and representative teams. Both Australia and Bohemians made an impression on each other, which resulted in the gift of two kangaroos (that may actually have been wallabies).

In 2014, a group of fans left Prague to retrace the 1927 tour, with the club helping to back the tour with one of the club's directors, Darek Jakubowicz, among the dozen or so travellers. They met Czech expats, officials of the cities, visited sports grounds and filmed a documentary of the trip. And while the club has seen many names, changes and fluctuations in fortunes, the fans seem to be a constant. Committed and slightly mad.

Despite the lack of conspicuous success in recent seasons, the fans stick by the club, singing constantly about Bohemians, kangaroos and the Dolíček, come rain or shine. The players appreciate it too, warmly applauding them after each game. Often first to acknowledge the fans is the aforementioned Patrik Le Giang. In 2021, he received a Merit Award from FIFPro for his contribution to charitable causes. Le Giang set up a foundation that auctions the jerseys of famous footballers and donates the proceeds to support children in need. He also took part in a project to renovate schools in Indonesia.

'If children look to footballers as role models, they should not see them as people with fast cars and a bundle of money. They should see them as someone who uses their influence for the community,' he said.

Like the fans helping the elderly, he is prepared to back fine sentiment with action.

'The overriding goal is to provide financial support to those who need it most. But in addition, we want to inspire young people to be better people and help those who need it,' he added.

'Football is a sport that unites people from all over the world; it is a common interest, a universal language, and a way of connecting with each other. No matter where we were born, how our skin looks, or what culture or race we are a part of – we all have a bigger calling in this life. Therefore, as players, I think our mission is far more important than kicking or catching a ball – there are other steps to be taken, and each one should help make the world a better place.'

It's heart-warming to see someone in the privileged position of a professional footballer focusing on the needs of those less fortunate.

Gól Bohemka Gól

Having re-established themselves in the top flight, what can Bohemians achieve now? The 2021/22 season was one of struggle, and since our visit, they plunged from mid-table into the relegation play-offs. Manager Luděk Klusáček was replaced by Jaroslav Veselý, who was tasked with keeping *Klokani* in the top flight. After an almighty battle, Bohemians defeated Opava over two legs to stay up. Hopefully, Veselý will continue next season, alongside veteran midfielder Josef Jindřišek, who, at 41, and after over 300 appearances, still represents the heart and soul of this club.

The contrast with Slavia Prague, their neighbours, is startling. Slavia's Sinobo Stadium is the most modern in Czechia, an all-seater amphitheatre made for Champions League football, with a hotel and a slick commercial operation. Yet it lacks the character of the crumbling Ďolíček, even if it does boast a fully functioning roof and the luxury of four sides.

Without a significant benefactor to invest in the squad and stadium, it's difficult to see how much the club can progress beyond mid-table in the Czech League, but perhaps they don't need to. If the fans here wanted to see a team win every week, they could always go down the road. But these fans have made a different choice. Winning isn't everything to these guys. Friends and fun are more important. That and not having to watch a game sitting next to arseholes. Plus, every now and then they get the sweet feeling of the underdog overcoming the odds, just as they did in February 2020, when they beat Slavia 1-0 at the Ďolíček, or January 2021 when they beat Sparta away 1-0. For some people, the game isn't all about money and glory. For some, the crack *is* the glory.

Liverpool

Founded:	1892
Stadium:	Anfield Stadium
Capacity:	54,167
Nicknames:	The Reds
Fans' Union:	The Spirit of Shankly

– STEWART McGILL –

UNLIKE SOME of the clubs covered in this volume, Liverpool do not really need an introduction. They are one of the most famous football clubs on the planet with a huge international following.

We were initially dubious about their inclusion in the first XI as they are owned by American venture capitalists who tried to take the club into the enormity of the European Super League. However, the reaction of the fans to that ludicrous idea, informed by a coherent philosophy aligned with cogent solutions, helped change our minds along with developments in the city and the fanbase since the Thatcherite assaults in the 1980s. Further, by no means every club in our first XI has an ownership aligned with the leftist philosophy of sections of their fans. The response of Liverpool supporters was also successful in changing the attitudes of the owners – at least in public – and in the way the club was run. For all this, and for the living spirit of the great Bill Shankly, a place in the first team is well deserved.

The City

Liverpool's wealth grew on the back of slavery, like that of the country as a whole, but more so. It was made a parish by Act of Parliament in 1699, the same year as its first slave ship, the *Liverpool Merchant,* set sail for Africa. Liverpool grew rapidly in the 18th and 19th Centuries due to slave trade profits but prominent Liverpudlians like William Rathbone, William Roscoe and Edward Rushton worked for abolition. *God's Fifth Column* is always at work, in keeping with the ideas of the book of that title by William Gerhardie, of whom a little more in the Post-Match Verdict. Gerhardie's fifth-columnists worked against the prevailing ethos of the age and its ethical deficits.

Opposing slavery was not without risk: William Roscoe, an MP who voted for abolition, was accosted by pro-slavery activists on his return to Liverpool after that vote and later saw one of his supporters murdered in a brawl. Eventually, a civic pride was felt in his principled stance and his name was given to Roscoe Lane and Roscoe Gardens in the city. Many more Liverpool streets and buildings are named after slavers, including the famous Penny Lane.

Liverpool was the fifth most visited city in the UK in 2019, much of it due to the enduring appeal of The Beatles, but Liverpool FC is also a major attraction.

Football is an underrated part of the UK's tourist business. London is the capital of UK tourism and it receives 500,000 visits per year that include watching a game live. The North West comes second in terms of number of total visits to the UK but a much higher proportion of visitors go there specifically for the football, 18 per cent compared to three per cent in London according to VisitBritain.

The average expenditure per visit for football spectators in 2019 was £909, much higher than the UK visitor average of £696 reflecting (i) the high value of these visitors to the UK and (ii) the absurd prices of football merchandise.

Football matters.

Liverpool and Manchester United received the most overseas visits. VisitBritain estimates that 1.5 million trips to the UK in 2019 included watching football. Of these 2019 visits there were an estimated 226,000 trips to Old Trafford and 213,000 trips to Anfield. Close rivals, even for tourist revenue.

Population

Currently estimated to be around 497,000, an increase since the 2011 UK Census figure of 466,400.

This reflects some of the city's recovery since the secular decline over recent decades. Liverpool's population peaked in the 1930s, with 846,101 recorded in the 1931 census. Until these recent increases, the city had experienced negative population growth every decade; over 100,000 people left the city between 1971 and 1981.

Whilst the story of the city's relative decline is reflected in the population figures it should be noted that (i) Manchester shows a similar decline in city population and (ii) that for both cities the decline reflects large scale movement to the suburbs rather than people having to leave the area completely for salvation in London, a trope that understandably annoys Liverpool people.

The city's population grew significantly through Irish migration in the 19th century, particularly during the Great Hunger of the 1840s. By 1851, 20 per cent of the city's population was Irish; 50-75 per cent of the current population are estimated to have Irish descent. Two of The Beatles, Lennon and McCartney, have good Irish names and George Harrison's mother was an Irish Catholic, George often visited his family who lived on Dublin's Northside.

The name Anfield is believed to come from Annefield in New Ross, County Wexford.

The first director of football at Liverpool FC was a Monaghan man, John McKenna. Liverpool's first manager was William Edward Barclay, a Dubliner, who was also Everton's first manager. The distinctive accent is also heavily influenced by the Irish infusion, though Welsh immigration also had some say in how the accent developed.

The Football

Anfield stadium was built in 1884 on land next to Stanley Park about two miles from the city centre. Everton used it before the club moved to Goodison Park after a dispute over rent with Anfield's owner John Houlding. Houlding was left with an empty ground and formed Liverpool in 1892. This story is well known in Liverpool and the chant 'You should have paid the rent' is still occasionally used to taunt Everton fans at the derby.

The capacity of the stadium at the time was 20,000, but only around 100 spectators attended Liverpool's first match at Anfield. Things moved on quickly. Liverpool's first English league title came in 1900/01 and they have won 18 more since. They have also won eight FA Cups, nine League Cups, three UEFA Cups and one World Club Championship.

And, of course, six European Cups, but they hardly ever talk about that.

Liverpool's successes have tended to come in bursts followed by fallow periods, though the astonishing 1973–1990 period was admittedly a very lengthy 'burst'. The legendary Bill Shankly took over in late 1959 when the club had been in the Second Division for over five years, something hard to imagine now. He took them up in 1962, they won the league title in 1964, the FA Cup for the first time in 1965 and then the league again in 1966. Then nothing until 1973. However, there was no clamour to get rid of Shankly, no entitled demands for success from angry supporters, no protests in the ground, again something hard to imagine now. The game has changed along with the attitudes of those who watch it.

A game-changer, literally, at Anfield came in November 1973 when they were beaten home and away by Red Star Belgrade. The tie was not quite the walkover for Red Star as it has become represented in popular memory, particularly the second leg at Anfield. (I saw the highlights on ITV, 10.30pm to 11.30pm – no live Champions League transmissions lasting four hours longer than the match in those days. This whole section must be staggering for younger readers.) However, it was the nature of the defeat that shocked and provoked change: Red Star Belgrade passed the ball in short triangles and moved into positions of advantage beautifully, depriving Liverpool of possession, getting them tired and silencing the Kop at Anfield.

Shankly said afterwards, 'The Europeans showed that building from the back is the only way to play.' He also said after the first-leg, 'They are a good side even though our fans would not pay to watch the football that they play.' I hate to argue with one of the few people I unreservedly idolise, but I think Shanks got that one wrong.

There was an immediate inquiry into the defeat in the fabled Boot Room, a meeting place where the Liverpool coaching staff would drink tea and discuss tactics, formed upon Shankly's arrival in 1959. The team did evolve to play differently, particularly in Europe, and quieting the crowds at away matches became a definite early objective. None of this happened under Shankly, who left suddenly and shockingly in the summer of 1974. Given Shankly's comment on the low entertainment value of Red Star's football, we can wonder if Liverpool would have changed that much had he stayed and would they have enjoyed such success. This could also provoke the largely sterile controversy over who was the better manager, Shankly or Paisley. The club undoubtedly had more success under the latter but with the foundations laid by the former. There are people foolish enough to rate Stevie Ray Vaughan a better guitar player than Jimi Hendrix, but even they would acknowledge that without Jimi there is no Stevie Ray.

And it was all a collective effort under both managers, more of this and the underlying philosophy later.

Between 1973 and 1990 Liverpool was up there with the top club sides in the world with a highly impressive run of success. Between 1990 and 2020 they enjoyed some intermittent success, including a European Cup victory in 2005 under Rafa Benitez, but they were overshadowed by their great rivals Manchester United for much of that period and few teams, players or managers from this period will be remembered as 'legends', an overused but descriptive word. However, Steven Gerrard and Luis Suarez are both contenders for the All-Time Liverpool Top XI, despite the latter's excessive hunger for the game and the former's punching of a DJ because he wouldn't play Phil Collins, the appalling musical taste deserving censure as well as the violence.

Since Jurgen Klopp took over in 2015 he has built a fine attacking side that wins trophies and Liverpool fans are at their most footballing content for three decades. He also seems to be largely in tune with the increasingly left-wing stance taken by the club's supporters. To understand the origins of this, we need to go back to the 1980s.

The Politics

In early April 2022, before the kick-off against Watford in the Premier League, a giant yellow flag was unveiled at Anfield that read:

'Seafarers are not a bank balance: United we stand.'

A reference to the recent mass sackings carried out by the ferry operator P&O.

In December 2021, a large banner saying 'Never Trust a Tory' appeared on the Kop, harmonising nicely with the 'Fuck the Tories' chant that is regularly heard across the ground. Arsenal supporter Jeremy Corbyn was feted by Liverpool fans with banners and the chant of 'Oh Jeremy Corbyn' to the White Stripes' 'Seven Nation Army'. 'Justice for Grenfell' banners have been displayed and one depicting the six most successful recent managers was definitely in a Soviet style, with a red star with yellow trim in the top left-hand corner.

All this began in the 1980s. Liverpool as a city and as a club had a tough decade, despite the sporting success. The trials of those times helped focus Liverpool's basic anti-establishment attitudes into a more developed set of left-wing positions and activism.

'Managed' Decline of the Not-Really-English City.

Tony Evans's excellent *Two Tribes* about the city and its football rivalries in the 1980s sums up the economic background succinctly:

'Britain's trading outlook switched from the Commonwealth and Americas towards Europe. The docks began to contract and industry relocated. Between 1966 and 1977, 350 factories closed or moved away from Merseyside. More than forty thousand jobs disappeared in the 15 years before 1985. In the year of the Heysel disaster Liverpool's unemployment rate reached 27 per cent. Nearly half the young men aged between 16 and 24, the age group that comprised the football club's most fervent fans, were on the dole.'

Liverpool council had an ongoing confrontation with the Tory government that hardened many attitudes on both sides. In 1983, the year that Thatcher won her second general election by a landslide, Labour won the city council elections with a socialist manifesto. It cancelled the 1,200 redundancies planned by the previous administration, froze council rents and launched an ambitious house-building programme targeting the city's most deprived neighbourhoods. Slums were knocked down, new leisure centres and nurseries were built and apprenticeships were created.

The council did not have the cash to fund its projects but one of Labour's election pledges had been to campaign for more money from central government. Roy Gladden, a then Labour councillor, says the council was confident it could secure the funds it needed given the deprivation in the city and the serious social need.

Initially, they were right. The Secretary of State for the Environment, Patrick Jenkin, visited Liverpool, was apparently shocked by the housing situation and awarded the city an extra £20m. But the council was rejected when it asked for the same money the following year. This kicked off a series of confrontations that culminated in the Labour Party purging the Militant Tendency members that were associated with the council's rebellion and the district auditor banning the Liverpool Labour councillors from public office for five years.

'They didn't seem to have the right kind of feeling,' according to Roy Gladden, a Liverpool councillor who it should be noted was never a member of the Militant Tendency, quoted in a BBC News Magazine report on *The Mersey Militants,* a radio show about the era.

'They were happy for us to have the factories and make the money that then got shifted to the south, to London. But when it came for that to be returned it didn't happen,' said Gladden.

This, along with other events in the 1980s helped confirm 'outsider' status felt by many in the city already, a 'scouse exceptionalism' that makes some uncomfortable. The musician Peter Hooton, then a youth worker, is quoted in the same BBC article:

'When Thatcher was in power, we felt that she looked at Liverpool and thought: "Well, they're not really English, are they?"'

Hooton also said, 'Liverpool has always seen itself as separate from the rest of the country. As a city, it has more in common with Belfast and Glasgow than it does with London. There was the big influx of Irish and, because it's a port, it's always been international. We look to America and Ireland – to New York and Dublin – more than we look to London.'

An interesting parallel with Hamburg there, another big port city whose inhabitants look more to London, and some maybe to Liverpool, than to the rest of Germany. Many Celtic fans also look to Ireland as the real spiritual home, though there are more nationalist elements at play with those sentiments.

Hamburg is different and so is Liverpool. The large Irish element in the population and the singular accent, quite unlike the rest of the area, have always marked them out as slightly 'beyond the pale' – a phrase that actually comes from the English occupation of Ireland: the pale was a fence that marked out the boundaries of the English settlements in rural Ireland; if you lived 'beyond the pale', you were no longer under the protection of English law, you were in 'savage' Ireland.

Attitudes had not changed much by the mid-19th century following the arrival in Britain of many Irish people driven there by the Great Hunger of the 1840s, the result of some savage behaviour by Britain. *Punch* produced this in 1862:

'A creature manifestly between the Gorilla and the Negro is to be met with in some of the lowest districts of London and

Liverpool by adventurous explorers. It comes from Ireland, whence it has contrived to migrate; it belongs in fact to a tribe of Irish savages, the lowest species of Irish Yahoo. When conversing with its kind it talks a sort of gibberish. It is moreover a climbing animal, and may sometimes be seen ascending a ladder laden with a hod of bricks.'

A similar contempt was revealed in a *Sunday Times* article, perhaps with a more class-oriented hatred after the Heysel stadium disaster in which a charge by Liverpool supporters led to the deaths of 39 Juventus supporters at the 1985 European Cup final in Brussels:

'Unlike Juventus, the majority of Liverpool fans who travelled to Brussels were recognisably and overwhelmingly working-class. Even without their team favours many would be instantly recognisable in their ragged jeans, training shoes and do-it-yourself haircuts.'

Before Heysel, but just after the riots in Liverpool 8 in 1981, provoked by some appalling racist policing, the supposedly left-of-centre *Daily Mirror* opined:

'They should build a fence around [Liverpool] and charge admission. For sadly it had become a "showcase" of everything that has gone wrong in Britain's major cities.'

And as Tony Evans describes in *Two Tribes*,

'Even the reliable Brian Glanville, so often a lonely sane voice in defence of supporters among the press was aghast (Liverpool supporters had mistakenly thought Abide With Me was over in a pre-season game and started to sing You'll Never Walk Alone). Liverpool, he wrote, were "cursed with some of the most savage fans in England."'

This was a time when football fans were generally demonised, but Liverpool supporters and their city attracted particular contempt. They were beyond the pale.

People in Liverpool felt that the government, on course for a major collision with the city council, would exploit the Heysel tragedy and the blackening of the city's reputation. Footballers at the time sensed it including two who played for Everton but were, and are, more politically aware than many players.

Peter Reid, Everton's captain for much of the 1980s and a Liverpool native, said that the assault on Merseyside was about much more than football, 'The Tories were trying to decimate one of the world's great cities. They wanted to destroy us.'

The Everton goalkeeper Neville Southall was equally clear – 'It wasn't about football to the Tories, it was an assault against working-class people and their culture.' (Both quoted in *Two Tribes*.)

The Thatcher government took English clubs out of European competition as a response to Heysel; UEFA responded with its own ban a few days later. This seriously damaged clubs like Everton and others who had earned the right to play in Europe or would have done so in the subsequent five years during which the ban applied. Perfectly innocent clubs, players and supporters suffered, and the name of Liverpool and the football club named after the city was further blackened. This did no harm to the government's totemic struggle against the council.

Liverpool was being abused economically and treated like it was the centre of an alien, aggressive culture in its own country. It wasn't alone in being brutalised economically by a government hell-bent on destroying both the organised labour movement and the mixed economy that had yielded so many benefits for working people in the decades after WW2, but it suffered particularly badly and rightly felt it was being treated like a pariah. After the riots in 1981 the Tory Chancellor Geoffrey Howe wrote in an official letter:

'We do not want to find ourselves concentrating all the limited cash that may have to be made available into Liverpool and having nothing left for possibly more promising areas such as the West Midlands or, even, the North East.

'It would be even more regrettable if some of the brighter ideas for renewing economic activity were to be sown only on the relatively stony ground on the banks of the Mersey.

'I cannot help but feel that the option of managed decline is one which we should not forget altogether. We must not expand our limited resources in trying to make water flow uphill.'

'Scouse Not English'

This practice of managed decline was classed as *autotomy*, the conscious abandonment of a damaged or diseased part of the body politic in order to preserve the healthy remainder, in a paper by Parker, Atkinson and Morales from 2017 in *Territory, Politics, Governance*, Volume 5, Issue 4. (In zoology, autotomy refers to the casting off of a part of the body, e.g. the tail of a lizard, by an animal under threat.)

They argued that the practice first emerged as a strategy of containment in Republican 'no go' areas at the height of the 'Troubles' in the early 1970s, despite its denial by a series of Northern Ireland ministers. The Irish connection keeps on arising when you talk about Liverpool.

Howe's paper was not made public until 30 years later but people knew at the time that the government was vehemently anti-Liverpool. It was anxious to ascribe the socio-economic problems of the city to underlying flaws in the character of the residents and their locally elected representatives rather than more long-running structural economic factors. This characterised their attitudes to ethnic minority areas such as Brixton as well: economic deprivation and discrimination had nothing to do with their problems; the areas were just full of people that could never be 'one of us', to use Thatcher's chilling little phrase.

Given the economic and political attacks on the city and its football, it's no surprise that Liverpool supporters became 'radicalised', not a term in use then, and turned against neoliberalism and the Tories who inflicted it on the country. Many also turned against the country: before the European Championship final in 2021, the *Liverpool Echo* reported that most of their readers said they would not be backing England against Italy in the forthcoming final.

'Just over half of readers who responded to our survey said they WON'T be backing England with many saying they were "Scouse not English."'

The Spirit of Shankly, and the Union

I talked to Jeff Goulding, Liverpool fan for decades, writer for the *This is Anfield* website, author of several books on Merseyside football, and former Militant Tendency man.

Jeff raised some interesting points about the complicated nature of the phrase 'left-wing club'. The people who run Liverpool may not be left-wing but a significant part of the community that supports and sustains the club is socialist inclined. This applies to a few of the clubs that we write about in this volume. The ethos of the fans and the man who made the modern club can influence the management though: the chairman between 2017 and 2020, Peter Moore, said he would always look at issues through the prism of 'what would Shankly say?' This could be marketing talk but the fact he said it has its own significance.

Jeff traced the shift to the left back to the 1980s in line with the analysis above. He said that the football and political establishments' appalling attempts to deny and cover up what actually happened at Hillsborough, combined with heinous attempts to attribute blame to the fans, formed a solidifying rather than causal factor in this movement.

Racism was not unknown amongst Liverpool fans in the 1970s and into the early 1980s, which Jeff acknowledged (it was actually much more of a societal norm than those of us who tend to romanticise that era like to admit). However, he did point out that the National Front and other organised racist groups never achieved any traction in Liverpool, acquired no toe-hold on the Kop and that Union Jacks have been given short shrift for some time at Anfield. It was made clear that this was not what Liverpool FC was about, even to young people who were unaware of it as the expression of any conscious political ideology. This had an impact on people growing up on the Kop.

The NF's toxic bigotry was classed as 'wool' or 'woolyback behaviour', i.e. something that pertained to people from outside Liverpool who didn't subscribe to the city's culture or traditions. The split between the city and the country – which includes smaller towns – and the prejudices they hold about each other are universals. City people tend to write the dictionaries, the reason why 'urbane' describes a courteous and refined manner, some Scousers would clearly subscribe to this view albeit they would express it in slightly less urbane language.

Jeff points out the importance of role models to the continuance of the Liverpool left tradition that crystallised in the 1980s on the terraces and in the streets. Young people in the ground will chant 'Fuck the Tories' and put up 'Scousers Hate Tories' banners. Many of them were not born at the time of Heysel and Hillsborough but they have been exposed to the narrative of those times from role models at football and elsewhere and that will influence their thinking. There is no doubt that people listen to those who they like and respect and will take on their views. As human beings we tend to become like the people around us; the club and the stadium, the faith and the place of worship, become a medium for the transmission of values. Had some of these younger Scousers been born a little further south and gone to Millwall rather than Liverpool from an early age, they would probably not be singing about the greatness of Jeremy Corbyn.

I asked Jeff why Everton had not developed a similar culture. He speculated, without any sense of crowing or red superiority – he's not that sort of guy and he has plenty of lefty Evertonian friends – that it could well be a derivative of the introspective psychodrama that Blues fans have suffered since the passing of the great team of the 1980s and the secular decline of the club on the field; all whilst the other giants of the North West, the Manchester teams and Liverpool, have enjoyed success. He didn't think Everton fans would ever adopt a right-wing position in conscious contradistinction to Liverpool's leftism the way some Rangers fans have in Scotland to differentiate themselves from Celtic. Toryism is a taboo across the city and there is no sectarianism as the embittering bitter factor in the uniquely poisonous Old Firm rivalry.

Liverpool and Everton fans do not get on the way they used to, though it was never really the 'friendly' rivalry romanticised by nostalgia. Interestingly, Jeff's analysis of this takes us back to Canetti and the importance of the stadium. Enforced segregation in all-seater stadiums now means that the mixing that used to happen in the derby matches can't happen and the 'otherness' of the faceless, dehumanised opposition at the far end is accentuated. It's nothing to do with Heysel and Everton being deprived of a place in the European Cup as some people speculate: there was no problem at the two cup finals they played against each other after Heysel in 1986 and 1989 and Everton fans showed nothing but solidarity after Hillsborough. Everton's increasing bitterness about the decline of their team is an important factor, as well as the confrontational aspects of today's stadiums. I speak as an occasional, distant Everton fan here – as you can imagine, much of this chapter was hard for me to write.

Jeff is a member of the Spirit of Shankly (SOS) group, the Liverpool Supporters Union as they describe themselves. Formed in 2008, SOS has become an increasingly important part of Liverpool FC as a wider institution, not just the company owned by American venture capitalists, Fenway Sports Group. The union was formed in opposition to the predatory Hicks and Gillett regime that took over Liverpool in 2007. They were labelled 'Sons of Strikers' by that odious regime (the union was originally called Sons of Shankly but this was quickly changed as it was not inclusive). SOS was instrumental in orchestrating the response to Liverpool's decision to join the European Super League (ESL).

According to Jeff, the club realised that they had made a catastrophic error when they were confronted by a unanimous, vitriolic and cogent rejection of the idea by a united fanbase led by the union. This may have been a derivative of the parent company in America, focused only on the bottom line, not listening to its executives on the ground in Liverpool. They were forced to engage with SOS to save some face and assuage some anger. Brilliantly, SOS had a series of solutions worked out already such as the creation of a shadow board of supporters with meaningful influence over existential issues related to the club and fan-facing matters such as the right to veto ESL entry, ground shares, and any name change proposals. All this has led to relations between the club, SOS and the wider fanbase being better than they have been for some considerable time. It will be interesting to see if this goodwill continues once Liverpool hit some hard times on the pitch again. It's easy to sing in harmony if you're winning.

What Was the Spirit of Shankly?

Shankly was a remarkable, charismatic figure, the sort of guy about whom my father used to say, 'You'd have to be a close relative of Adolf Hitler not to like him.' His philosophy of football – and life as he saw the two as intimately connected – is summed up by the following quotes. The first is the more famous:

'The socialism I believe in isn't really politics. It is a way of living. It is humanity. I believe the only way to live and to be truly successful is by collective effort, with everyone working for each other, everyone helping each other, and everyone having a share of the rewards at the end of the day. That might be asking a lot, but it's the way I see football and the way I see life.'

This has an emotional appeal that connects with many more people than does a detailed examination of dialectics by Marx, and I speak as a big fan of the latter. Bob Paisley reflected this attitude when he was asked about how he felt winning the European Cup in 1977, an achievement that eluded Shankly.

'Bill built the house, I just put the roof on.' This collective mentality obviously has an appeal to the left-wing mindset, and is a good way of concluding debates about whether Shankly or Paisley was a better manager.

One of Klopp's assistants appeared on a BT documentary about the history of the Anfield boot room and quoted something that he had just read in a German historical book that he felt resonated with the ethos of Klopp's Liverpool: 'Without the tailor, the King would be naked.' The legacy of this club is in the good hands of people that understand both history and the spirit of Shankly.

The second quote is less well known but is my favourite of Shankly's sayings, and that of Goulding as well:

'If I became a bin man tomorrow, I'd be the greatest bin man who ever lived. I'd have Liverpool the cleanest city on earth. I'd have everyone working with me, succeeding and sharing out the success. I'd make sure they were paid a decent wage with the best bonuses, and that we all worked hard to achieve our goals.

'Some people might say, "Ah, but they're only bin men. Why do we need to reward them so well for a job anyone can do?" But I'd ask them why they believe they are more important than a bin man? I'd ask them how proud they'd feel if this city became the cleanest in the world? And who would have made them proud? The bin man.'

Two short paragraphs that say a lot about the dignity of labour, respect and the application of basic human decency. They also tell you a lot about Shankly, including the fact that he wasn't shy about his abilities. But why would he be? Apart from the success on the pitch, he remains one of the great role models across any walk of life and his spirit lives on in this great football club.

Conclusions

It's hard not to like this current Liverpool set-up. The team is great to watch, successful and fight like hell for each other; the management model worked out with the union may not be perfect but it's a huge improvement on the regular British paradigm; the manager seems a thoroughly decent guy and the fanbase have admirable values.

Not all is perfect. Going to Liverpool as an away fan in the 1970s and 1980s was not a comfortable experience, as anyone who made that trip will tell you. By no means everyone who supported the club in those days was a comrade showing solidarity. It seemed like the whole town hated you, including the police. Actually, especially the police. I'm sure that there are still plenty of fans who like to give rugged welcomes to the visiting supporters but the pitched battles of those decades do seem to be a thing of the past. The ambushes? Probably not.

The great thing is that the wider club works to eradicate vestiges of the bad old days. After some fans came out with the chant about Chelsea rent boys early in the 2021/22 season, Klopp met Paul Amann, founder of Liverpool LGBT and fan group Kop Outs. After the meeting, Klopp said any supporters who sang the song in earnest were 'idiots', while those who participated without knowing the background should find another way of supporting the team. This ethos of the club also militates against the hideous chants about the Munich Air Disaster that were ubiquitous in the 1980s but are no longer heard at matches.

There is a sense of Scouse exceptionalism that can offend some on the left as being a form of jingoism undermining solidarity. I can understand this and spoke to a couple of Everton fans I know about it, both very firmly men of the left for whom I have a great respect. They both questioned the whole notion of a left-wing football club to an extent, and whether something so fundamentally tribal and adversarial as football could amount to anything other than a performative version of identity politics. I think this is too cynical and underestimates the commitment of many Liverpool fans, and others that we cover in this book, to the wider cause. Would we have seen Liverpool fans flying banners saying 'Justice for Grenfell' at Chelsea if they were parochial Scouse nationalists? Or chanting about Jeremy Corbyn?

It's quite possible to love your team and support them with the irrational, biased passion that afflicts all football fans but still see a bigger picture. Liverpool FC have a huge domestic and international following. Their fans espousing left-wing ideas and causes has to be seen as a good thing if you are on the left. Tens of thousands of chanting role models at Liverpool certainly did Corbyn no harm before the 2017 general election. It couldn't do too much for him after those electoral gains of 2017 prompted a series of establishment attacks to undermine his credibility and character: fan power has limits.

* * *

Don't Buy *The Sun*

– Vincent Raison –

One of the things I admire about the city of Liverpool is that all those years after Murdoch's tabloid rag defamed Liverpool fans over the Hillsborough disaster, people still largely adhere to the Don't Buy *The Sun* Campaign. There's been no forgiveness. Why would there be? No 'let bygones be bygones'. No 'I only read it for the sports section' acceptance. Crucially, there's been no forgetting what they did, and what they continued to defend for long after it was apparent their spiteful, vile coverage was based on lies.

For our younger viewers, a quick recap: 96 people died in a fatal crush at an FA Cup semi-final between Liverpool and Nottingham Forest in 1989. The independent enquiry concluded that no Liverpool fans were in any way responsible and that the main cause was police negligence, which had been subsequently covered up. Yet four days after the tragedy, before many families had even had the chance to bury their dead, 38 of whom were under 19, *The Sun* saw fit to publish untrue allegations on its front page blaming the fans, along with some rank fabrications of the most horrendous behaviour. The hurt they caused is unimaginable.

In an article for *The Spectator*, Boris Johnson accused Liverpudlians of wallowing in 'victim status' over Hillsborough. What he failed to understand is that their campaign to achieve justice for those who died was not about victimhood, it was about truthfulness and principles, which would explain why he failed to recognise it.

The day of 'The Truth' headline began a city-wide boycott. Sales of the paper dropped 40 per cent overnight on Merseyside. To quote Davey Brett from vice.com:

'Depending on whose estimates you believe, the city of Liverpool has cost Rupert Murdoch either a "shit ton" or a "fuck load" of money.'

The boycott has without doubt cost the publisher millions. Copies were burnt in the street. Stickers in cafes and pubs declaring 'The Sun not welcome here' were stuck on windows. The Hillsborough Justice Campaign and Total Eclipse of The S*n kept up the pressure. Apologies came and went but no one was in any doubt – all the newspaper wanted was their market share back. The editor at the time, the odious Kelvin MacKenzie, claimed he was duped by his sources, a Tory MP and a senior police officer, but privately admitted he had been ordered to apologise and was not sorry at all. He had form publishing made-up stories and was utterly unrepentant at having done so. After discussions with the Hillsborough victims' families in February 2017, Liverpool FC barred the paper's journalists from reporting on their matches at Anfield and denied them access to the players and staff for interviews.

Then, in MacKenzie's second spell at The Sun later that year, he published a hideous article about Everton's Ross Barkley, along with more inexcusable insults aimed at Liverpudlians, the contents of which are too deplorable to repeat. Mackenzie was suspended before his contract was terminated by mutual consent, some 28 years too late. Everton banned the paper from Goodison Park and their training ground, too. 'The newspaper has to know that any attack on this city, either against a much-respected community or individual, is not acceptable,' the club said in a statement. While they were defending their player, they were also standing by their city.

The Sun wasn't alone in publishing what was essentially a police conspiracy story to hide its own guilt, but it went further and it went harder. We've all seen how the right-wing media taps into people's prejudices and sells them back to its readers. It's a lucrative business confirming ill-informed stereotypes and bolstering bigotry. Such is the poisonous effect that Rupert Murdoch has had on journalism around the globe. World leaders have felt unable to stand up to him, eagerly courting his approval instead, lest he ruin them. But the city of Liverpool stood up to him.

Murdoch has built a media empire without any moral consideration to restrain it. Caught with its pants down over the hacking scandal, News International suffered a few resignations and the closure of the *News of the World*, only to be replaced by *The Sun on Sunday*. Business continues as usual. Except on Merseyside, where the cancer called Rupert has been told to 'do one'.

How sad is it, though, that football clubs have more integrity than the succession of politicians from all sides who make their compromises with *The Sun* because of its influence?

Detroit City

Founded:	2012
Stadium:	Keyworth Stadium
Capacity:	7,933
Nicknames:	Le Rouge
Ultras:	Northern Guard, Keyworth Casuals,
	The Jolly Rouge

– VINCENT RAISON –

THERE'S A real sense of the American Dream turned nightmare within the history of Detroit. It was a gleaming success story, the centre of car manufacturing, that most American of industries, combining creativity in engineering and design with blue-collar sweat. Detroit blasted sweet soul music into almost every radio in the world and launched global icons like Marvin Gaye, Diana Ross, Stevie Wonder and The Jackson 5. By 1960, it was the richest city per capita in the whole United States, a glowing symbol of American confidence.

But by 2010, Detroit had lost more than 60 per cent of its population, with factories closing, its industrial base rotting, a city plagued with crime, poverty, unemployment and racial antagonism; its decline as spectacular as its rise. The City of Detroit would soon file the biggest municipal bankruptcy in American history, with debts of over $18bn, and had become synonymous with urban decay.

And it was against this backdrop that Detroit City Football Club was born. In a bruised and battered town that was climbing to unsteady feet once more, ready to defy the odds and revive itself.

It says a lot about Detroiters that it has succeeded in becoming a destination for tourism once more.

In 2012, five guys got together to form a football club and help support its community through sport. They were an immediate grassroots success. One of the founders, Sean Mann, and his wife may have had to mow the pitch the night before matches, but from these humble beginnings the club quickly developed an identity of its own, a progressive fanbase, and became a part of the regeneration of a city. Supporters in their hundreds became supporters in their thousands. And those supporters were unlike the fans of Detroit's other sports teams. They were committed to noise and smoke and inclusivity.

Success in the lower leagues meant City needed a proper stadium and in 2016 an investment drive, supported by local legend Iggy Pop, raised over $700,000 for them to secure and renovate Keyworth Stadium, in Hamtramck. In 2017, the club won the NPSL Midwest Regional Championship. In 2018 they hosted St Pauli at the Keyworth, an event that signalled they had not just arrived in football, they had become part of the global leftist family.

Let's get the soccer thing out of the way. Soccer is an English word derived from association football and invented to differentiate proper football from rugby football. It is still used in America to differentiate it from American football. It has fallen into disuse in the UK, just like 'gotten'. For some reason, Brits like to take the mick out of Americans for using a word we created. We're a strange bunch.

Managed by former Ipswich Town and LA Galaxy coach Trevor James, who once worked under Bobby Robson, they joined the National Independent Soccer Association in 2020 and turned professional. Two years of boasting the league's most notorious fans coincided with two championships. In 2022, they began life in the USL Championship, the second tier of American soccer – a truly remarkable rise.

The Fans

It's almost as if the Northern Guard Supporters were waiting for DCFC to happen. Founded by the Butcher brothers, Gene and

Ken, they went to the club's very first match armed with drums, smoke bombs, flares and flags in an attempt to create a similar atmosphere to those created by European ultras.

It is very unlike the support of America's other sports, which tend to be seated, a little dull and not usually on fire.

Another difference is the politics, which while born out of community support, is undeniably lefty. This, from the Northern Guard website:

'We come from all backgrounds, beliefs and traditions. We vehemently reject racism, sexism, homophobia and anything else that makes anyone feel unwelcome in our stands. The only two things we hate are hate and Oh*o. No matter where you come from, if you support City, we support you.'

I'm not sure the Ohio thing is ironic, given the popularity of their 'Fuck Ohio' scarves in the stands, but as previously mentioned, humans have a terrible habit of loathing their neighbours, who are often the people most like them. The 'profanity scarves' have now been banned from the ground, causing fan groups' concerns about censorship and sanitisation of their support. But aside from the Buckeyes, everyone is welcome and, like many of the clubs in this book, their politics is connected to music.

'The lefty thing came from the punk, ska and skinhead communities,' Matt from the Keyworth Casuals told us. The Casuals provide 'a bridge between the football club, activism and the music scene', he said.

It's interesting that the fans look to mainland Europe rather than the UK for terrace inspiration, despite the adoption of some very British chants.

'It's much more German or Italian,' said Matt. 'The Northern Guard are choreographed. The chants aren't organic.'

Even St Pauli fans are having a conversation about whether chants should be spontaneous, like in the UK. It's true, support is much more organised on the Continent. Consequently, it continues for 90 minutes, and doesn't experience the post-half-time-pie-and-pint lull. Having said that, the Northern Guard do sing the Millwall anthem, 'No one likes us, we don't care,' as well as Manchester City's 'We're ruining football and we don't care,' albeit for different reasons to the Mancs.

Plus they will 'Tetris' in the stands, linking arms and shuffling side to side while singing the melody to the video game. And many will wear costumes or skull masks. As Ken Butcher explained, 'We wore face masks that looked like skulls because we kept hearing that the city of Detroit was dead. Well, if we are dead, then we're gonna be the walking dead.'

It's hard to gauge whether opposition supporters really don't like Detroit fans, but it's almost certainly true that they've never seen anything like them before. They might seem tame compared to say, Galatasaray, but they're in a league of their own at their level. Never mind smoke bombs, Americans are not that used to swearing at sports grounds. But the atmosphere is more like a party than a riot.

Black Arrow Award

The player of the year in US sports is known as the MVP (Most Valuable Player). But at Detroit City, the MVP award is known as the Black Arrow Award. 'The Black Arrow' was the nickname given to Gil Heron, the first black player to turn out for Celtic, who played for the Detroit Corinthians and Detroit Wolverines as well, where he was top scorer in the NASFL in 1946. Gilbert Saint Elmo Heron was also father to Gil Scott-Heron, the poet and musician most famous for his landmark poem *The Revolution Will Not Be Televised*; a classic filled with wit, cultural references and restrained acid anger at the position of black people in American society, and a forerunner for rap music.

Spotted by a Celtic scout when the Glasgow giant was touring North America, he signed for the Bhoys in 1951. He scored on his debut, but only made half a dozen appearances before moving on to Third Lanark. Nonetheless, he made quite an impression. Not everyone gets a nickname.

Born in Jamaica, he also played cricket at a decent level while in Scotland before returning to the US and becoming a published poet, like the son he would not see between the ages of two to 26. He died at 86 in Detroit in 2008. DCFC honours a man they see as one of their own with this award.

Detroit Sport

Soccer has a curious place in the American sports scene. From here in the UK, it's hard to imagine the Beautiful Game being behind NFL, baseball, basketball and even ice hockey in the affections of a populace. Football is the most popular sport in the world by far; it's an absolute dominator. That's because it's the best sport in the world by far. Sorry, not sorry.

To see how different America is from the rest of the world, you only have to look at its sports. There is a sense in America, at least this is what I felt when I lived there, that America *is* the world. But football is the world's *lingua franca* and it's barely spoken there. While there is some interest in American sports in Europe, globally it is pretty irrelevant. And to most Americans, so is soccer. It's not the common language that divides us. It's balls.

And it's in this landscape that Detroit City is making its mark. Detroit already has four major sports teams: Detroit Lions (NFL), the only franchise operational for the entirety of the Super Bowl era to not appear in the Super Bowl; Detroit Tigers (baseball); Detroit Pistons (basketball); and the Detroit Red Wings (ice hockey), the most successful of the Detroit outfits. But the matchday experience of all these teams is far removed from that of the Keyworth.

'Detroit City has ruined other sports for me,' said Matt. 'I went to a Red Wings play-off game. I can't sit down [to watch sport]. The Tigers was cool because baseball is just a drinking thing. It's in the background. It's like a picnic. But I can't watch NFL.'

US sport seems to be predicated on its ability to facilitate TV advertising. They all have short bursts of activity that can just be halted while the business of capitalism does its thing. You can't do that with football. You can't stop the game to advertise Coca-Cola. Every little run, movement, tackle, pass and shirt-pull is more important than Coca-Cola.

There's hardly any singing at any of the other sports, unless you count 'Defense! Defense!' (*sic*) as singing. Which I don't. The only other musical expression you'll hear at the ball game is the national anthem, played and honoured at every US professional sports stadium in the country. You can get away without singing it, but woe betide you if you don't stand for it. There was more bravery in Colin Kaepernick's knee than in a million hand-on-heart gestures in the bleachers of America.

Patriotism is a powerful presence throughout the country. When in a foreign land, it's only right to respect local customs, though as a lefty, I found displays of nationalism do feel a little off, especially when they were allied to an adoration for the military, as I experienced at the Philadelphia Phillies. It's disconcerting to see such unquestioning veneration for an institution that not only protects America, but has killed so many civilians – in Vietnam, Iraq, Afghanistan and elsewhere – causing so much misery around the world. Just as it is to hear the loons at home defending the British Empire doing the same from Ireland to India and beyond. So, in a book featuring clubs that largely tend to eschew expressions of nationalism, such as St Pauli, where national flags are not allowed in the stadium, it is jarring to know that such a rebellious club as Detroit City has to play 'The Star-Spangled Banner' before games. I was told they have no choice. That they have to, 'by league mandate, but it is played at the earliest allowable time, which is before the broadcast starts and even before the majority of spectators have arrived'.

The irony of that anthem is that it comes not from the War of Independence, but from the War of 1812, a footnote in America and Britain's history, that basically ended in a draw (between the US and Britain, alongside Canada): a war in which the British, of all people, fought alongside Native American tribes to try to halt America's expansion into indigenous lands.

The Jolly Rouge supporters' group don't speak for everybody, but their Independence Day tweet of 2020 in support of Black Lives Matter was notable: 'This country has way too far to go before it's worthy of celebration.'

America and Antifa

America's relationship with anti-fascism is peculiar, which, given all of the above, may be expected. It's a conservative country in which both the main parties are right of centre and both are beholden to the military-industrial complex. But it is by no means a homogenous nation. In a country of over 300 million, there are a lot of left-wing voices, often drowned out by a conservative mainstream media, quite apart from the rabid outlets like Fox News. In antifa (pronounced an-TEE-fa, in the US), the far-right have a catch-all bogeyman they can demonise, without reflecting on what that means.

'You're either with us, or against us,' has been used by many on the political right, such as Mussolini and George W. Bush. It's a reductionist tactic that denies society's shades of grey and discourages scrutiny. But if you take that to its logical extension with fascism, you're either antifa or you're pro-fascism; you're pro-Nazis. Yet it seems completely acceptable, even mainstream, to be anti-antifa, without following through on what that actually represents.

Despite what the more unhinged commentators on the right might say, American antifa is not an organisation, but a movement of many unaffiliated groups who oppose right-wing extremism and white supremacy. And although the modern movement began in the 1980s with Anti-Racist Action, it was almost dormant until Donald Trump came to office in January 2017. Eight days after his inauguration, Trump signed an executive order banning people from six Muslim-majority countries from entering the United States. Hours later, Marq Vincent Perez burnt down the Victoria Islamic Center in Texas (for which he received 24 years for committing a hate crime). The left was threatened by the activities of the right in America, probably more than at any time since the McCarthy-era communist witch hunts, but it was not alone in feeling threatened by extremists when there was one giving them succour in the White House. The rise of Trump emboldened the far-right, and antifa groups rose to oppose them, to counter-protest extremist marches and make it harder for white supremacists to organise events.

In a country where even liberal is a dirty word, soccer seems to be a sanctuary for leftists, relatively speaking.

Aside from Detroit City, the top flight of the sport in America, Major League Soccer (MLS) has a number of anti-fascist supporter's groups, at Portland Timbers, Seattle Sounders and CF Montréal (née Montreal Impact).

The Timbers Army try to create a European atmosphere at Portland games, with singing and *tifos*. They even have a *Fanladen*, a tribute no doubt to the Hamburg paragon. The Timbers Army's use of the Iron Front symbol – three arrows – breached a ban on political symbols the MLS brought in in 2019. The Iron Front was an organisation in Germany opposing totalitarianism in the 1930s. Consisting of social democrats, trade unionists and liberals, they opposed Nazism, communism and monarchism. However, the Timbers Army fought the ban by arguing that the fascism, racism and sexism they opposed were not political but related to human rights. Normally filling their ground with noise, they staged a protest by remaining silent at a nationally televised match against Seattle until the 33rd minute (to commemorate 1933, when the Iron Front was disbanded), when they belted out *'Bella Ciao'*, the glorious Italian anti-fascist anthem. Amazingly, after the league met with supporters, they reversed their decision and allowed the Iron Front flag to fly again.

Seattle fans joined in with the protest. While the ban was in effect, the banner saying 'Anti-Fascist | Anti-Racist | Always Seattle' remained, though some fans were removed for displaying that message at an away game in Vancouver in 2017. Unbelievable, Jeff.

Detroit's own Keyworth Casuals were heavily influenced by Brigada 71, the supporter's group of the New York Cosmos, currently plying their trade in the National Independent Soccer Association (NISA) – the third tier of American soccer. The Cosmos is a famous name from previous attempts to promote proper football as a major sport stateside. In the 1970s, they could name Pelé, Franz Beckenbauer and Carlos Alberto in their side, albeit all in the twilight of their careers. The club was reborn in 2010 and again attracted big names, though this time in non-playing roles, which was probably best given that Eric Cantona was 45 when they played their first match – at Old Trafford for Paul Scholes's testimonial – and Pelé was 71.

The Casuals' Matt came across Brigada 71 when he came to New York to see St Pauli play. He discovered that they were pretty much the same group as New York St Pauli. This is how they describe themselves on the Brigada 71 website:

'We are Cosmopolitan, we are anti-fascists, we are committed to keeping the rising racist, homophobic, transphobic, & xenophobic tide away from our club and our community. Punk football, and football for all.'

Brigada 71 collect money to fund their *tifos*, flags, smoke displays and away days, but also to support Clapton CFC's membership drive, St Pauli's *Viva Con Agua* fundraiser as well as topical collections, for instance to support victims of the white-nationalist attacks in Charlottesville, Virginia.

It's worth remembering the sheer diversity of America and not generalising on the basis of the loudest voices. There are 'very fine people', not necessarily 'on both sides' as Trump declared after the Charlottesville rally, but there are very fine people.

Franchise or Club?

There are further peculiarities to the structure of American sport. Teams at the top tier of sport are not 'clubs' as we in Europe understand them. They are franchises, who pay an enormous fee to be half-owned by the league they're in and sign over the rights to their brand. They can then be moved to another city if the league feels they are not generating enough income. It's hard to imagine Everton, say, moving to the West Midlands to become the Dudley Blues, at the behest of the Premier League. And that is because the very heart and soul of Everton FC resides in the city of Liverpool, at Goodison Park. The fans would go ballistic and it would never get off the ground. By moving a team/franchise from New York to California it suggests sports clubs either have no heart and soul, or if they do, they don't matter.

We did of course have Wimbledon, who were moved by their owners to Milton Keynes. (And if you're a south London pedant like myself, you might say the same of Woolwich Arsenal, who moved to north London.) But nonetheless, it's a very different approach to the organisation of sport in the US, and Detroit City has more in common with the origin stories of football clubs over here. Some guys got together and made a team and local people felt proud enough of them to come and support them. But it gets complicated, because, having risen from the fourth tier of football to the second, there's only one place left to go: MLS. And that means they would be vulnerable to being moved elsewhere – even Ohio.

And it would be ridiculous. Detroit City cannot exist anywhere other than Detroit. And, should MLS really want to expand into Detroit and move another franchise there, they would find that the entire soccer fanbase of the place would still be going to see City instead.

Here's what the Northern Guard had to say on the subject:

> 'We would be lying if that wasn't a concern. That's the make-up of the land in the United States. If you have something successful there's always going to be someone that wants a piece of it or the whole thing. [DCFC] though have shown us they really care about our opinions and thoughts especially when it comes to any corporate aspects. Just this past month we successfully got the club to end a relationship with a sponsor who we thought didn't fit the overall culture of the club.
>
> 'As it stands right now, if DCFC were to make the jump to MLS it wouldn't be DCFC anymore. It would be a centrally-owned MLS franchise with big money investors who could be moved at any time.

'But the club is very much rooted in the community and maintained their own IP when making the jump [to the USL Championship] – they are very much still a club.'

Millionaire investors have been sniffing around Detroit, but so far the club has been safe from the sharks. At least, as far as anyone knows. From a DCFC fan on social media platform Reddit:

'The current ownership group consists of five guys who are just guys who wanted to start up a soccer club. To make the jump to pro, they had to bring in an investor. I don't think anyone outside of the ownership group knows who this mysterious benefactor actually is. Supporters generally like the idea that anyone can start a club, not just the super-rich, although we somewhat sheepishly welcome the support of our mystery millionaire.'

And as mentioned above, the sensibilities of the fans are respected by the owners.

'There's also a very big social aspect to the club. City announced a new sponsor this year who went against the values of the supporters (big MAGA guy), and a lot of them flipped out. City's response was to drop that sponsor. It really was incredible to see, and showed that the owners really do care about the opinions of their supporters. The closest similar club I can think of is St Pauli.'

It's really heartening to hear that money doesn't rule everything in American sport. There are principles that are held dear. Another principle held at DCFC that isn't shared by the rest of the sport is the issue of promotion and relegation. In most US sports it doesn't matter how badly you suck (see Detroit Lions), there are no consequences, other than a disused trophy cabinet. You still make loads of money and are still back at the table next season for more. The reason is bound up with capitalism. Why would investors pump millions into NFL teams if there's a chance a bad year could substantially degrade the worth of a franchise? If you keep it a closed shop, everyone is happy, except those outside the shop. And if you want in, you have to await league expansion and pay millions of dollars to join.

Ironically, attracting new talent to NFL franchises is among the most socialist transactions in America. Young stars don't come up through grassroots clubs, they play for their college. And every year the team with the worst record gets to pick the best college player, to try to give the league a chance of equity. It's truly remarkable. It's not possible in Europe as we don't have that same relationship between education and youth sport. But it is in many ways preferable to the current set-up in the UK, where the biggest clubs hoover up as much talent as possible, with little thought as to how many will be spat out, unqualified to do anything else, and are often finished in the game in their teens. And when smaller clubs do develop fine young players, the Elite Player Performance Plan, adopted in 2011, ensures that the richest clubs no longer have to pay the market rate to poorer clubs, which has seen several grassroots clubs close their academies. So when it comes to developing talent, it's the UK that bows to the moneyed elite, not the US.

It is however sad that at some point Detroit City may face a choice between playing at the highest level in their country, or retaining their integrity and identity. I'd hope, and expect, them to choose the latter, but it does MLS no credit that it's set up to discourage grassroots football from flourishing and challenging the game's most successful sides (apart from in the US Open Cup, which has been going since 1914 and is set up much like our FA Cup). I don't know which is more American, submitting to the greed of capitalism, or fighting for the ambitions of underdogs.

Actually, no, I do.

Dulwich Hamlet

Founded:	1893
Stadium:	Champion Hill
Capacity:	3,334
Nicknames:	The Hamlet
Fans:	The Rabble, Dultras

– VINCENT RAISON –

WE'LL GO on to discuss what we mean by 'left-wing' later in this chapter, but now we're all the way down to the sixth tier of English football to look for real political engagement in the national game, uncompromised by the vast commercial operation of top-flight football. Lots of clubs throughout the Premier and Football Leagues do fantastic charity and community work, without tying their colours to any particular political mast for fear of dividing the fanbase. Because even Marcus Rashford's successful and wholly laudable campaign to shame the government into feeding vulnerable children has attracted the ire of some, who risibly suggest he 'stick to football', instead of being an exemplary human being.

There have been many great socialist managers over the years: Matt Busby, Bill Shankly and Brian Clough, for instance. Their ideals still echo in some supporters – Fans Supporting Food Banks, for instance, a joint initiative of Everton and Liverpool fans, inspired by Celtic's Green Brigade, is a great example of progressive football activism. But both Liverpool and Manchester United are global brands, profit-orientated behemoths, and their initial support for the European Super League project, which could have decimated grassroots football to provide an eternal cartel for the world's richest clubs, reflects badly on their motives. Many Liverpool fans are of the left though and remain inspired by the wisdom of Shankly (see the Liverpool chapter on page 94).

One of the differences between the UK and Germany, Italy and Spain, is that we've never had a fascist government. Nor have we been occupied by the Nazis, like Belgium, Czechia and France. However flawed our democracy is, it has never been taken away from us. So anti-fascism could be considered less relevant than anti-racism here. Being anti-fascist in England means being opposed to a small group of fringe lunatics who have no power beyond their offensiveness. Racism has been the most prominent language of far-right expression in the UK for decades, though a number of anti-democratic moves from our current government provide legitimate cause for concern.

It took a long time for football to challenge racism in its midst, but in some ways it has tackled it better than wider society, certainly better than, say, the Metropolitan Police. There is still work to do, but you can say that racism in football is generally unacceptable now, when in the 1970s and beyond it was common and barely remarked upon. Most clubs support anti-racist initiatives, and some support anti-homophobia stances, but down at non-league level you'll see fans batting for refugees, food banks and being openly against Islamophobia and transphobia. That's where you'll find Dulwich Hamlet, Whitehawk, Clapton, West Didsbury & Chorlton, FC United of Manchester, and Eastbourne Town – fan-owned clubs run by volunteers that set their own agendas.

The Hamlet

Battling against the odds to keep their ground and fighting for promotion would be enough on the plate of most football clubs. But National League South outfit Dulwich Hamlet are not most clubs. Thanks to a politically and socially engaged supporter base – and a board that listens to its fans – they back a number of good causes. Their place in the sixth tier of England's football pyramid may represent the pinnacle of their 127-year history, but in many respects they are in a league of their own.

Dulwich have never been an ordinary club. Their proud history in non-league football includes four FA Amateur Cups and four Isthmian League titles. Their Champion Hill ground was used in the 1948 Olympic Games. And they had the last non-league footballer to play for England. The name of Edgar Kail, who scored two goals against France on his England debut, is still chanted at every game, though the last of the 427 goals he scored for the Pink and Blues was in 1933.

Their crowds began to grow around 2013, with people drawn to a warmer, less confrontational football atmosphere and away from the millionaire showroom of the Premier League. One fan in particular saw an opportunity for the club to appeal to a less traditional fanbase. In February 2015, the Hamlet played a friendly against Stonewall FC, Britain's top gay football club, thanks to the initiative of Dulwich superfan Mishi Morath, with all the proceeds going to the Elton John Aids Foundation. Sadly, Mishi passed away in 2019, but his legacy is a club that always tries to 'do the right thing'.

'We do get labelled "lefties", or just plain weird. Let them label us,' said Mishi. 'All I see are Dulwich Hamlet fans united as one, not deliberately being political, even if some of us are. Just doing what is right, and working with our local community. Making all welcome, regardless of race, religion, sexuality, gender or colour is what all football clubs should be naturally striving for.'

A lifelong socialist, Mishi was born into Dulwich Hamlet, growing up on the East Dulwich Estate and being taken to games as a kid. He found himself at home at Champion Hill, where his ideas to promote anti-racism and anti-homophobia, as well as forge ties with like-minded clubs around Europe, such as Altona 93, St Pauli's lower-league neighbours in Hamburg, were enthusiastically embraced.

His energy and outlook made the Hamlet an exemplary community club and among the most inclusive football clubs around. Indeed, they were named the Football Foundation Community Club of the Year at the National Game Awards in 2016. And it's a direction driven by the fans, as club director Tom Cullen told me.

'It comes from the terraces to the boardroom. Which isn't that far, to be fair,' he said. 'We're all fans.'

Leafy Dulwich is an unlikely location for politico-football pioneers. Dulwich Village is one of the most affluent areas in London, whereas East Dulwich, home to Champion Hill, is in the full bloom of gentrification. But it does retain its strong sense of community in a solidly Labour constituency.

In 2017, the club played a fundraising match against Assyria FC to raise money for the Southwark Refugee Forum and the British Red Cross Syria appeal, raising thousands of pounds. They also collected donations for the Dulwich2Dunkirk campaign, providing food for refugee camps in Northern France. In 2016, they teamed up with The Bike Project to gather second-hand bikes to donate to refugees, giving them much-needed independence while on a low income in our expensive capital city.

But the club also collects money for The Royal British Legion and Help For Heroes around Remembrance Day, facts that are often overlooked by their detractors. After all, they lost several players in World War II.

But the club itself has faced existential difficulties; problems that even threatened its survival. In 2014, their ground was sold to property developers Meadows Residential, who four years later locked the club out of the ground. Dulwich were forced to groundshare with their rivals, Tooting & Mitcham, a situation that would not have been sustainable for long. Sadiq Khan and Jeremy Corbyn both lent their support to the campaign to save the club, as did Conservative MP Tracey Crouch. During this period, however, they gained promotion to the National League South for the first time amid delirious scenes, after a play-off penalty shoot-out against Hendon.

Battles with property developers rarely end well for those opposing them, but after some careful negotiations, they were allowed back into their ground to continue their great work on and off the pitch.

The last eight years have seen Dulwich's crowds grow from a few hundred to regularly selling out their ground, with 3,334 souls cramming into Champion Hill. For a club at this level of football, that is remarkable. There are many reasons for this. One, I've already mentioned: the disillusionment with top-level football. Another is the Champion Hill experience. It includes families and dogs, as well as local craft beer and food producers. On days when there's room, you can walk around the ground with your drink, to join 'The Rabble' behind the goal to sing their numerous anthems. Abusing opponents is not encouraged, though reading the keeper his Facebook updates can prove more disconcerting to a goalie than any insult.

The absence of aggression is a breath of fresh air amid all the nonsense of the beautiful but sometimes spiteful game.

The third reason for the Hamlet's rise is the manager, Gavin Rose. After more than ten years at the helm, Rose has lost none of his drive to make the club progress. And none of the club's work for good causes would have been possible without his support and participation. He's seen numerous players pass through Champion Hill on their way to careers in the Football League and he's overseen two promotions and the club's transition from relative obscurity to one of the best-supported clubs in non-league football. Born in nearby Peckham, Rose has previously said it doesn't get much better than growing your local club, success coupled with a conscience also takes some beating.

The fans have made many friends along the way; most notably with Altona 93 in Hamburg, with whom they share a strong bond, and with Red Star in Paris, whom they played a supporters' friendly match against a few years ago, thanks in part to Mishi.

As for the future, the club has seen off a storm – two if you count Covid – and still have an outstanding manager, a good squad and a fanbase with a focus on social issues and having a good time. In 2019, they added a women's team that is thriving in their new home. And while the club may say they are not political, they make clear their offering is for everyone – a statement that shouldn't be political but sadly is.

What is Left?

'We're not a left-wing football club,' said Scolly, another of the club's directors and the vice-chair of the Dulwich Hamlet Supporters Trust. 'We just try to do the right thing, like Mishi said. Is collecting for refugees "left-wing"? Isn't it just humanitarian?

'It's a very big part of the club that everyone is treated equally, everybody's welcome, everybody's included. We don't make judgements about anybody. If you seem to be doing some good, you're tagged left-wing. That has to shift.'

Scolly was not just echoing Mishi but Bill Shankly too, who said, 'When you hear people running down fellas that are socialists I think they are wrong. They don't know what they are talking about … I'm talking life. I'm not talking about politics in the true sense of politics … I'm talking about humanity. People dealing with people and people helping people.'

Chairman Ben Clasper is similarly puzzled at the pejorative labelling of the club. Having seen his sober dedication and professionalism on Discovery+'s Peter Crouch-led documentary *Save Our Beautiful Game* I was a little surprised at just how passionate he was about everything Hamlet. Mind you, that was after we'd had a couple of pints. He told us how they offered the use of their fairly enormous top floor of their main stand to a local food bank and were told, 'Thanks, but it's too small.'

'Too small! That shows just how much food banks are needed in modern Britain. But, if we help a food bank, we're considered left-wing. When did food become left-wing?'

Yet, food banks are seen as a left-wing concern. Helping people in need should be normal, not political and not tribal.

David Rogers, a volunteer at both the men's and women's matches at Champion Hill, put it like this, 'We want everyone to be welcome. But having said that, we do a lot of things that marry up to a left-wing stance, like refugee collections, anti-homophobia and anti-transphobia initiatives. But that's just the fans. If fans go to the club and say we want to do this, they usually say, "OK."'

David got involved after moving down from Manchester and getting turned off Premier League football by silly prices and soulless stadiums. He came to watch the Hamlet with a mate and, 'It was a good laugh, basically. I ended up coming down all the time and getting involved with the initiatives they have here. Really good stuff, like helping refugees. Doing massive trips to Calais with van loads of goods to help people out. It was when there were pictures on the news of people washing up on the beach. We thought, right, we need to do something about this. We put feelers out and come matchdays we were filling tables and tables with the stuff. Coats, boots, waterproofs. A pair of Superman trunks. We did three trips to Calais.'

It begs the question: what do we mean by left-wing? Do we mean radical socialism? Is collecting food and clothes for people in need radical in any way? Or do we simply mean concerned with equality and for the disadvantaged in society? In which case, sorry Dulwich, you're bloody lefty bastards.

But if you find yourself criticising them for what they do, there is a word for you too.

Neighbours

There's a toxicity at Premier and Football League grounds that is absent in non-league football. The rivalries can be nasty and should players fail to excel, it can result in some pretty rank abuse, the sheer importance of three 'massive' points overriding basic human decency. What matters is the win; what matters is the bragging rights; what matters is lording it over someone else. It's no wonder so many have been turned on to a level of football where fans can simply enjoy themselves and have a pint on the terraces surrounded by people who do not appear to be arseholes.

Dulwich have definitely benefited from those who have tired of the upper levels of the game throughout London. Many fans of their larger neighbours in south-east London – Crystal Palace,

Millwall and Charlton – find themselves at Champion Hill leaving anger and local arguments aside.

The taking of the knee has become a gesture open to interpretation since its quite straightforward origin – protesting racial inequality and police brutality in America in 2016 before NFL games. After many clubs decided to take the knee in England during the 2020/21 season in support of the Black Lives Matter movement, others, including Millwall, decided to put a halt to it after it attracted boos from their own fans. They wanted a 'less divisive' gesture to express their solidarity with anti-racism, such as linking arms, holding a banner promoting equality. BLM and the taking of the knee had Marxist connotations, according to some on the right-wing. For the players, it was clearly simply an anti-racist message, unless *Das Kapital* has made a surprise incursion into the dressing rooms of England. Yet England fans booed their own players and were given succour by the government and right-wing press. But when Hungary fans booed England and the Republic of Ireland players for taking the knee, it became impossible to say it was about disputed economic theory once they followed it up with monkey chants. When Wales were booed in the Czech Republic the Welsh fans responded by chanting 'Racist bastards!' at them. Racists aren't the only ones who enjoy freedom of speech.

At Dulwich Hamlet, the taking of the knee is met with warm applause. At Charlton Athletic, it's performed so quickly that anyone that wants to boo has to be quick, and anyone who wants to have a word with them has to be quicker. When Millwall hosted Crystal Palace live on television in Jan 2022, Millwall fans booed Palace players taking the knee loudly before the game.

'I wondered, "Is there a purpose to this anymore?"' Scolly asked himself. 'But [The booing] reinvigorated me to think, "Yes, there is a point to this."'

Danny Mills

One Dulwich player who also believes there's a point to the knee is striker Danny Mills, whose work for the charities Show Racism

The Red Card (SRtRC), Shout Out For Mental Health and Kick It Out Players Advisory Board saw him named on the 2021 Football Black List, as one of the most inspirational black educators.

'Of course it's still needed,' he said. 'Because we're not where we need to be. Look at what happened at the Euros. Look at the abuse on social media.'

But Danny was also keen to point out that taking the knee is not solely about racism.

'It's about solidarity with all those who have suffered discrimination.'

Danny is a classic No.9. Tall and strong, he's the focal point of the Hamlet attack, scoring goals and bringing others into the game. His league career started at Peterborough United, but he's had hundreds of games at National League level, including more than 170 for Whitehawk, another left-leaning club, on the East Sussex coast. I asked him whether the club they played for made a difference to footballers.

'I can only speak for myself but it was a factor in signing for Dulwich. [I asked myself,] "What does this football club stand for? What do they represent?" And I've really bought into their ethos.'

So much so that Danny is now the equality and diversity officer at the club. But it was the pandemic that led him to seek other ways to make himself useful.

Show Racism the Red Card is the UK's leading anti-racism educational charity. It was established in January 1996, thanks in part to a donation by former Reading, Newcastle, West Ham and Portsmouth goalkeeper Shaka Hislop. He was moved to act after being racially abused by a group of people while he was filling his car up with petrol in Newcastle. His wife and young daughter were inside the car. When they realised who they were insulting, they changed their tune and asked for an autograph. It was then that he realised footballers could make a difference in challenging racism in society.

Danny gives workshops in primary schools, secondary schools, universities and to adult groups, using football, telling Shaka's story to get over an important lesson and get kids to think. They see a short film featuring people like Harry Kane, Trent Alexander-Arnold and Harry Maguire.

'Once they know you've been a footballer, you've got the room,' said Danny. 'You let them know they are in a safe space to ask questions. They get to define racism, talk about stereotypes, unconscious bias, and get to challenge their own way of thinking. They surprise themselves. It's an eye-opener. And there's a need for what we do. A need for this dialogue.'

It's hugely valuable work in the battle against bigotry.

The Rabble

Having been a football spectator for many decades in the Football League and then later the Premier League, it was a breath of fresh air to go to The Hamlet. Humour, friendship, beer and football are among the pillars of a good life in my view, and they are all present on the terraces of Champion Hill.

With three bars all selling decent beer, unlike most Premier League grounds, the pre-match pint is often taken at the ground. As are the post-match pints. It's noticeable that the crowd can be a bit quiet in the first half until the effect of those pints inspires song.

'Tuscany! Tuscany! We're the famous Dulwich Hamlet and we look like Tuscany,' goes the puzzling chant from The Rabble.

A local objector to planning permission for the Champion Hill ground claimed that the proposal should be rejected because, from his window, the area 'looks like Tuscany'. It's not something you hear a great deal in south London, but the NIMBYism has been immortalised in song and reflected in the waving of Tuscan regional flags at games.

Away days to towns like Margate, Bognor Regis, Eastbourne and Canvey Island are bound to be enormous fun, taking in fading English seaside towns, great beer and welcoming locals. Like a holiday with a 3pm kick-off thrown in.

Players and clubs often get their own bespoke songs, in contrast to the one-size-fits-all approach of many clubs further up the football pyramid. Met Police FC got: 'Repressive state apparatus, you're just a repressive state apparatus.' While Canvey Island heard: 'You're not a proper island! You're not a proper island!'

The opposing goalkeeper is more likely to be accused of voting Liberal Democrat than be called a cunt. 'Hang the lino, hang the lino!' is about as threatening as they get.

English irony isn't for everyone in the meaty world of football, but it is another thread of non-league football that differentiates it from the upper echelons of the game.

Matchday: Welling United 1 Dulwich Hamlet 3, February 2022

With recent Saturday games at Champion Hill being sell-outs, I opted for a midweek local derby away day on a Tuesday night. Not that there's any derby tension with Welling, a mere ten miles away in south London, which is a shame in a way, as the febrile atmosphere of a derby match is one of the greatest things in football.

As Welling is home to two micro-pubs (shops converted to pubs), nothing could be more certain than a visit to both before an evening kick-off. I met Pompey Dunc, an inveterate groundhopper and Hamlet fan, in The Hanger during happy hour for an excellent pint of £3 cask ale before heading to The Door Hinge, which was filled with Hamlet and Wings fans. Not that Welling is a hotbed of support for Paul McCartney's post-Beatles project, but Welling United are known as 'The Wings', presumably due to the winged horse on their badge. The Wings fans were affable, buoyed by a recent good result, but haunted by a general decline in the club's fortunes.

Welling have had some notable managers in the past, such as former England international Paul Parker and Republic of Ireland international Liam Daish. But perhaps none as prestigious as the manager that evening, Peter Taylor, who was caretaker manager of England for one game, in which he named David Beckham as captain for the first time. Here he plied his trade in more modest surroundings, the crumbling Park View Road ground, which

Welling share with Erith & Belvedere FC. He has since been sacked and replaced by Warren Feeney. Having spent most of this century in the top two levels of non-league football, they were in danger of slipping out of the National League South to the seventh level of the English football pyramid for the first time since the 1980s.

It was a good turn-out on a wet Tuesday night from The Rabble, who probably outnumbered the home crowd. Pints and burgers accompanied kick-off and the Hamlet, resplendent in their pink away kit, looked on top even before long-serving defender Quade Taylor's strike from outside the box put them one up early on. After half an hour, Dulwich were two up, through a sharp finish from striker Chike Kandi, an ex-Chelsea youth who's found his feet in non-league. Early in the second half, Taylor got his second, from close range, before former Dulwich hero Dipo Akenyimi pulled one back from the spot. The 3-1 win put Dulwich back into the play-off spots and left Welling further in the mire, with some gloomy but stoic faces among the Wings fans in the pub after the game. 'Might not see you next year, lads,' said one, sadly, exiting the Door Hinge door. They will meet again shortly, as Dulwich slipped into mid-table and Welling managed to avoid relegation by a comfortable two points.

The Future

Every club in the world strives to reach the highest level they can and fulfil their potential. It's conceivable that Dulwich could win promotion to the National League in the not-so-distant future, further than they've ever been before and one step below the Football League. It would be an incredible achievement for a club that not so recently lacked a home and whose entire future was in doubt. But even as they plan for such a contingency, there is a sense of dread. Because in the mad world of non-league football, it would be a financial disaster for them.

As much as 50 per cent of Dulwich's income comes from booze sold at the game. But if they get promoted, they will no longer be allowed to sell alcohol within sight of the pitch. So they can be as successful as they want, but they had better not try to enjoy it.

Wages would also increase hugely, if they were to attempt to compete at that level and sign players capable of keeping them there. Ground improvements would entail considerable cost in addition, making success on the pitch a distinctly double-edged sword. It's a crazy situation. Why can't UK football fans be treated like adults and be allowed a pint while watching the game? Sadly, we all know the answer to that and it's a sad indictment of our culture.

Will 3,000-plus fans show up if they can't drink? Will anybody sing without the aid of pints? Given that the main reason Dulwich thrives is that it's fun, success could ruin them. What a sad and strange state of affairs it is that a lack of booze could have a devastating effect. Though given the nous, dedication and creativity of the people who run the club and volunteer for it, you wouldn't put it past them to find a way forward.

Clapton CFC

Breaking away from the original Clapton FC (founded 1878) and starting again from the bottom of our impressively large football pyramid, having also lost your historic home, couldn't have been easy. But Clapton Community FC are exceptional in many ways. The club's away shirt, inspired by the International Brigades and the flag of the Second Spanish Republic has 'No Pasarán' stitched into it – They Shall Not Pass – the anti-fascist slogan of the Spanish Civil War. The club sold 11,500 of them, 5,500 of them in Spain; an extraordinary amount for a club that struggles to get 100 fans to games in the 11th level of the National League System.

After a Clapton Ultras' boycott of Clapton FC, due to a long-running dispute with owner Vince McBean, who tried to close down the charity that ran it, they set up their fan-owned breakaway club. They won the right to return to London's oldest senior football ground, the Old Spotted Dog in Forest Gate, and through the hard work of their community they have rolled back decades of neglect to ready it for an emotional homecoming for the 2022/23 season.

McGill and I watched a men's game at their temporary Walthamstow home, nicknamed The Stray Dog, in January 2022, catching an impressive 6-0 victory in the Alec Smith Premier Cup, a trophy they would go on to win. 'Don't mention Dulwich here,' I told McGill as we tucked into the delicious spicy potato samosas on sale at the ground. 'I hear they're not fans.'

When I returned from the bar with a couple of pints, McGill had already made friends with Sam, a journalist with the *Socialist Worker*. Sam introduced us to other fans and proved a great host, despite Stewart immediately spilling that I follow Dulwich Hamlet.

The team looked very good for this level, and destined to progress through the pyramid. The fans are proudly anti-fascist, and, unusually for a UK club, fond of the bit of pyro. However, as they were in somebody else's ground, they were on their best behaviour.

The singing and drumming were fairly constant but once a few beers had gone down, the anti-Dulwich Hamlet songs came out. It's quite peculiar that of all the teams they could choose to diss, they would choose the one most closely aligned to them, even if Dulwich claim to be apolitical. Clapton, to their credit, nail their colours firmly to the mast. But it is sadly symptomatic of the left all over that division is more common than unity. And sadly, in the UK, it's one of the reasons why we so often have a Tory government.

But did that mean we couldn't have a pint and a laugh together in the Dog & Duck afterwards? Certainly not. That would be going too far.

There's a lot to admire at The Tons, including the equal status and support for the women's team, who also won silverware in 2022, winning the Capital Cup and gaining promotion to tier six for the 2022/23 season. They had a great run in the FA Cup as well, where, despite being in the seventh tier, they made their way to the third round. There, they were beaten by Plymouth Argyle, in front of dozens of noisy travelling fans who had made a 460-mile round-trip journey to support them.

Cosenza

Founded:	1914
Stadium:	Stadio San Vito-Gigi Marulla
Capacity:	20,987
Nicknames:	*I Lupi* (The Wolves)
Ultras:	*Cosenza Vecchia 1989, Amantea Ultras*

– STEWART McGILL –

AS WE were putting together the idea of *The Roaring Red Front* we asked people on social media and in real life which teams they would like us to cover. Many more replied with Cosenza than I expected, and as we were keen to walk down the unbeaten track with this project we decided to head down to Calabria. It was a good choice, as this was one of our more interesting, enjoyable and exhausting trips. Cosenza is a singular place with some very intense football fans. The football was terrible, the worst game we saw by some distance and the fans made their views very clear about it in a genuinely extraordinary manner that we have never seen before, nor would want to see again.

Cosenza: the Town

Cosenza is in Calabria and way down south, around the instep of the Italian boot. The city centre's population is around 70,000, the metropolitan area has around 200,000 people. The Old Town is the seat of the Cosentian Academy, one of the oldest centres of philosophical and literary studies in Europe, and the town hosts the University of Calabria. The university has approximately 25,000 students so is an important element of the town.

The city centre population reached a peak of around 105,000 in the early 1980s but has been falling steadily ever since, at an average of 2.1 per cent a year during the 1980s, though that rate of decline has become much steadier in recent years.

Unemployment in Calabria as a whole is around 16 per cent, youth unemployment around 49 per cent. Italian economic figures have to be treated with some caution, a recent study showed that the 'shadow economy', i.e. the black market, was worth as much as 12 per cent of the country's official GDP. It's probably more than that in Calabria; however, you don't feel like you're in a wealthy place in any part of the Cosenza that we saw, particularly the Old Town.

In the recent municipal elections, the centre-left won the second round in Cosenza with 57 per cent; Salvini's fascist Lega candidate received 2.8 per cent of the vote, so well done to Cosenza there.

The median age is 47, similar to that of Italy as a whole. I'm writing this in Argentina, where the median age is 31 and you notice how much younger people are in the streets. Europe has an ageing population, particularly Italy and Germany, the latter's median age being 46.

The Football

The current organisation was founded in 2011 through a circuitous route involving more than one fiery rebirth of phoenix clubs of the original Cosenza Calcio 1914. They were actually founded in 1912 but the 1914 reference was to the year of their first historic match. This club spent much of its time in Serie B, getting very close to the top flight in 1992 but never really threatening after that heart-breaking season.

They did actually win the Anglo-Italian Cup in 1983. The Anglo-Italian Cup was an event featuring English and Italian clubs that existed intermittently and in several incarnations between 1970 and 1996. It was an odd competition but is the only one that Cosenza has won, so I'm glad that it existed.

In 2003 Cosenza 1914 was suspended from the Italian league after a series of financial irregularities. Eventually a stable new club was established in 2011, Nuova Cosenza Calcio, and started in Serie D, working their way up to Serie B by 2018. They were saved from relegation to Serie C for the 2021/22 season due to tax offences by Chievo: Cosenza were the best positioned relegated side so avoided the drop. Cosenza managed to stay in Serie B at the end of the season with a narrow victory in the play-offs against Vicenza.

In the middle of an unnecessarily long process to buy a glass of wine in Napoli in 1986 the barman looked at me and smiled with a mixture of mirth and contempt for an agitated foreigner, 'You see in Italy, everything is complicated.' The paragraphs above will confirm that drop of wisdom (the barman and I bonded a little later over our uncomplicated love of Diego Maradona).

We were not drawn to Cosenza because of the football, it was solely the reputation of their fans. Cosenza fans were covered extensively in Tobias Jones's excellent book *Ultra* about the 'underworld of Italian football'. Maybe this was why so many asked that we write about Cosenza.

Matchday: Cosenza v Cremonese, December 2021

First, the important pre-match warm-up, and this was crucial to the Cosenza trip. Vince travelled by himself to Cosenza on the Friday before the game. I was up in Napoli talking to Napoli United (see Extra Time for what developed from that conversation) and was going to join him on Friday evening. He found a place called the Bulldog Ale House in the middle of Cosenza's new town: the facade featured three pictures of a thirsty looking bulldog and advertised that it featured more than 200 beers. In the UK, this would probably not attract a lefty like Vince as the bulldog has become associated with bone-headed racist nationalism. However, as Cádiz's working-class hero Andy Capp showed us, the same symbols can evoke very different feelings across different cultures. This place was for people who liked what they saw as British-style beer and a particular element of British culture.

Cosenza is not a place that attracts many visitors and it's unlikely that those who go there on business frequent this place, so Vince must have stood out. He was approached by a middle-aged Italian skinhead dressed like someone from Woolwich in 1980. Despite the vaguely menacing sound of all this, it was the start of a beautiful friendship. This was Silverio Tucci, guitar player with the Oi! band Lumpen. Silverio and his twin brother, Mattia, the band's bassist, are huge Cosenza fans.

Vince writes more about Lumpen later.

There is a group of St Pauli skinheads who are as anti-racist and anti-fascist as the rest of that club's supporters. Skinheads in the UK are now associated purely with racist aggression. It's interesting how it's more complicated in Europe, with people like Lumpen harking back to the original days of a movement that was multi-racial, loved ska and represented a fusion of white working-class and Jamaican cultures. The 'soft power' of the English language and British culture is also striking: Andy Capp; the ubiquity of the graffito 'ACAB'; the enduring appeal of the skinhead culture; the fact that one of the bands in the 1980s ska scene that influenced Silverio was called 'Totally Pissed'. It's not just the likes of Shakespeare and Chaucer that have influenced international culture from these islands, and Totally Pissed would have been a great title for a sonnet or Canterbury Tale.

Silverio and Vince hit it off due to a shared love of beer, music and football, three strong international languages, and agreed to meet at 11am the next day with me at Silverio and Mattia's traditional Calabrian restaurant to meet some friends and have a few drinks before the game. We definitely managed a few drinks.

Pre-Match Entertainment

Silverio greeted us with a nice, though very Calabrian, version of 'The Wild Rover' on guitar with one of his restaurant staff helping out expertly on percussion on the counter; these are clearly well-trained people. He then took us over to a bar just opposite their restaurant and as he got the drinks in I asked him why Cosenza had this left-wing, anti-fascist edge. He said that it was unusual in Italy. A significant number of Italians were inclined to support fascism. Nobody could be really sure why but Cosenza had rejected that culture and mentality for a long time and the team's support reflected that. Silverio put it down to the presence of the university and a couple of influential professors at the time of the Red Brigades in particular.

The squat movement is very important in Cosenza and many of the club's supporters have been very active in that movement. In an interview in 2019 given to *The Brooklyn Rail*, a Cosenza fan that we met later that Saturday in the stadium, Roberto, gave a longer historical perspective on why Cosenza is different:

'Across some overgrown train tracks from the Hotel Centrale is the Rialzo social centre, in a squatted abandoned rail station. It was established in 2007 as a *centro politico occupato autogestito* (self-managed occupied political centre, or CPOA), and brings together cultures of the many lands now disgorging their disenfranchised and usurped to Italy and Europe, the kids at Rialzo have not forgotten Salvini's past.'

Roberto was one of those 'kids' and told *The Brooklyn Rail*:

'Salvini is racist against African people but also racist against people from the South.'

He points to a door painted brightly with the words *Cosenza Meticcia* – mixed, akin to the Spanish word mestizo. 'Calabria is multicultural,' he says. 'So many peoples passed through over the centuries–Greeks, Romans, Arabs, Normans, Spanish, Albanians.' Going back to ancient times, he recalls that the Bruzzi or Bruttians, the local Italic tribe, resisted Rome. 'We in Cosenza inherited that mentality,' he says wryly.'

The fascist *Lega* and the even more fascist *Fratelli d'Italia* regularly poll around a combined 40 per cent of the intended votes in Italy. It's heartening to see that Cosenza is different as well as a proud city of the south that rejects everything that Salvini represents.

Silverio in particular is keen that we have plenty to drink, not for the first time we struggle to pay for our drinks but we show a rugged determination to get to the bar as often as we can sneak one in. There is a group of leftist friends of Lumpen and Cosenza there from various parts of Italy. One makes the mistake of saying that he has a bit of a friendship with some Portsmouth fans and a resultant liking for the club. This sends me and Silverio into a chorus of 'No-one Likes Us', the Millwall anthem, in drunken response. Behind the alcohol-infused bad singing, part of me realises that Jimmy Greaves was onto something: I'm in the deep south of Italy singing Millwall songs with a left-wing Calabrian skinhead wearing a Harrington jacket to a northern-Italian Portsmouth sympathiser – this is truly a funny old game. And the reach of British working-class culture is huge. I start to wish the class had more confidence to shake off its shackles ... but somebody gets the vodkas in and Silverio needs a bit of help with 'Antifa Hooligans' by Los Fastidios.

At some point in the next few hours, people remember that there is a game on and we are all bundled into a couple of cars to take us up to the stadium. Silverio has to stay and prepare the restaurant so his twin brother and Lumpen bassist Mattia is our guide. He's a more sober and quieter version of Silverio, nothing to do with alcohol intake, just in general. The Lumpen crew went to the *Curva Nord*. We bought tickets for the *Curva Sud* as that's where we heard the action was. Not particularly true at the moment but going to that part of the stadium did give some interesting insights, so I'm glad that we did.

The Game

We met my friend Sara from Napoli at the game who very kindly came down to translate for us. We also met Roberto, the young squatter quoted above, and a white-haired old guy with a bit of an ageing Trotsky look about him who came over to chat. This guy was not very keen on the ultras over on the much more busy and lively *Curva Nord*: he pointed with derision at them exclaiming in English, 'Them, they are not us, they are system.' The *Curva Sud* ultras tend to see themselves as more of a radical, street-based activist protest group. Again, much of it based around the squat movement, as opposed to the *Curva Nord* crew, whom they view as more concerned with conventional politics and therefore a bit of a sell-out. The left as a whole is not known for its ability to unify against a common enemy. Left-wing football ultras are not immune to these fissiparous tendencies.

This guy stayed and chatted for what seemed like most of the second half, not bothering to watch the game. As he left he asked Sara which team she supported in Rome. She replied with some indignation that she came from Napoli. This far south, even a good Napoli girl like Sara is a bit of a northerner, in more ways than one as we will see.

Cosenza had five loan players in a team that looked as ill-acquainted with the basic art of passing to someone on the same side as they did with each other. They also showed no passion, a total failure to play 'with their balls hanging out' as they say down in Calabria. Cremonse won 2-0 with ease, three points on their way to promotion to Serie B at the end of the season. The few fans who made it down from Cremona celebrated raucously with the players. Cremona is 625 miles from Cosenza, so fair play to those who made the trip. If they did come in a taxi as per the old terrace taunt then it would have been a pretty expensive one.

The Cosenza ultras in the *Curva Sud* were not happy. They were led by a small, intense guy with a beard and a megaphone who became steadily more agitated as the game went on. At the end, he and his crew took off to the front of the terraces and began haranguing the players. The players were gathered in the middle, probably consoling themselves with words such as, 'It's ok, your loan period will soon be over.' The players then started walking slowly to the *Curva*. I asked Sara what the guy was shouting over the megaphone but she couldn't understand much of it. Dialect differences in Italy can be significant even over small distances and Napoli is almost 200 miles from Cosenza: when the Cosentinos were talking to each other in dialect she couldn't really understand much of it all. That's the last time I employ a northerner.

The players came to within about 20 metres of the *Curva Sud*, stopped and listened for around five excruciating minutes as the angry megaphone excoriated them. The rest of the ultras threw in the occasional insult but were mostly content with the megaphone doing the abuse. This was extraordinary. We have seen a lot of football between us and plenty of abuse directed at players by angry fans, but never a team obeying fan orders and standing silently whilst being advised by a supporter of their failings as footballers and as men. We found out more about what actually happened the day afterwards.

Post-Match Discussions

After the end of the game, we walked back to the twins' restaurant and complained about the football. We asked the guys about the split among the leftist fans and they explained it was partly politics and partly 'business'. In this part of the world that can be euphemistic for organised crime: Calabria's *Ndrangheta*, once seen as a poor relation of Sicily's Cosa Nostra, has risen to become not only Italy's most powerful mafia but also one of the largest, most sophisticated and feared criminal organisations in the world, with deep inroads into many aspects of Calabrian life. The guys were clearly not keen on talking about this in any level of detail and nor were we. Let's just leave it with saying that the causes of the split amongst the fans are multifactorial.

We all went out to attend a pretty large demonstration in the centre about its housing problems where we saw Roberto again and the White-Haired Trotsky. He came over to us smiling and said, 'Vesuvius. Working-class!' I thought he was making some reference to the working class being about to explode and asked about it, but Sara said, 'No, he doesn't speak much English, he just came over to repeat some of the words and phrases he does know.' But she was still smouldering with Trotsky a little bit, after he called her a Roman.

We left the demo with Silverio angrily remonstrating with a cop about the relatively mellow policing of the demonstration. We were feeling better but the name of the 1980s ska band in Cosenza that inspired Silvio, Totally Pissed, still had some relevance to our situation, so we decided to sit down and eat somewhere. We managed to get a couple of pints of Cosentino Guinness in before supper, though. Cosenza, despite being a small Italian city, has a pretty good beer and stout situation. You can begin to understand why the band chose that name.

Cosenza Vecchia

Trotsky had a Cosenza Vecchia (old Cosenza) t-shirt on and the phrase clearly had some significance beyond a celebration of the city's ancient district, so we went there for a look on the Sunday after the game.

The old town is a few minutes' walk south of the new town across the Busenta river. It's authentically very old and has a certain desperate elegance clinging to it, but even when viewed at a distance from the cathedral that wearily overlooks it, Cosenza Vecchia looks like its last lick of paint was applied during the mid-Renaissance. All the money has clearly been spent on the new town.

We walked through the broken and very quiet streets. The grey weather added to the sense of abandonment. Despite being in the far south Cosenza has its own microclimate and is not a place to find some winter sun. I remembered thinking the previous evening, 'If I wasn't so heavily sedated I'd be feeling pretty cold here.'

We were about to leave the area when I saw a bright yellow garage about 30 yards ahead with Che Guevara's image on it, painted in a very post-Renaissance style. This was one of those strokes of luck that you need when doing research. As I walked to get a picture of the Che garage it took me past the clubhouse of Cosenza Vecchia, the name for the *Curva Sud* ultra group, and the angry guy with a beard and megaphone was just walking out of it. We recognised each other and smiled and we started to chat through Sara.

He was a much nicer guy outside the stadium. He apologised for not coming over for a chat with us the day before – the football had made him just too angry. We asked what he had said to the players: he looked embarrassed and rightly so. He had shouted to the captain that he had better come over with the team right now and listen to what the fans had to say or they would find him and beat him up. Football can often bring out the worst in people and this is a pretty grim instance of that phenomenon. The guy clearly felt bad about it but that doesn't diminish the gravity of what he did. Probably sensing our ill-concealed shock he asked us into the clubhouse for a cup of coffee.

I had a look around the books in the small shop to the side while Vince and Sara talked to the old guy who was making the coffees on the front desk. The books formed a heavyweight and contemporary collection of leftist Italian revolutionary works along with a few magazines. As I was looking through these publications I heard Sara and Vince having a good laugh out front. The old guy had been telling them about all the good works that Cosenza Vecchia did in the community and one of the young guys had interrupted – 'No we don't, we just sit around here taking drugs all day!' provoking much laughter and denials from the old man who, while also amused, remained determined to make his point. I believed him, but looking at the eyes of some of the people in there, I didn't disbelieve the younger guy either; frankly if I lived in Old Cosenza I'd probably be tempted by something stronger than the local Guinness.

We had a last chat with megaphone guy, who told us about some of the difficulties of life in this part of town, how they continued to fight for improvements but that it was difficult to effect real change in a fundamentally conservative society. He also explained why the *Curva Sud* was so quiet the day before: you needed to show your green pass, your proof of vaccination, to get into the ground and a lot of *Sud* guys just didn't trust the state enough to get a vaccine. This may also explain Trotsky's dismissal of the *Curva Nord* as 'system'. We asked him about the problems with the Curva Nord fans. He said he didn't like the situation, thought it was a bit stupid, but like Silverio's crew didn't really want to talk about it. We respected that.

Sara made her apologies and said that she had to return to Napoli and would head off to the railway station. This kicked off a very Cosentino incident. Sara's mother was rather horrified that she was going to Cosenza and asked her how she was going to get from the railway station to the hotel. Sara said that she would get a cab if needed. Her mother replied, 'There are no cabs in Cosenza!' which Sara attributed to a bit of Neapolitan disdain for the country bumpkins down south. However, her mother had a point: there are in fact only three cabs operating in Cosenza, servicing a metropolitan population of 200,000. This has led to a culture of people arranging lifts for each other. I noticed that when we had to get to the match that there was no talk about getting a cab. The most sober guys in the neighbourhood were commissioned to give us a lift up to the ground.

They were very keen to get Sara a lift to the station but she kept on saying she was fine and could walk. This kicked off a not atypical lengthy chat and debate – I love the south of Italy but lengthy chats and debates do seem to be provoked by very tiny things – and I started to worry if she was going to make the train. A guy did show up in a car but Sara politely declined and eventually we were able to say our goodbyes and walked away. Sara appreciated the gesture but there was no way she was going to get in the car with a guy she didn't know, particularly as she was not taken with the attitudes displayed to women by the men 'down south'. She's from Napoli, a city that receives serious abuse from northerners as being a southern backwater slum, something she despises along with any sort of prejudice, but she still wasn't getting into that car.

It's not wholly unknown for Neapolitans to refer to Calabria as 'Calafrica'. Maybe we all need some sort of south that affirms our sense of our own civilised values in comparison. I resolved to read Borges's *The South* again in the hope that I might understand it this time.

(To be fair, Calabria does have some way to go regarding women's rights. The cultural traditions dictating that women should stay at home and take care of their husbands and children still have traction. The national statistics office of Italy noted that in 2021 day-care availability nationwide was a scarce 25 per cent; in southern Calabria, a mean nine per cent.)

Conclusions

We had a great time and met some genuinely interesting people in a part of the world that is far from any track beaten by tourists. The passionately angry response to the team's failure emphasised further that the ultras of left-wing clubs do care about the football; it's not just about the politics and the party on the terraces. Like all fans they want to see the team at least play with some passion for the club they love and the absence of that was a huge factor in the anger that followed the game.

Elais Canetti in *Crowds and Power* wrote about the ancient arenas forming a closed ring from which nothing could be allowed to escape. All the rage and rebellious attitudes to authority would only be tolerated if it stayed there, contained in a space in which it didn't really matter. Tobias Jones in *Ultra* writes about how the disappointment of the failure to get promotion in 1992 drove many ultras into new activist projects. Their focus shifted from the club under the slogan 'The struggle isn't at the stadium anymore.' Jones writes, 'Many of the Cosenza ultras were trying to break the ring, to allow the idealism of the stadiums to energise the streets.'

However, Jones also writes that many ultras gave up because 'they glimpsed the impotence central to the experience of being a fan'. All the choreographed cheering, chanting and rhythmic hand clapping left nothing behind after a game, and you don't have any real influence over the outcome of the contest; you are fundamentally impotent, just an observer a long way from the action. He's right. Being a football fan is often a disappointing affair that incites a sense of impotent rage, even the fans of successful clubs do spend a lot of time moaning. However, what happened at the end of the Cosenza game shows to a certain extent the converse, the appeal of the ultras in that they can provide a potential collective voice to those who don't get listened to very often.

Most of us in our working lives and elsewhere can feel a certain lack of autonomy and power: we have to take orders from people and things over which we have no control can shape our lives. If you live in a place like Cosenza where youth unemployment is so high, and particularly in an abandoned place like Cosenza Vecchia, you're not going to feel any control over your own life or that if you talk that anybody will listen. If you become an ultra then as well as affording some meaning to life and a sense of belonging, you also have the possibility of gaining a part of a collective voice that is heard. You can assert yourself through that voice and it matters. This is partly what megaphone guy was doing: he and his group were able to get those players to stand for five minutes and listen to them. Irrespective of the morality of how they forced that compliance, irrespective of the results of the actions, this was an assertion that 'we matter and we will be heard'.

Similar sentiments lie behind the banners of Boca Juniors fans asserting that they are the 12th man in the game and the top exponents of that position in the world. This may seem presumptuous to many, but it's a justifiable assertion by fans that they are part of the event. They make a massive contribution to creating the vibe and the spectacle needs them. They matter. And the people of Cosenza matter, as does their quirky town. One day, watching the team might become as entertaining as the city.

* * *

Lumpen

– Vincent Raison –

When Cosenza Calcio walk out onto the pitch at the Stadio San Vito-Gigi Marulla they do so accompanied by the joyful noise of local Oi! band Lumpen and their thrilling version of 'Sloop John B' – 'Sembra Impossibile'. When times were good they'd have 20,000 vocalists singing at the tops of their voices, echoing off the blocks of flats above the *Curva Nord* and the Calabrian hills in the distance behind the *Sud*.

It was a surprise to hear hardcore punk in southern Italy. I had no idea it was such a *thing* here. For those unfamiliar with Oi!, it's an offshoot of punk rock that started in the late 1970s, when some of those punk pioneers – Sex Pistols, The Clash, Buzzcocks and The Jam – found themselves riding high in the UK charts. Oi! bands, disaffected by the rush to monetise the new sound, were not aiming to become posters on your kid's bedroom wall. They wanted to make loud, urgent, high-energy rock music that spoke of working-class rebellion, police harassment, oppression, and yes, 'Antifa Hooligans'.

Oi! took on board the roots of punk from the Ramones and MC5 to the Pistols and added a kind of soccer-chant pub rock from acts like Eddie & The Hot Rods and Dr Feelgood, with a throwback to glam too. But for all the tasty ingredients it remained uncompromising and angry enough to stay resolutely out of the mainstream.

Music often has surprising ancestors. 'Sloop John B' itself was made world-famous by The Beach Boys and covered many times. But it's actually a Bahamian folk song, set in Nassau, of unknown but fairly ancient origin. Now it escorts a Calabrian football team onto the pitch in the second tier of Italian football, through the medium of Oi!

I was 15 when the Pistols' 'Anarchy In The UK' was released and, with the dogmatism of youth, was certain that no worthwhile music existed before it, unless it was by David Bowie. Gigs were visceral and inspirational, but also dangerous. At every punk gig there would be skinheads and that would mean you might have to run for your life on the way home. Quite why remains a mystery. We liked the same music, but had different hair, though of course there are deeper reasons why a guy wants to beat the shit out of someone who is different from them.

As Oi! attracted a skinhead following, I was suspicious of the punk spin-off when it emerged. The original skins were into ska and rocksteady; the late 1970s skinheads were into far-right politics and violence. That was underlined by the seminal Oi! compilation album, *Strength Through Oi!* If you forgave the Nazi-referencing title as a half-decent pun, the sight of a threatening Nicky Crane on the cover spoke volumes, even though his Nazi tattoos had been airbrushed out. He was a notoriously violent skinhead I lived in fear of back then, until he was jailed for racist violence. After a lifelong campaign of hatred against black people, Jews, communists and homosexuals, he renounced his former life and came out as gay. Funny old game.

But it was not the Oi! musicians who were far-right fuckwits. Indeed many, like The Oppressed, were loudly anti-fascist. As skinhead culture spread throughout Europe, America and Australia, a movement known as SHARP (Skinheads Against Racial Prejudice) emerged to distinguish anti-racist skins from the far-right connotations of white supremacist arseholes like Skrewdriver.

Lumpen have been active in Cosenza for more than 20 years and have played all over Europe, sharing stages with bands like Sham 69, Angelic Upstarts and Peter and the Test Tube Babies. They started out in the ska scene – a common love among left-wing football fans. There's a real anglophile nature that goes back to the original 1960s skins, with button-down Ben Shermans, braces, jeans and Doc Martens.

As described above, we were lucky enough to run into Lumpen's guitarist, Silverio Tucci, who gave us a taste of raucous Cosenza hospitality. He was a fitting ambassador for the city, the music and the football, all of which he loves passionately. Before they were Lumpen, they were Cosenza ultras, with the *curvas* providing a counterpoint to the right-wing ultras that were, and are still, prevalent throughout Italy.

When Lumpen was formed, they wanted to make their position clear given the ambiguity around the skinhead scene. The cover of their 1999 album *Demo* showed a Russian soldier raising the Soviet flag in Berlin. Although they are not Stalinists, they thought it important to make clear which side of the divide they were on.

As they told the skinhead culture blog, *Creases Like Knives*, 'Lumpen is just a group of skinheads who like to go drinking in pubs and who like to go to football ... but we are, and we will remain, socialists. We are people who have chosen a political idea.

'Growing up in this environment made it much easier for us to be what we are. Cosenza has always been very sensitive to anti-racism and anti-fascism, so for us it was fertile ground on which to grow. And that's the context in which Lumpen was born.'

When I first saw this heavily-tattooed skinhead walking towards me with a pint in his hand, I had no clue that within the hour we would be swapping tales of the things we loved that we had in common: The Undertones, football, socialism and beer. Nor that the city that was a part of him would become a part of me too.

* * *

Livorno

– Stewart McGill –

Livorno are the senior leftist team in Italy but as we were planning our travelling the club had lost its stadium and looked to be in danger of ceasing to exist, so we decided to go to Cosenza instead. Livorno have made an impressive recovery since then, are now back in their original stadium and at the time of writing are one home play-off game away from promotion from *L'Eccellenza*, Italy's regional fifth level, to Serie D.

Livorno was the birthplace of the Italian Communist Party in 1921, formed when Amadeo Bordiga and Antonio Gramsci led a split from the Italian Socialist Party. The football club was founded in 1915 and became a founder member of Serie A, the top flight of Italian football. In 1943 the Amarento, as they were known due to their maroon shirts, were runners-up in the league but have spent much of their history yo-yoing between the top three flights of calcio, winning Serie B twice, among six promotions back to the top flight.

Livorno's political stance has often led to clashes with the right-wing ultras of other clubs.

Fighting has been a feature of matches against Roma, Lazio, Inter, Milan and Hellas Verona.

Livorno has its own rough crowd. In 1999, the ultra group Brigate Autonome Livornesi (BAL) was founded, bringing together disparate groups of fans under their skull-and-crossbones emblem.

On the terraces they celebrated the birthday of Stalin. And they declared, 'The struggle of our lives is that of the working class, of anti-fascism and anti-capitalism, and so it will be in eternity.'

BAL goaded Milan fans and insulted Silvio Berlusconi in particular. They were not shy of violence, leading to banning orders far in excess of those issued elsewhere in Italy.

Their leader, the former boxer Lenny Bottai, was reported to have attacked a coachload of Sampdoria fans – on his own. Livorno's *Curva Nord* bears a huge Che Guevara flag alongside anti-fascist symbols, Cuban flags and Soviet slogans.

BAL became hate-figures for the Italian right before their eventual dissolution in 2003 under the weight of the constant bans of their members.

Livorno's fans have formed a so-called 'triangle of brotherhood' with fellow left-wing fan groups at Olympique de Marseille and AEK Athens. They have also forged connections with Celtic, a pact they call 'United Against Fascism', plus links with Adana Demirspor in Turkey and Omonoia Nicosia in Cyprus.

Livorno's brand of unreconstructed revolutionary socialism may not be to everyone's taste, but we are delighted to hear of their recovery and look forward to seeing them as they take the long march back to Serie A.

Red Star

Founded: 1897
Stadium: Stade Bauer
Capacity: 8,000
Nicknames: *L'Etoile Rouge; Les Audoniens*
Ultras: Gang Green, Perry Boys, Spliff Brothers

– VINCENT RAISON –

WHEN PEOPLE think of football in Paris, they tend to think of Paris Saint-Germain, with its Eiffel Tower badge on a shirt that's in almost every sports and souvenir shop in the world; of Mbappé, Messi and £200m-worth of Brazilian glamour boy in Neymar. But there are other football clubs in Paris: Paris FC, a club with right-wing fan affiliations in its past, and Red Star FC, a football club with a long history and deep sense of integrity behind it. Its modest, but loyal supporters represent a club and fanbase with principles, currently plying their trade in the Championnat National, the third tier of French football.

Red Star represent Saint-Ouen, the racially diverse, working-class neighbourhood they play in, a *banlieue* just over the *peripherique* from central Paris, by the docks on the Seine. Saint-Ouen is mostly famous for its flea market, *Les Puces*, one of the largest antique markets in the world. It is part of the Seine-Saint-Denis *départmente* of greater Paris, a hotbed of football talent; often referred to by its administrative number, *quatre vingt treize* (93). Around 26.5 per cent of the population of the 93 district are immigrants, by far the largest proportion of any Parisian neighbourhood. Red Star reflect and embrace this diversity. Many of the fans are left-wing and actively anti-fascist. They're a noisy bunch too.

There are only six miles between PSG and Red Star, but in every other respect, they are light-years apart. You could be forgiven for thinking that PSG is the one with the noble past, but you'd be wrong. They were only founded in 1970 and only became regulars at Europe's top table once Qatar Sports Investments bought them in 2011 and turned them into a football Disneyland.

Red Star's story begins in 1897, making them one of the oldest football clubs in France. Founded by one of the most venerable names in world football, Jules Rimet, they had won the Coupe de France five times before PSG was even a twinkle in a billionaire's investment fund.

Rimet, who lent his name to the original World Cup trophy, was president of FIFA for 33 years, from 1921 to 1954, and was one of football's great visionaries. His father was a grocer who brought his family to Paris when Jules was 11. At 24, he formed Red Star, a club that, in accordance with Rimet's ideals, did not discriminate on the basis of class, a principle the club still honours today.

Red Star moved to their current home, Stade Bauer, formerly known as Stade de Paris, in 1909, having begun life at the Champ de Mars, near the Eiffel Tower. The stadium's inaugural game was against English amateur club Old Westminsters – the Pinks, from whom Dulwich Hamlet (see page 126) got the pink in their kit from. Between 1920 and 1934, Red Star won the French Cup four times, secured professional status and became founding members of Ligue 1, France's top flight.

The post-war years were bleak ones for Red Star. Although they mostly bobbed between Ligue 2 and the third tier, they would occasionally reach the heights of Ligue 1, albeit briefly. Their last season in the top flight was 1974/75. This century saw them almost go bust in 2003 before they reached the nadir of their existence – the sixth tier of French football, between 2003 and 2005. Since then they have revived, winning promotion to Ligue 2 in 2014/15 and 2017/18 before relegation back to the third tier the following year.

Patrice Haddad, a film director and the club's president since 2008, has big plans for the club and their crumbling stadium. Fans remain broadly in support of his efforts to place Red Star at the centre of the community. 'I want Red Star and Stade Bauer to become a social and economic lung of [Saint-Ouen],' he said. But as we will see, fans are wary of foreign investors and fearful of them hijacking their club.

Even if current attendances are small due to only one stand being open, Red Star still have a number of ultra groups that cram onto the terrace and make their presence felt. They have friendships with Red Kaos at Grenoble and while they may be among the more chilled of ultras, they have a fierce rivalry with Paris FC. And while PSG has taken all the glory, Red Star has seen stars of their own pass through Bauer, including Abou Diaby, Moussa Sissoko and Steve Marlet. But Red Star has a glory of its own; one that can't be bought or traded. The club has an identity. The club means something.

Rino Della Negra

The connection to anti-fascism is not a new look for Red Star. It was fully cemented during the Second World War. Rino Della Negra was born in Vimy, the son of Italian immigrants. He was a talented right-winger who could also play in goal. When he signed for Red Star in 1942, they were Paris's flagship football club, but before he could even play a competitive match for Les Audoniens, he was wounded and captured by the Nazis. The German military had been governing Paris since June 1940, but there was underground resistance to their brutal rule. Jews were forced to wear the yellow Star of David badge, and were barred from certain professions and public places. A million Parisians left the city for the provinces, where there was more food and fewer Germans, but Rino stayed to fight and disrupt.

Secret anti-Nazi groups and networks were created, some loyal to the French Communist Party (PCF), others to General Charles de Gaulle in London. Initially opposed to fascism, the

159

PCF's attitude to the war shifted according to directions from the Soviet Union, much to the dismay of many of its members, who left after the Nazi-Soviet pact of 1939. The PCF organised some resistance but individually many communists worked to undermine the fascists regardless of the prevailing wind. They wrote slogans on walls, organised an underground press, and occasionally attacked German officers. Reprisals were harsh. After the Germans invaded the Soviet Union in June 1941, the PCF followed Stalin's orders to all communists to engage in the armed struggle against the Nazis.

Rino joined the French Resistance through the Manouchian Group, the most active Resistance unit in Paris. Named after their commander, the French-Armenian poet and communist activist Missak Manouchian, the group were a sub-group of the FTP-MOI (*Francs-tireurs et partisans-main-d'œuvre immigrée*), an immigrant outfit fighting for France. They formed a network of communist freedom fighters who carried out attacks on Nazi targets. Rino went underground with the 3rd Italian FTP-MOI detachment in the Paris region, commanded by Manouchian himself. In November 1943, an operation to seize a German cash courier went wrong. Rino took a bullet in the leg and was captured along with Manouchian. On 21 February, 1944, he was executed by firing squad. He was 20 years old.

Before his death, his final message to his brother read, 'Hello and goodbye to Red Star.' His sacrifice remains hugely symbolic to Red Star fans. His brother, Sylvain Della Negra, was there to see the club unveil a plaque to his memory in 2004.

Doctor Bauer

At the time of Rino Della Negra's death, Red Star's home was known as Stade de Paris. In fact, its official name remained that until very recently. But long before that fans always referred to it as Stade Bauer. Indeed, the stadium stands on Rue de Dr Bauer. But who was Dr Bauer?

Jean-Claude Bauer lived around the corner from Red Star's stadium with his wife Marie-Jeanne, a nurse, at 3 Rue de

Blanqui. During the Spanish Civil War, he lent his services to the Centrale Sanitaire Internationale. When World War II broke out, he joined up, only to be captured by German troops. After he escaped, he came to Saint-Ouen and worked at the nearby Claude Bernard Hospital. Both he and Marie-Jeanne participated in the Resistance.

On 2 March 1942, he met a Resistance colleague, Jacques Solomon, in a bar on Rue Tronchet. Solomon was assistant to the philosopher Georges Politzer, the head of a group of communist intellectuals and consequently was being followed by a special brigade of the Paris police. He was arrested and handed over to the Gestapo for interrogation, as was Marie-Jeanne. On 23 May, he was taken to Mont-Valérian, along with Solomon, Politzer and others, and shot as a 'Communist Jew' at the same place where Dino Della Negra would be killed two years later.

Marie-Jeanne was transported to Auschwitz, which she somehow survived. Returning to Saint-Ouen she found her house bombed and that her brother had also been killed.

The Rue de La Chapelle on which Red Star's stadium stood was renamed for Dr Bauer after the War and people began calling the Stade de Paris, Stade Bauer. Fans made it clear to me that we were not in Paris, we were in Saint-Ouen. 'Paris is 50 minutes' walk away,' I was told. And as such, Red Star's stadium represents not Paris but resistance.

Stade Bauer

Red Star's ground since 1909 was used as a football venue during the Paris Olympics of 1924. It was also the home of the French national rugby league side during the 1930s.

With the decline in fortunes of Red Star, the stadium suffered, falling into disrepair. So much so that when they were promoted back to Ligue 2 in 2015 and 2018, they were forced to play their home games away from Bauer for safety reasons. Home games were played at Stade Jean-Bouin, near Parc des Princes, Stade de France and even in Beauvais, 80km away.

Clearly the situation was unsustainable if the club wanted to progress and have any future. They would need a ground that would be available to them in higher divisions. An initial scheme for stadium development was rejected by fans, and plans to move to a new stadium were also abandoned. Red Star had to be in Saint-Ouen. In May 2021 an agreement was reached for the city of Saint-Ouen to sell the ground to a private company, Réalités Group, to rebuild Stade Bauer as a multi-purpose stadium. The distinctive triangular block of flats, *Planète Z*, that overlooks one of the goals will remain, while two new stands will be built to accommodate a total of 10,000 fans. Red Star will continue to play games at the Bauer while work takes place on-site, with an 'English-style' build introduced that will keep fans close to the pitch. In addition, the Bauer Box would be developed, incorporating apartments with green roof terraces, plus shared workspaces, shops, health services, entertainment and a restaurant in the north stand, overlooking the pitch.

'The stadium is going to be completely rebuilt. It's going to be amazing,' said Paul Ducassou, Red Star's communications director. 'It's a new era for the club. It's a big, big change. We can stay here during the rebuild, we can stay if we get promoted and we can sign good players because we're staying here. Ten thousand seats, so a small stadium for the first or second division, but with a fantastic atmosphere. That's why we want to stay here in our city. If you love football you know what fans can be for a club. It will be fantastic.'

Paul's enthusiasm for the development and Red Star's future is uncontainable and you can see why. Seine-Saint-Denis, the *départmente* Red Star inhabit, has produced many professional football players, maybe the most in all of France, including icons like Kylian Mbappé. It's currently impossible for them to hold on to emerging stars, but, if their swanky new stadium can lead to promotion, the future of Red Star will start to look very different. Bauer has been named as a training ground for the 2024 Paris Olympics, in a nice slice of symmetry with the previous century.

'The new stadium will allow us to grow and shine. The club's vocation is to celebrate football that is close to the people,' said the president, Patrice Haddad.

Of course, not everybody is pleased. Change can be uncomfortable. One fan group withdrew from the process, the corporate vibes of the pitch-view restaurant being too much for them. It is symptomatic of the move from public to private ownership. While the city owned the ground, there was no money for investment. In order for a company to want to spend millions of euros on development, there has to be a substantial return. Such is capitalism; such is reality.

The club has been wrestling with a solution for a long time. This is the one they found. Paul's hope is that the development will not affect the thrilling atmosphere the fans generate on matchday. McGill asked whether it might lose something, as he felt Arsenal had in their move to the Emirates Stadium back in London.

'The big difference is that our stadium will be in the same place. I went to the Emirates, and nothing happened in the stands. Nothing. The fans worked on the project with the city of Saint Ouen, because it is passing from a public to a private stadium. They need a say. At Arsenal they can sell out with tourists, they don't need the input from the fans. With 10,000 seats, we don't need that. We can fill that with people from Saint Ouen and North Paris.'

777 Partners

Since our visit, though, a new development has pushed a wedge between fans and the club. In April 2022, it was reported that Red Star are to be bought out by an American Investment fund, 777 Partners. Patrice Haddad agreed to remain as club president at the club after the club announced they had 'selected 777 Partners as its project features ambitious sports development goals backed by adequate investments, all the while being respectful of the club's identity'.

Haddad said that apart from their funding he chose them because of 'their understanding of the club's singularity'.

A Miami-based alternative investment fund was always going to be a hard sell to the fans and at the first game after the announcement had to be abandoned after fans protested by throwing flares on the pitch.

Paul told us the fans had been invited to meet with the directors, along with 777, but had refused to. As far as the club are concerned this investment is the culmination of everything they have been working for in the past 15 years: the development of the Bauer; securing a training centre at Marville; and now the funding to get them back into Ligue 2. All their collaborations had been carefully chosen so as not to mar their reputation as outsiders, nor their approach to innovation.

'We have chosen a long-term entrepreneur that has never sold any of the companies in which it has invested since its creation,' he said.

We can only hope Red Star will not be just an asset on an investor's spreadsheet, but something of more than monetary value.

777 Partners have multiple sports and business interests, including full ownership of Genoa, a substantial stake in Sevilla and plans to acquire Standard Liège and a chunk of Vasco da Gama. Whether the sale is finalised and whether they will be able to satisfy the fans remains to be seen. Fans are concerned that Red Star will simply be part of a network of clubs, and that its rich seam of local talent will benefit Genoa, Sevilla and Standard Liège, not themselves.

Red Star Lab

Something else separates Red Star from other clubs. If Jules Rimet is credited with founding Red Star in 1897, then Patrice Haddad must be credited with founding the Red Star Lab in 2008. The Lab is a cultural and artistic laboratory that encourages children to find their creative passion. Local kids join Red Star with the dream of becoming professional footballers, but in addition to their football education they have access to workshops in different disciplines such as theatre, cinema, design, photography, street art, podcasting, writing, dance, radio, video, music and more. Supervised by professional educators and artists, kids are encouraged to produce a collective work. Their natural curiosity is stimulated, broadening their horizons and gathering the tools to their own economic freedom, should football not work out for them.

But the Lab echoes the spirit of the club's founder, Jules Rimet. Initially, the club included other sports – cycling, tennis and fencing, for example – but it also had a literary club. Red Star even had a library in its early days. It always saw sport and culture as parallels. The Lab is now based at the club's training ground at Marville and their motto is, 'Work the body, feed the mind.'

On joining Red Star, each kid is presented with a small, beautifully bound book that describes what the club represents and how it is, 'apart in French football, in all respects ... a secular and urban club, raw and romantic, a pop culture club. This is where you signed, this is the history to which you subscribe.'

Paul Ducassou was kind enough to send me one, which I treasure. It mentions Balzac, Hugo, Stendhal, Flaubert, Maupassant and Zola. And, of course, Jules Rimet. It really is a club like no other.

At the head of Red Star Lab is the creative director, David Bellion, a former Red Star player, who also starred for Manchester United and Bordeaux. As far as I know, no other club has a creative director. But then again no other club does as much to prepare kids for a life outside the game.

If M. Hadded founded the Lab, then David is responsible for growing and developing it into the institution it is now. David has a love for English football from his time in the UK and the first project he oversaw was inspired by his time at Sunderland, where fans produced a fanzine called *Sex and Chocolate isn't as Good as Football*. He asked friends to help guide a group of children to produce a Red Star fanzine; an artistic director, a journalist from *GQ* and a photographer who followed Red Star. The kids were forced to think about writing, photos, layout, artwork, editing and production, possibly for the first time. And then a sponsor agreed to print about 1,000 copies.

'The kids were very happy, because they saw their work transformed into something they could hold,' said David. 'Always at Red Star Lab we aim for something that could be a business or become a finished product. They stood at the stands and did old-school selling. There was no price, it was up to the supporters to give what they wanted. The supporters liked it, they gave one euro or five euros, and the kids saw how the economic model works.'

Other projects have included stadium architecture; fashion, using old Red Star shirt stock; a trip to Berlin for the anniversary of the Wall coming down; a tournament in Israel – a challenge with added significance for a lot of kids from Arabic or Berber backgrounds. They did a food project based on the diet of athletes, taught English through football, designed their own football boot in conjunction with a local bootmaker ('and genius,' added David) and learnt about public speaking.

Friends and sponsors eagerly support the work of the Lab, because it helps children, he says. Foot Locker, Vice, Kappa and LinkedOut – the digital network that helps homeless people find jobs – all back the Lab.

I asked David if there was anything like Red Star Lab anywhere else. As a player, David came through the same academy as Zinedine Zidane and Patrick Vieira – AS Cannes. There you either made it, or you didn't. There was no cultural programme to help you towards an alternative, even though the odds are stacked against you becoming a professional footballer.

'We may be the only ones who do this, but I wish everyone would take our programme, steal our programme,' he said. 'Honestly, I don't think I can be proud we're the only one. It's sad.'

'Maybe one, maybe two, maybe no players make it as a professional in a year. What about the others? For me, the victory is the boy or girl who we helped go in a direction that they like. When you're young and want to be a professional, you love football so much it takes up so much of your mind. You don't think, "I could be a chef, or a photographer, or a street artist." Can you imagine the pleasure of a guy coming back to us after ten years and saying, "You remember that photography class? Well, I'm a photographer for a magazine now." That is a victory.

'They all want to be footballers, but we want to give them another door, so if one door closes, there are others.'

Sadly, at most football clubs, the only alternative to success is the exit, which is often a crushing experience for a young person. But at Red Star, they rightly believe that such widespread rejection does a disservice to youth.

Matchday: Red Star v Stade Briochin, February 2022

Clearly we had to stay in Saint-Ouen to get a flavour of the neighbourhood. The walk from the Gare du Nord to Mob Hotel was instructive as we left the spacious boulevards and grand architecture for the low-rise, narrow streets of the *banlieue*. It felt different and looked different. It felt less like a brochure and more like a place where people lived.

We were pleasantly surprised to find our hotel was adorned with pictures of Karl Marx and staffed by hip, welcoming young people. It turned out that the hotel supports the club by advertising at Stade Bauer. When I mentioned that it had pleased me to see that, they replied, 'Red Star is our team!'

Before the game, one thing was certain. We would have a beer in Olympic de Saint Ouen, an old-school bar lying in the shadow of Stade Bauer, steeped in decades of support for Red Star. Stickers from around the football world adorn the wall. Red Star shirts and scarves hang proudly. The beer is cheap and the camaraderie tangible. This is a second home for Red Star fans.

Spotting the club shop opening its doors, I popped over. I could not in all honesty buy my son yet another football shirt and look my wife in the eye, but a Red Star scarf for myself would surely be fine. What I didn't know was that the shop was opening its doors for the very first time and I was one of the first customers. Consequently, I was given a bottle of Red Star IPA, a collaboration of Red Star FC and Brasserie Urbaine de Saint Ouen. As a self-confessed beer snob, I was delighted to find it was a really excellent ale, freshly brewed just over the road from Stade Bauer.

We met with Paul Ducassou, who talked excitedly about Red Star and showed us around. Paul had fallen for Red Star in the right way: as a fan, in the stands. McGill and I decided to watch the game from the *Première Est*, to be with the fans rather than the directors, and experience the Bauer in all its glory. It was a shame we weren't allowed to drink beer, but it was fantastic to stand and cheer with fans who sang without pause for 90 minutes in support of their team, and to notice a strong female presence in the crowd. The quality of the play contrasted with their position in the lower half of the third tier of French football. Their passing and control showed great technique, but they lacked a cutting edge in the final third, at least on this occasion. Some defensive fannying about on the edge of their own area led to a shooting opportunity that Briochin took to go 1-0 up in the first half, through Ahmad Allee, yet it didn't dampen the mood.

In the second half, Red Star dominated but were vulnerable to the counterattack. Their top scorer and playmaker, Damian Durand, seemed curiously out of sorts. But with 20 minutes to go, Owen Maës cut in from the left to tee up Pape Meïssa Ba to equalise. At last, we could hear what it was like to celebrate with Red Star fans. Though they had been behind most of the game, there hadn't been anything but 100 per cent support and the team were clapped off after the 1-1 draw. Maybe this time we picked the wrong match. They won their next two home games 3-0 and 5-2.

Olympic was too crowded for us to return to, so we went to Bar Moderne nearby, where we chatted to some Red Star fans, good guys from Bretagne who now lived in Saint-Ouen, some of whom had misgivings about the Bauer going into private hands. And we met some affable but very drunk Celtic fans. Everywhere we go we run into Celtic fans. Along with St Pauli fans, they are the lifeblood of lefty groundhopping. They are also often very, very drunk.

Parisians have a reputation for unfriendliness which we didn't experience in the slightest. Quite the opposite, in fact. But then we weren't in Paris. We were in Saint-Ouen.

Je te Reverrai

I used to think it was impossible to love more than one football team, particularly as I was first introduced to the terraces of my local team at around six-years-old and spent decades with eyes only for her. But when, for me at least, money and rage poisoned modern football, I found the pleasures of non-league football in the UK turned my head. Then trips to St Pauli and Rayo Vallecano with McGill made me realise that the faithful husband had turned into something of a slattern. At least I was still picky though, even if I was no longer exclusive.

David Bellion described Red Star as a 'romantic' football club and it's easy to see why. Everything about the club intrigues and inspires admiration. From its origins to its history; from its place among the Resistance, to its place at the heart of its community, doing something concrete to help the young people that surround it to lead better, more fulfilled lives. It's deserving of applause.

And now there is this sense that Red Star could be on the verge of fulfilling its vast potential. With so much talent on its doorstep, inspirational leadership and passionate fans, anything is possible. I long to see them back in Ligue 1, where perhaps they belong; their grit and integrity striking a counterpoint to the glittering success of their oil-rich neighbours. Because they would only want success with honour. Glory earned, not bought. Though with American investors at the doorstep, the supporters have questions.

The fans remain politically engaged, but they will go on supporting, win or lose, as long as they feel the club is still theirs and not some investment fund's financial asset. They don't need to buy championships, marquee signings or celebrity footballers. They just need a red star on a green shirt, and a club that means something, that represents their values, that reflects their belief in a fairer world.

Palestino

Founded:	1920
Stadium:	Estadio Municipal de La Cisterna
Capacity:	8,000
Nicknames:	*Los Árabes; Los Baisanos*
Ultras:	N/A

– STEWART McGILL –

I LOVE Latin American football and a couple of years ago caught a game online between O'Higgins and Club Deportivo Palestino. A team with a classic Irish name playing a team named after a famous part of the Middle East, in Rancagua, the southernmost tip of the Inca empire. No wonder Latin America is the home of magical realism.

The existence of a club in Santiago de Chile named Palestino and founded by Palestinian immigrants is fascinating and we were keen to cover them in this book. It's probably fair to say that Palestino stand for a cause beloved by many on the left rather than constituting a left-wing club. However, this does attract support for Palestino from leftists in Chile. The club is interesting in itself and this is a momentous time in Chilean politics in which it looks as if an uprising by the people could have delivered sustained success and improvement. For all these reasons, Palestino scrape into the first XI.

And I had the opportunity to speak to one of Chile's top politicians and a big Palestino fan, Daniel Jadue, the communist mayor of the northern Santiago district of Recoleta. The Spanish word for mayor is Alcalde: like many words in Spanish it derives

170

from Andalusian Arabic, our world is the product of many migrations over many centuries.

The History

Some say Celtic don't play in Ireland, but they play for Ireland. Similarly, Palestino don't play in Palestine, but they do play for Palestine. When they won the Copa Chile in 2018, Palestine President Mahmoud Abbas sent a personal letter congratulating the team on their victory and inviting the players and coaching staff to the country. As Abbas pointed out, Palestino are more than just a football team. They represent both the nation of Palestine and the 'just cause for freedom, justice and peace'.

Many Palestinians fled during the Crimean War of the 1850s due to fears of Russia taking over the Holy Land. Some found their way to Santiago de Chile and established a strong community there, attracting other Palestinians after the traumas of the World Wars. Chile is believed to be home to the largest Palestinian community outside the Arab world, numbering at about 500,000 people mostly from the historically Christian towns of Belen, Beit Jala, Bethlehem and Beit Sahour. The vast majority of Palestinians in Chile are Christians, despite Palestine being majority Muslim, but this in no way diminishes the national feeling of Palestino fans. There is a painting of the Al-Aqsa mosque on the walls of the Palestino stadium in southern Santiago, the third most holy site in Islam. Indeed, many prominent members of the Palestinian resistance have been Christian. It's not a religious struggle.

The club was founded on 20 August 1920, when they participated in a colonial competition in Osorno. In 1952, Chile first set up professional leagues and Palestino, nicknamed *Los Arabes*, were accepted into the second division which they won to secure promotion to the top flight.

The Football

They won the league in 1955 and again in 1978. Their last success before the cup win in 2018. But the appeal lies outside the football.

Apart from the politics there is something inherently cool about fixtures such as Palestino v Colo-Colo, the top Chileno side named after a Mapuche freedom fighter (see below for how some Palestino fans stand for Mapuche rights in Chile and see their struggle as one with that of the Palestinians), and Palestino v Club Guarani, the Paraguayan side named after the indigenous people whose yellow and black colours were inspired by Penarol of Uruguay and the emblem of Francis Drake. Again, no wonder Latin America is the home of magical realism.

Elias Figueroa is the club's most prominent former player; after returning to Chile from success in Brazil and Uruguay he led Palestino to the league title in 1978. He was named one of the world's best living footballers by Pelé in 2004, and was voted the eighth-best South American and 37th-best player of the 20th century in 1999. Their most well-known former manager by far is Manuel Pellegrini, who managed the club between 1990 and 1992 before moving on to clubs such as Real Madrid and Manchester City.

The Shirt Scandal

One of the club's main priorities is to raise awareness of the plight of Palestinians in the occupied territories and to continue to seek freedom, justice and peace. This erupted into a political scandal in 2014.

In January of that year, it was decided to add to the club's traditional red, green and black colours an alteration to the number design on the back of the shirts: the '1' was to be shaped like the outline of Palestine before 1948, when Israel was created. Jewish groups in Chile and elsewhere were outraged and saw the act as deliberate provocation. The Chilean Jewish community branded Palestino's shirt an act of 'smugness'. The Zionist lobby in Chile is very influential, as Daniel Jadue discovered, which we'll come to shortly.

Palestino's shirts even came to the attention of the Israeli government, which stated that the kit amounted to 'provocation with the evident intention of denying Israel's existence'. A state diplomat, Itzhak Shoham, met with representatives from the Chilean embassy to express Israel's 'surprise and concern' and hoped that Chilean authorities would step in. The first formal complaint was made by the Jewish chairman of first-division side Nublense, Patrick Kiblisky. He believed that, 'We cannot accept the involvement of football with politics and religion.'

Palestino, evidently feeling the pressure, made their defence via their Facebook page: 'Palestino and its symbols have existed in our country since 1920, 28 years before the establishment of a state of Israel in Palestine.' They went on to deplore what they viewed as the hypocrisy of discussing disputed territory while 'endorsing illegal settlements and the wall of segregation in Palestine'.

Palestino concluded by reinforcing their belief that 'for us, free Palestine will always be the historical Palestine, nothing less'.

Christine Legrand, writing for *The Guardian* during the scandal, visited the Patronato quarter of Santiago, where many of Chile's Palestinians live and work. It's close to the San Jorge, Chile's oldest Orthodox church, built by Palestinian migrants in 1917. One local cafe owner Legrand spoke to described himself as a 'third-generation Chilean' and said that many of the elder members of the community still converse in Arabic.

He explained that there are real links to the Palestinian homeland for the migrant community and, as such, Palestino's shirts are representative of those people rather than anything more sinister.

The Football Federation of Chile fined Palestino $1,300 (£800) following Kiblisky's complaint. Despite protests by Palestino, the fine stood. The club eventually complied and paid the fine without appealing, though Legrand notes that some of the Palestino players tattooed the original map of Palestine on to their forearms.

The controversy provoked acts of solidarity from other Chilean clubs, notably from the two biggest teams, Colo-Colo and Universidad de Chile. Palestino played them both shortly after the eruption of the shirt controversy. Universidad de Chile's home fans held up a banner with the Palestinian flag that read '*Palestina Libre*', while Colo-Colo supporters unfurled an enormous banner featuring the Palestinian flag on one end, the Mapuche flag on the other, and the map of historic Palestine filling in for the letter 'i' in the word *Resiste* printed in bold in the centre. Chilean football can be very tribal and antagonistic, but this display anticipated the unity and solidarity displayed during the *Estallido*: football fans are by no means all a bunch of incorrigible tribalists doomed by their stupidity to internecine violence through the power of the football circus.

The club still maintains its proud Palestinian links, though the map has disappeared from the back of the shirt. There is a Palestinian flag on the club website as well as sponsorship with the Bank of Palestine, while Palestino president Maurice Khamis Massu is a member of the Belen 2000 Foundation which awards scholarships to children in Palestine and sends doctors there to work.

As Chilean radio commentator Sebastian Manriquez told *These Football Times*:

'It's impossible to deny that the Tino Tino [Palestino] is a club like no other in the league. Most Chilean fans recognise the contributions of the Palestinian diaspora in Chile and the historical background that Palestino seek to represent. The majority of Chileans support the Palestinian cause, and because of that I would say, despite the fact that Palestino is not one of the most popular teams in the tournament, their fans are the most respected and supported in Chilean football.'

Chile's Estallido Social, or October Revolution

The *Estallido Social*, literally Social Outburst, was a series of massive demonstrations and riots that originated in Santiago and spread to all regions of Chile mainly between October 2019 and March 2020. The spark was an increase in the price of Santiago's underground railway fares. Like many neoliberal cities poor people have been priced out of the city centre and have to travel a long way to work so this was a big deal in itself, but it was very much the last straw, albeit a weighty one. Chilenos had been discontent for some time about the cost of living, inequality, the impact of privatisation and the fact that so many were dirt poor in a rich country. Many in the wealthy global north were shocked by the *Estallido Social*. Chile looked like the Latin American success story. It's important to look behind the GDP per capita figures. The appropriate Spanish word for it is *profundizar*.

The *Estallido* culminated in two highly significant votes. On 25 October 2020, Chileans voted 78 per cent in favour of a new constitution. On 19 December 2021, a former student leader and 35-year-old leftist was elected president of Chile with 56 per cent of the vote against a right-wing candidate who venerated the memory of Pinochet, the murderous fascist and friend of Thatcher who ousted the democratically elected Allende government in 1973.

Palestino expressed support for the aims of the *Estallido*, along with much of Chileno football and society, including Manchester City's goalkeeper Claudio Bravo Munoz on 19 October 2019:

'They sold our water, our electricity, our gas, our education, our forests, the Atacama Saltworks, our glaciers, our transportations to the private sector. We do not want a Chile of a few people, we want a Chile for all. Enough.'

Football also assumed a psychological significance to the *Estallido*. Chileans take the game very seriously: a picture of fans of Colo-Colo, Universidad de Chile and Universidad Católica together at a Santiago demonstration wearing their club shirts, and embracing, rather than beating the hell out of each other, became a symbol of unity in the conflict against the government.

I was in Santiago at the start of 2020, by chance. Chile is one of my favourite places and we had booked to spend the last few days of a family holiday in South America there, for a 'restful' couple of days. This is an extract from some thoughts I wrote down at the time. They tell you something about the prevailing atmosphere and the background to the *Estallido*.

Tear Gas and Burning Churches

We returned to Santiago de Chile for the first time since 1992. Like most big cities since then the skyline has grown tawdry with ugly skyscrapers but the most remarkable difference was in the proliferation of political graffiti – it's pretty much everywhere – and how often the graffiti contained the good old fashioned British 'ACAB.'

We mentioned this to our tour company guide Anna, a very nice, middle-class and middle-aged lady: she smiled and said it had appeared everywhere since the uprising in Chile began in October 2019. She knew what it indicated but asked in her very nice Chileno accent: 'is it "All Coppers Are Bastards?"' We laughed, it was odd to hear a quintessentially British yobbo phrase enunciated in such a beautiful way.

A few days later Anna was again our guide as we were taken to the airport. The previous night my son and I had taken part in the regular Friday demonstrations against the Chilean regime. The demonstrations are part peaceful but often turn violent. The 'Pacos,' the police, are hated and with some justification (hence the popularity of ACAB – a tribute to the soft power of British culture–and *'Paco Asesino'* as graffiti).

We talked to Anna about the events of the previous night in which some demonstrators had burned down a church, the Iglesia San Francisco de Borja in Santiago, that had become the preferred place of worship for the Chilean National Police Force. Anna was only sorry that one of the guys responsible had been caught and feared for him.

So, a nice, respectable middle-class lady concerned about the perpetrator of the seemingly hideous act of burning down a church, and in a Catholic country. How did Chile, previously the right-wing's poster boy

for Latin American stability and the triumph of the
neoliberal model, get to here? The story has huge lessons
for all of us, everywhere.

Wealth and Inequality

People across most countries were shocked when
the riots kicked off: Chile was an OECD country, a
stable democracy, the place that provided a model
for development of the rest of Latin America etc etc.
Chilenos weren't.

Chile is a rich country full of poor people.

While the country's per capita income would give
Chileans over $2,000 a month, most make $550 a month
or less. A 2018 government study showed that the richest
Chileans had an income nearly 14 times greater than the
poorest. Chile is the most unequal of OECD countries,
with an income gap that's about 65% higher than the
OECD average.

Now that's not seriously high by Latin American
standards, Chile has mid-range inequality by the
standards of the region and many Chilenos are well-off
compared to other people in South and Central America,
but the fact the country enjoys such wealth and shares
it so badly is the driving force behind the protests. This
was largely the point of the book 'The Spirit Level' a
few years ago: the inequality in itself is the problem, it
leads to a deep and wounding sense of unfairness, a sense
that institutions of the state are not impartial, that the
whole system is rigged in the interests of the rich aided
by their marionettes in parliament. All these factors
innervate levels of discontent irrespective of absolute
levels of poverty compared to the lower-paid in peer
group and neighbouring countries.

Victoria Murillo, Director of the Institute of Latin
American Studies at Columbia University, said that

political scientists had long warned about the growing disconnect between Chile's political elite and the rest of the population. She noted that a 2017 report from the United Nations Development Program found high levels of discontent due to unequal access to healthcare and education, and further inequality in the way people were treated once they accessed the services. Ordinary Chileans, the report found, felt that the elite were treated better and this had led to pent-up anger.

'There was a sense that something could explode for a while,' says Murillo. The breadth and depth of the discontent is obvious from the protests. They were spontaneous, had wide-ranging demands – a new constitution, better health services, lower education costs, improved pension pay-outs – but found common ground in rallying against the elites. While in other Latin American countries there are many fronts to the protest, says Murillo, 'what's interesting about the Chilean case is that it's everyone against the elites'.

Murillo likens the protests in Chile to what is happening in the US with the 99%, which is to say everyone but the wealthiest 1% of the population. People are protesting against levels of inequality that Chile shares with its neighbours, but it is Chile's prosperity – much higher than that of its neighbours – that is pushing Chileans to protest. 'The people know that the money is there, that they can have better education, or health care,' says Murillo.

Another Guide

Our guide to Cajon del Maipo, a beautiful canyon outside Santiago, was a young guy, Pablo, studying to become a teacher. We chatted around the subject of the protests but after a little while his t-shirt rode up and we saw the ACAB tattoo on his arm.

So then we started talking. Pablo basically said that the protests were no surprise to most Chilenos. He described the inequality as a time bomb that had been ticking for years that had finally gone off, the transportation fare increases in Santiago being the catalyst (politics fans may see some similarity between this and basic Marxist analyses). Pablo believed that the average Congressman in Chile was paid 300 times the minimum wage: not true as far as I can make out, but the perception is important, the Chilean minimum wage is pitifully low and Congressmen do pretty well out of salary and kickbacks etc.

He had his leg broken by the Pacos a few months earlier, battered by truncheons as he lay on the floor after being hit at a demonstration. He was now fit again and was planning to attend the regular Friday evening event in central Santiago. We said we would also be going and joked about meeting him there: he advised us to be very careful, 'the repression is very brutal'.

Please note at this stage that both Pablo and Anna are even by Chilean standards incredibly nice, welcoming, warm people. (I loved Anna from the moment she found out we were Irish: 'oh we like the Irish, they're more like us'.) These are not cold-eyed bitter fanatics bent on killing the bourgeois enemy, these are decent people responding in a wholly understandable way to a very bad situation that had become desperate.

The Demonstration

We went to the demo early Friday evening, with keffiyehs and lemon juice (lemon juice can help repel the effects of tear gas, there are some benefits to having spent some of my childhood in the North of Ireland in the late 1960s and early 1970s). Like many such occasions there is a peaceful, 'party' element in which people march, sing songs (some from the old struggle against the Conservative Party's friend, Pinochet) and shout slogans. Just around the corner from this main focus was the aggro, a bunch of mostly young people, by no means all guys, attacking the police who responded with water cannon and the occasional rounds of tear gas. I pass no judgement on this: violence, and the threat of violence are instrumental in forcing change and these people are in desperate need of change.

And we joined the aggro. The hatred for the police is visceral and unquestioning, throughout the night the attacks on them were unrelenting and of course the Pacos' Church was burnt down. The demonstrations are now very organised: many people have hard hats and serious gas masks; the demonstrators have their own medical squads and teams charged with disabling the tear gas canisters once they are released; there are stalls selling catapults, gas masks and eye protection (many demonstrators were blinded by police anti-riot bullets in the early days of the protests); many people patrol the area carrying a spray that acts against the effects of the tear gas, a couple of times I was very glad for the help of these young people in spraying my eyes and inside my keffiyeh, it stings like hell but is better than the effects of tear gas.

I'll always remember a young guy who emerged from the heart of the aggro, coughing and spluttering like hell after the gas got to him; he knelt down, coughed up some serious liquid from the lungs, took a swig from the water we offered him, had the eyes sprayed by a *compañero* and went straight back in there. That's what the Pacos are fighting; and they know it, the protestors will tell you that the police get dosed up on cocaine for the demonstrations, one of the factors behind their inhuman brutality.

Matchday: Universidad de Chile v Palestino, April 2022

Due to various family and other commitments I could not get over to see Palestino at home but hoped to get to the game against Universidad de Chile, La U, Chile's second team behind the huge Colo-Colo.

La U normally play their home games in the Estadio Nacional, the place where many were taken by the military after the coup in 1973 to be tortured and shot, including the great Chilean folk singer Victor Jara. I didn't really want to go there so was glad that this game had been moved to Unión Española's stadium in the north of the city. Unión are one of Palestino's big rivals alongside Audax Italiano, the team for Italian immigrants. The match-ups amongst these three are known as the *Clásico de Colonias*.

Tickets were only available online: I could not buy any as the site would not accept my UK vaccine pass nor any of the various passes that I needed to get into Chile (a separate book could be written on travelling in a plague year. Suffice to say at this point that Chile was the toughest country to get into by far). I took off for the long walk up the *Avenida de Independencia* to Unión's ground to see if I could get tickets. The centre of Santiago could pass for a European city, and many of the people look very European. If you take a walk out of the centre along a long straight avenue like *Independencia* you know you're in South America – the buildings look different, the people have much darker skins and look more indigenous. Indeed, parts of northern Santiago could pass for Central America.

Sadly, Santiago has a homeless issue and the smell of putrid urine assaults you pretty much everywhere outside the centre. A significant cause of homelessness is that the minimum wage often fails to cover housing costs. You can understand why there was an *Estallido*.

There was no chance of buying tickets at the stadium and the game was only for supporters of La U, no away fans were allowed and I was a fan from very far away. I had a good crack with the security guys who wanted me to admit that I wasn't actually a supporter of Universidad de Chile – 'Come on, we can tell that you hate La U' – but sadly this was not a game I was going to be able to get into. Worth mentioning here that whilst the country may have its problems, Chileans are up there with the nicest, friendliest people on the planet. Well worth a visit, despite it being a little tougher to get into than Gallipoli in 1915.

I went to the stadium on a pretty and warm early Saturday evening anyway. Seeing the long increasingly angry queues forming outside the ground actually gave me a sense of relief being at a game without the pressure of having to get into the ground on time. The spectators were overwhelmingly young men with blue Universidad de Chile shirts on. Many of the guys had the mestizo faces common in Santiago's working-class suburbs. My security guard buddies had a point – I didn't look like a fan of La U.

I waited outside one of the main entrances, about ten Pacos and two angry German Shepherd dogs were controlling the queue and letting people into the stadium intermittently. Ten minutes before the game there were thousands still outside and they were agitated. This is a population emboldened by the *Estallido* and the antagonism felt towards the police spoke through their eyes as well as the angry shouts. Every time someone was pulled out because of ticket irregularities, and this happened often, they would argue with the heavily armed cops without any fear. The police would always bring the dementedly barking German Shepherd dogs with them for these confrontations but the fans weren't concerned and kept arguing. One guy took a nasty and gratuitous nip on the arm from one of the dogs but kept on debating the validity of his ticket with the Pacos. All this made me worry slightly for Chile: this is a population that isn't afraid anymore and the ruling classes know it. When are they going to get the army and the police to step in again?

When the game began at 5.30pm there were still thousands of La U fans outside; they didn't all get in until 5.50pm. Not quite so bad as Rayo Vallecano but not too far off. Football fans everywhere suffer from the desire of clubs to sell season tickets and they make it difficult for the fans who can just afford to go occasionally or don't have the time to see every game. This is one of the curses of modern, business football. Bohemians in Prague was the only ground we went to where you could pay with cash on the day at the turnstiles, but that was a glorious trip back to the 1970s.

I walked back down south to the centre of town. Luckily, I found a Peruvian restaurant showing the game on live TV so I caught most of the second half there. The ground was about three-quarters full but it looked like a great party which made me even more annoyed about the failure to get in, maybe I could have become a U fan after all. However, a minority of them were shining laser pens into the face of the Palestino goalkeeper when he faced free kicks and corners. Laser pens are really common in Chile as people supporting the *Estallido* would use them against the police to disrupt their equipment. During the riots in 2020 we felt left out in not having any. It was a little disappointing to see the weapons of revolution being misused against the wrong people, not for the first time.

The game itself was a terrific 0-0. Chilean football remains underrated and is often a great spectacle with end-to-end action. It's tough, the tackles go flying in and not many of the players would last 90 minutes in the Premier League. I felt a little like David Elleray when he retrospectively officiated the famously dirty Leeds v Chelsea Cup Final replay in 1970: 'He'd be off! And him!' (Elleray famously refereed a TV recording of the match in the late 1990s and said that the teams would have shared six red cards and 20 yellows.)

It's no substitute for being there but I left the restaurant well fed, reasonably content and thinking, 'Next year in Palestino.'

El Alcalde, Daniel Jadue

Jadue is the mayor of Recoleta in northern Santiago, a Palestino who came very close to being the left's candidate for the presidency in 2021. Jadue is a busy man so it was very kind of him to see me. I must also thank the great Carlos Ronaldo in Santiago who worked so hard to get me the meeting. Carlos is a Communist

Party member who was imprisoned after 1973 and then moved into exile in the north of England until the end of the Pinochet regime in the early 1990s. Carlos is one of those unassuming good guys who make you feel there is hope. Meeting him was one of the highlights of my trip.

Jadue is the grandson of Palestinian immigrants to Chile. Since 2012 he has been Mayor of Recoleta. In this capacity he has presided over the creation of 'people's pharmacies', a series of municipal-run drugstores to provide patients with affordable medication. Jadue gets around 65 per cent of the vote in Recoleta. The Communist Party has three places in the Chilean cabinet and also holds the mayorship of central Santiago through Irací Hassler. Things have most definitely changed in Chile.

Jadue began his political career with organisations related to the Palestinian Liberation Organisation and joined the Chilean Communist Party the day after the Oslo Accord was signed. He is a big Palestino supporter and agrees that the club has been crucial to sustaining the Palestinian identity of the diaspora in Chile. Celtic has similarly been crucial to the continuing identity of the Irish population in Scotland. However, Jadue was quite adamant that Palestino was not a left-wing club. The owners were right-wing rich people and many of the supporters were of the right as well, something with which Carlos agreed heartily. They may support the Palestinian cause, but they were not of the left. He did acknowledge that, because of the name and the association, some leftists were attracted to the club; and he is right, as we'll see in the next section. Personally, he didn't feel welcome there anymore because of his support for the *Estallido*, or October Revolution as he prefers to call it for obvious reasons.

Jadue was looking good in the opinion polls in the spring and early summer of 2021 and looked likely to get the nomination as the presidential candidate of the left, but in the end he lost to Boric, who took 60 per cent of the vote. Some residual concern about the communist 'brand' could have affected the result along with the inevitable allegations of anti-Semitism that will be directed at any pro-Palestinian politician who looks to be on the brink of power anywhere. The Simon Wiesenthal Centre made the expected allegations against Jadue that were invoked during the campaign. Strangely enough, just as I was thinking this, Jadue mentioned Jeremy Corbyn's visit to Chile the previous month to attend Boric's inauguration ceremony. Jadue talked about the strength of the Zionist lobby in Chile, which he believed was as powerful in Chile as it was in America. The great Salvador Allende was also accused of anti-Semitism.

Jadue was optimistic about Chile's prospects and was not fearful of a renewed military takeover: the Chilean people had shown during the October Revolution and its aftermath that they were not going to be pushed around anymore and that the right would have a serious fight on its hands if they used the military to exert power again. From what I saw at the Universidad de Chile game and in the 2020 demonstrations, he was right about emboldened people with little fear. He was less optimistic about Palestino and had no faith in the board to do the right things to take the club beyond the mid-table mediocrity that beckons this season.

Let's hope Jadue continues to be right about the future of Chile and wrong about Palestino. Despite his reasonable strictures about the club not being of the left, I will always be a supporter. The chance meeting described in the next section will help explain why.

Jadue's message to the wider left was interesting and direct: 'Get out of your institutions, get off social media, and get onto the streets and talk to people.' He still gets out and talks to people on a regular basis, despite being a very busy man as mayor, and 65 per cent of the vote is tough to argue against for any party.

Intifida Antifa

I went to the Plaza de Dignidad in Santiago to pay my respects to those that fell fighting the regime during the *Estallido*. This part of downtown Santiago was the centre of the struggle. The place now has a certain feel of the Bogside about it with a series of murals remembering the fallen and reminding people that the struggle is not yet over. I saw a group of people flying Palestine flags, wearing Palestino shirts and painting the plinth of the old Bernardo O'Higgins statue with the Palestinian colours.

I saw a guy with a great t-shirt featuring a stylised image of Leila Khaled, a Popular Front for the Liberation of Palestine fighter who made a big impression on me as a young man in the early 1970s and remains a major icon of the Palestinian struggle. I asked him where he got the t-shirt. He began to reply in good Spanish but I knew he wasn't local and asked him if he spoke English. Turned out he was an American Communist from Kansas – he definitely wasn't there any more – who was studying in Chile and it was one of his university mentors who was painting the plinth with Palestinian colours.

These guys also had some large banners that celebrated the struggle of the indigenous Mapuche people as much as that of the Palestinians. Daniel Jadue said that the Mapuche struggle was the same as that of the Palestinians, they had just been waging it for a few hundred years longer. It was great to see Palestino fans out there fighting for Mapuche rights and it gave additional context to the expression of solidarity extended to Palestino by Colo-Colo fans. Colo-Colo was a great Mapuche fighter against colonialism, an outstanding role model for a mestizo nation.

I talked to Sam's mentor, Inyaki. An inspiring young guy in a Palestino shirt from a Bulgarian family that has emigrated to Chile in the late 1990s. He was a member of the Chilean Young Communists and had become a Palestino supporter due to his support of the Palestinian cause. This had led him organically and seamlessly into wider left-wing politics and into support of the Mapuche struggle. Chatting to Inyaki gave me a sense of universal wellbeing. He was such a fundamentally decent young man with nothing but good in his heart. It reminded me of why I got attached to leftist politics in the first place: working for the triumph of people like Inyaki against the likes of those that would support and rationalise fascists like Pinochet because of lies that they brought 'stability and a better economy'.

Inyaki's group is known as Barra Intifida Antifascista, linking the common name for an organised football group with the Palestinian uprising and the wider struggle against fascism.

All of which helped confirm me as a Palestino fan and tells you why, despite the perfectly rational caveats imposed by the conversation with Daniel Jadue, Los Arabes sit on the Roaring Red Front's first XI.

Conclusions

I was disappointed that I didn't get to see the game and that I didn't get to see Palestino. Despite indicating that they would see me when I got into Chile, the club responded to no communication when I was in the country.

I went down to the Palestino stadium in a rugged district called La Cisterna, deep in the south of Santiago. The paintings of Al-Aqsa on the walls remind us that the club may have been founded by Christian Palestinians but the mosque remains a powerful symbol of the country and its resistance. I asked to be let in to have a look around but the security guy explained I couldn't because the players were training. I explained why I was there and he kindly asked me to sit down while he called up and asked someone in management if I could get in for a look.

I was waiting for a long time and had a chat with the guy, probably in his early 60s like me. He explained Chile's problems as being due to too many immigrants. Another disappointment. But the tendency to blame immigrants for the problems caused by neoliberalism is unfortunately universal. The left has to try to understand these attitudes and to confront them based on that understanding, rather than just condemn with the ecstasy of sanctimony, to employ Philip Roth's great phrase again. Chile has experienced some major demographic shocks over the last few decades. Santiago's metropolitan area population was around 4.5 million when I first went there in 1989; now it's around 6.9 million, a 53 per cent increase. Chile's total population was 12.9 million; now it's 19.1 million, a 48 per cent increase.

Much of the growth has been organic but immigration has been a factor and around seven per cent of the total population are immigrants from other Latin American countries, including Haiti. Some communes like Santiago Centro and the nearby Independencia record 28 per cent and 31 per cent of the population as Latin American immigrants.

These people were attracted to Chile by its relative prosperity and political stability. However, if over the decades high levels of immigration emerge as one more factor pressing down on real wages and come to be seen as a reason for increasing inequality, that political stability will become threatened. That being said, Chile's *Estallido* was aimed at the right targets: those in power. But there is no doubt that there are many Chileans who are uneasy about immigration. High levels of immigration that are not coupled with protection of wages and conditions can be problematic – the Brexit debate and its outcome demonstrated that.

I didn't get into Palestino in the end. The PR guys came out to apologise and later on they offered to talk, but I was a little annoyed at being continually ignored, to be honest, and preferred to keep my memories of Palestino associated with the likes of Jadue and Inyaki. And I had to get across the Andes to Buenos Aires.

* * *

Palestinians and Football

– Vincent Raison –

'Keep politics out of football' – that favourite mantra of the apolitical is a laughable ambition in Palestine and Israel. Everything is political. The Israeli-Palestinian conflict seeps into every corner of this land, with the hopelessly uneven paw prints of British colonialism smeared all over it.

Football arrived in Palestine in the late 19th century, but in the interests of brevity, we're going to skip to the first time a global international body recognised Palestine, after the creation of Israel in 1948.

In 1998, FIFA gave that recognition, allowing its national team to compete in FIFA-sanctioned competitions at least a century after the game kicked off there. As well as the national team, the Palestinian Football Association administers domestic football in Palestine, including the West Bank Premier League, the Gaza Strip Premier League and the Palestine Women's League, plus the Palestine Cup and the Yasser Arafat Cup. The West Bank Premier League turned professional in the 2010/11 season, but thanks to the conflict, the Gaza Strip Premier League has only been able to complete its championship seven times.

There have been countless ways in which the conflict has impinged on Palestinian football. In the past, travel restrictions imposed on Palestinians in the West Bank and Gaza Strip, along with the difficulty of obtaining exit visas from Israel, meant that the national team had to draw on players from the Palestinian diaspora, from Chile, Lebanon and the United States, to complete their World Cup qualifiers. In November 2006, the final match of their Asian Cup qualifying campaign against Singapore was cancelled due to the Palestine team's inability to travel. The AFC and FIFA decided not to reschedule the match despite protests, and Singapore was awarded a 3–0 win. Try taking the politics out of that.

While there have been several incidents of players being unable to travel to away matches, there are constant issues with travel within Israel, where checkpoints can make short distances take hours. Striker Ziad Al Kourd was allowed to go and play for his country in Qatar, only to find his Gaza Strip house demolished when he got home. Another international player, Ayman Alkurd, 29, was killed by an airstrike on his building. Others have been detained, accused of terrorist offences or belonging to terrorist groups. Two teenage West Bank footballers were shot in the feet at a checkpoint in 2014 and would never play again. The chairman of the Palestinian Football Association, Jibril al-Rajoub, said he felt Israel was determined to destroy Palestinian sport, with stadia and infrastructure repeatedly damaged. It's perhaps little surprise that

Palestine launched its own amputee football team in 2021. Based in Gaza City, they hope to compete in the 2022 Amputee World Cup in Istanbul.

Where can we find hope in this most polarised of disputes? It's hard to imagine, but in football, with all its passions, such a thing can be found. Because there is more Israeli-Palestinian integration on the football field than elsewhere in society. As Dan Friedman explains on forward.com, an independent news site aimed at Jewish Americans:

'Contemporary Israeli soccer leagues are entirely composed of multi-ethnic teams (with one notable exception) ... The success of Arab and Jewish teams fielding multi-ethnic teams is that, along with pharmacies, soccer fields are one of the few venues where Arab and Jewish Israelis mix in general society. The exception is the lamentable and disgraceful racism of Beitar Jerusalem and how – like other European clubs with fascist origins – it is tolerated, still, by national institutions.'

That was from his review of *More Noble Than War: A Soccer History of Israel and Palestine* by Nicholas Blincoe, a book named after a Palestinian chant, 'Football is more noble than war'. If only our differences could be constrained to the field of play. 'Football is war,' said former Netherlands manager Rinus Michels. If only war was football, instead of madness. Because on the pitch, Israelis and Arabs can play side by side, for the same cause.

Sakhnin is a small Arab city in Israel's Northern District, with a mostly Muslim population plus a sizable Christian minority. Its football team, Bnei Sakhnin, is one of the best in the Israeli Premier League and the vast majority of its support is Palestinian. Bnei Sakhnin won the Israel State Cup in 2004, the first team from an Arab city to do so and the first to play in the UEFA Cup. The fans enjoy a friendship with ultra groups at Hapoel Tel Aviv, St Pauli and Wydad Casablanca. While the current squad contains a Palestine international, as well as players from Africa, Europe and Brazil, the majority of the squad is Israeli, loudly supported by Palestinians. The current captain is Beram Kayal, an Israeli international and former fan favourite at Celtic and Brighton & Hove Albion. In the Israel national side, he plays alongside a number of Arab-Israelis of Palestinian origin, including their star striker, Mu'nas Dabbur, currently playing in the Bundesliga for Hoffenheim. Israel's captain, Bibras Natkho, is Muslim.

One of the more famous footballers in Palestine though is the first captain of Palestine's women's team, Honey Thaljieh. Now retired due to injury, she pioneered the women's game in a warzone, despite considerable opposition as well as enormous difficulties. Now working for FIFA, she became a tireless campaigner for the Peace Through Sport movement and an Ambassador for the Homeless World Cup. Nowhere is her work more meaningful than in her home country.

The 'notable exception' to Israel's multi-ethnic teams that Dan Friedman mentioned, Beitar Jerusalem, are Bnei Sakhnin's bitter rivals. With notoriously anti-Arab supporters, their games are often plagued by fan violence. In 2021, the Ministry of Economy and Industry temporarily revoked the licence of Bnei Sakhnin's ground, Doha Stadium, after they beat Beitar, claiming they had exceeded their allowed capacity. After the 2-0 defeat, Beitar's manager, Erwin Koeman, brother of Ronald, got the sack. Critics felt the closing of the stadium was politically motivated. Beitar is the biggest club in Israel. Benjamin Netanyahu is a fan but even he has criticised their fans as racist. We will return to Beitar later in this book, but it is worth remembering that, though they are significant, they do not represent all football in the region.

But also, we must recall that football itself is an exception. In a country that Amnesty International, B'Tselem, Harvard's International Rights Clinic and Human Rights Watch have all concluded is committing crimes of apartheid against Palestinians, sanity prevails for 90 minutes a week, plus any time the referee adds on for stoppages. How mad is that?

Boca Juniors

Founded:	1905
Stadium:	Estadio Alberto J Armando (*La Bombonera*)
Capacity:	54,000
Nicknames:	*Los Xeneizes; Los Bosteros*
Ultras:	La 12, but they're all ultras

– STEWART McGILL –

BOCA JUNIORS are one of the great names of world football and have a reputation as being the 'team of the working-class' or the 'team of the people'. This is why they will often appear in lists of international left-wing clubs. Often, it has to be said, with limited evidence. There was just a feeling that Boca should be in there because of the working-class association.

'Feeling' is the important word here and it shouldn't be underestimated when it comes to political discourse. Many people adopt political positions and choose sides based on feelings about what is right and fair rather than deep analysis of the logic and coherence of alternative views. Even the political creeds that appear based on cold, rational calculation of optimal outcomes have elements of an emotional act of faith about them.

Marx became famous for his incredibly detailed work on 19th-century capitalism and how it developed, but was driven to this analysis by the vaguely utopian, existentialist mindset on display in his *Economic and Philosophical Manuscripts* of 1844. The scope and depth of his economic and historical analysis are astonishing but would his influence have survived if he had written only that?

He connects most when he sounds like an angry Old Testament Prophet:

'All that is solid melts into air, all that is sacred is profaned, and man is at last compelled to face with sober senses his real conditions of life.

'Proletarians have nothing to lose but their chains, they have a world to win, workingmen of all countries, unite!'

There are strong elements of feeling and faith in all creeds and this is especially true of Peronism, the uniquely Argentinian political movement that is still a driving force for the Argentine left. There's a restaurant called Perón Perón in Buenos Aires in which the graffiti decorating the walls celebrate Boca Juniors, the Peróns, and Peronist-left politicians like the Kirchners. Every hour the Peronist March is played and everyone joins in banging the table; it's a great rabble-rousing tune, irrespective of your views on Juan and Eva Perón, the two very problematic icons of the movement.

So Boca are in the first XI not only because they are a great club with an interesting history in itself, but because they are associated with the working-class and the liberation of that class is the objective of much left-wing thought. It's also because the debate about whether Boca are a left-wing club provokes some interesting questions. Here we again get into issues about what being 'left-wing' actually means: is it driven by elements of visceral tribal identification? The working-class v the posh elite? Boca v River Plate? And how should the left project its emotional appeal? Whatever its failings and oddities, Peronism has endured as a serious political force with mass appeal – it has 'legs'.

And Boca have had some hellish good players over the years. Any excuse to talk about them.

The History

In 1905 a group of young men of Italian and Greek heritage met in the Buenos Aires barrio of La Boca to form a football team. The area is strongly associated with the mass Italian immigration to Argentina so the Greek influence may be a bit of a surprise, but not to those Greeks who regard the country as having invented everything. Ireland also likes to claim a ubiquitous hand of its people and the nation will be glad to know that the first trainer was a Paddy McCarthy from Tipperary. The founders were students of McCarthy at the Club Atlético Gimnasia y Esgrima of Buenos Aires.

Tipperary's county colours are blue and gold and the Irish romantics amongst us might like to think that this was the origins of the famous Boca kit. It's unlikely, to be honest, but we can cherish the possibility. Interestingly, the current Tipperary GAA jersey looks just like that of Boca Juniors.

The use of the English 'Juniors' in the name reflects the influence of the British in Argentina at that time, particularly in the development of the nation's football. River Plate, rather than Rio de la Plata, Racing Club, Newell's Old Boys. This is a phenomenon across much of South America, not just Argentina: at the time of writing, Boca's next game in the Copa Libertadores will be against Club Always Ready of La Paz.

Boca reached the Argentine top flight in 1913 when it was expanded from six to 15 clubs. This was the season of the first official Superclásico against River, with the latter winning 2-1. After a few mediocre seasons, Boca won their first Primera División title in 1919 and began a serious run of success. They won their fourth title in 1924, winning 18 matches out of 19 and scoring 67 goals (average of 3.5 per game) whilst conceding only eight.

Boca's ascent to superstar club status was confirmed by their European tour in 1925 across Spain, Germany and France. They won 15 out of 19 games and Real Madrid were amongst their victims.

The club have enjoyed several 'golden ages' since then, notably the 1960s and 1970s and the Bianchi period across the late 20th and early 21st century.

Boca is ranked third in terms of international club titles behind Real Madrid and Al Ahly of Egypt. FIFA in December 2000 ranked Boca as the 12th-best club of the century, a place held jointly with Liverpool, Internazionale of Milan and Benfica.

Style of Play and *La Garra*

Boca are traditionally known as the hard-running, hard-working team, in contrast to River Plate's more elegant technical style. This probably reflects the image of Boca as the working-class boys from the working-class area against *Los Millonarios* of River Plate, the guys who made good and left La Boca and moved to a posh part of town up north. People who know Argentine football better than me will say that there is something to this distinction, but Boca have also had gifted and hugely venerated players like Rattin, Maradona and the awesome Riquelme over the years. However, hard-working and aggressively enthusiastic players like Carlos Tevez are also loved by the faithful and probably better represent the spirit of Boca (which is not to deny Tevez's huge talent).

La Garra means 'claw' in Spanish. In South American football it is most associated with Uruguay's '*Garra Charrúa*', the Claw of the Charrúa. This is about tenacity and courage in the face of adversity, never giving up and never being faced down by bigger opponents. It's the spark of the defiant underdog. You can see why this concept is embraced by Uruguayan football, a nation of 3.5 million people that historically has punched well above its footballing weight.

The Charrúa were the indigenous people that lived in the area before the Spanish invaders. They fought like hell to defend their land but were finally crushed and largely exterminated in a brutal massacre in 1832. That their name lives on in the characteristics that Uruguayans have chosen to embrace as the spirit of their football is testimony to the strange, ambivalent attitude of South American culture to the people that they brutalised. The fact that Chile's biggest club is named after a Mapuche chief is another example.

I've always associated *La Garra* with the Uruguayan game but when I met the top Boca-supporting journalist, Marcelo Antonio Guerrero, in La Boca before the game against Godoy Cruz in April 2022, he told me about the importance of *La Garra* to Boca. This says something about Boca's self-image as the working guys who need to fight to achieve. Whilst the concept of *La Garra* may be mostly about a mental fortitude, it can manifest in a willingness to commit violence in pursuit of the cause on the field. I first heard about Boca Juniors in 1971 when there was a serious pitched battle at the end of a Copa Libertadores game at the end of a home tie against Sporting Cristal of Peru. It erupted when the Uruguayan referee refused to award a penalty to Boca in the game's dying seconds. In the spirit of massive understatement, it's fair to say that the Boca players took it badly. At the end of the ensuing running battle, the referee handed out 19 red cards, which puts the Leeds v Chelsea 1970 Cup final in some genteel shade. Tragically, the mother of one of the Cristal players was so traumatised watching the game on TV that she had a heart attack and died. That's some *Garra*. Don't let people tell you that violent over-reaction and tantrum-chucking is a new part of the game.

La Boca

La Boca is a barrio at the mouth of the River Matanza in southeast Buenos Aires. Buenos Aires and Argentina as a whole received many immigrants from northern Italy in the 19th and early 20th centuries, particularly from Genoa. Many of these immigrants settled here and the club's nickname is *Xeneizes*, old Genovese dialect meaning basically 'sons of Genoa'. Boca has always seen itself as a little different. In 1882, after a lengthy general strike, the barrio declared itself independent and the Genoan flag was raised. This independence did not last long, but you will still see plenty of graffiti and restaurant signs proclaiming *Bienvenidos a la Republica de Boca* when you arrive there. Boca has a bit of a reputation for radical politics, and elected the first socialist member of the Argentine Congress, Alfredo Palacios, in 1935.

Boca is famous for the homes made of corrugated iron scavenged from the local docks, some painted in very bright colours, which also differentiate the area in a city of mostly sombre tones. The most prominent and most brightly coloured street is

'El Caminito', and it's the area around here that now attracts most of the tourists.

Outside the tourist blocks, Boca remains a tough Buenos Aires barrio with the usual problems, wrought by poverty and insecurity. I had my phone stolen by one of the city's very competent pickpockets on the underground on the way to Boca and had to report it to the police for insurance purposes. A couple of cops kindly took us to the Boca police station through some streets that will always remain well off the beaten tourist track. One was a Chelsea fan, one was Liverpool. On the way to the nick we discussed the merits of those sides and their respective title chances. This is an odd little planet.

La Boca is very densely populated, with its 46,000 inhabitants representing around 9,000 people per square kilometre compared to London's 5,700 and Hong Kong's 7,140. It's a lot bigger on matchdays. The size of Boca is basically irrelevant to the club's 'catchment area'. Around 40 per cent of Argentines identify as fans of Boca; River has only 26 per cent.

Matchday: Boca Juniors v Godoy Cruz, April 2022

Getting tickets for Boca Juniors is not easy. Sales were handed over to supporters' groups a few years ago. The waiting time for membership is around six years now.

Not all season-ticket holders go to all the Boca games and many will have agreements with a hotel or broker. If the supporter doesn't go to a game, he or she lends their card to the broker for a price, the broker changes the necessary details on the card and passes it on to the purchaser, adding their own percentage. With nearly half the county supporting Boca and the club's international fame there is a healthy demand for tickets and they are not cheap. I went through an agency called Wander Argentina run by an American lady who lives in a Boca area and has connections. They are a pretty reliable source. All this is a terrible system peppered by corruption but unfortunately you have to work your way around it. You won't get a ticket by yourself unless you are very well connected or lucky.

Marcelo Antonio Guerrero, Muy Boca

Marcelo's a prominent football journalist and Boca fan – you can check him out on the Muy Boca website. I contacted him on the morning of the game day via Twitter and he very kindly agreed to meet me near the stadium a couple of hours before the game.

Marcelo was adamant that Boca is 'the team of the people' but certainly acknowledged that neither Boca's management nor a significant majority of its fans could be described as of the left. Boca fans comprise a large part of the country and vote for a variety of political parties.

He also mentioned that in Argentina political distinctions between left and right were often blurred – things are very different there, as we will discover. However, Boca has itself maintained a distinct, working-class Italian identity and a sense of being something different and unique within Argentina. This sense of belonging to a place and a tribe slightly apart is something common to many of the teams we cover.

He suggested that maybe we look next at Independiente, whose president is Hugo Moyano, former head of Argentina's biggest union, the Confederación General de Trabajadores, the CGT. The CGT was a keystone of Peronist support and this took us onto a discussion of this peculiarly Argentine political phenomenon named after former leader Juan Domingo Perón, though the image and memory of his wife Eva is just as important to the folk memory and continuing emotional appeal of the movement.

I asked Marcelo about Peronism and its relation to Boca and the working-class movement. He explained that Perón passed a lot of labour reform laws that helped the Argentine trade-union movement and, of course, Eva was seen as being on the side of the poor. Marcelo believes that Perón was a Boca fan; he was certainly immensely popular with Boca supporters: in his heyday they would chant, *'Boca y Perón, un solo corazón,'* – 'Boca and Perón, a single heart.' This working-class area with a history of radicalism certainly believed that Perón was on their side. The reality, as we will see below, is a little more complicated.

198

Like many Argentines Marcelo seemed a little weary of all politics right now. Argentina's perpetual crises have done the same to many and he talked quite movingly about how his father, a former trade unionist and true believer, had lost that belief and come to think that no real change was possible. Perón did not hold much sway across the terraces of Boca any more. People were more interested in just football. However, he did say that Rosario, Argentina's second city and home of Rosario Central, my favourite team and that of Che Guevara, was one of the last big centres of Peronism in Argentina. I have seen a couple of Perón banners when watching Central on TV and made a mental note to visit Rosario as well as Independiente on my next visit.

I asked Marcelo the regular Maradona-v-Messi question and the answer was more nuanced than I expected: Messi had the longer and more successful club career but Maradona had produced the goods for Argentina, particularly in 1986, whereas Messi had failed to do so until the most recent Copa America victory. He also mentioned that because Messi had left the country so young, assessments were clouded because he was seen by many as not really being proper Argentinian.

On Maradona or Riquleme he was very clear: Riquelme was the much more important player for Boca, Maradona was Boca's most famous and vehement supporter. Marcelo's two favourite players were Osvaldo Potente and Roberto Mouzo, two Boca stalwarts from the 1970s. I think we always favour the players we saw when we were young and everything was simpler, including getting into a ground to watch a game.

We exchanged fond farewells – I hope Marcelo remembers his promise to get me a press pass for Boca next time I am in BA – and we took off for the game. Marcelo is not an enthusiast for this current Boca team. I was about to find out why.

The Game
Wander Argentina includes a drive to the ground there and back as part of the package. My driver Leila is a fan of both Boca and

classic rock and gets somewhat angry when some Lionel Ritchie dirge sullies her radio and she changes stations quickly. I often feel at home in Argentina, consistently my favourite country to visit. This feeling is accentuated more when Leila drops me in Avenida Regimiento de Patricios, from where I have to walk the slow last 500 metres to the stadium. The San Patricios were a group of Irish guys who left the US cavalry in the 1840s to join the Mexican army fighting against America's land-grab invasion. The San Patricios are celebrated all over Latin America, particularly Mexico and form one of the reasons why St Patrick's Day is such a big deal there, and in Argentina as well. Good to talk about Irish soft power rather than British for a change.

It's a cliché, but there is a genuine sense of party around the ground. I stand out as one of the few people over 40, not wearing a Boca shirt, and I am proper Celtic-fringe pale, so don't look local, but there is absolutely no sense of any trouble or antagonism. The only tension lies in the presence of the riot police on the sidelines, all of whom have well-practised hard-man stares. There have been no away fans allowed at Argentinian domestic football for some time but the police like to be ready and present.

My electronic card pass works perfectly to get me into the ultras standing section. I was asked to show my documents, so was grateful that I packed my passport last thing before I left the hotel. In Argentina it's sensible to assume that at some point you're going to be asked for your papers: parliamentary democracy has ruled for nearly 40 years but the legacy of the country's dark 20th-century history lives on, and the habits of the security forces die hard.

La Doce

I get in early but the stadium is very busy already and people are sitting down on the terraces waiting for the game to begin, something I didn't expect. I stand right at the top in what seems to be a place where some of the older guys hang out. They are all standing up: old guys, old school. The huge banners at the other standing end proclaim the Boca fans to be the best 'Number 12' in the world. For younger readers, in the old days players were numbered 1-11 and the substitute was number 12. Boca fans call themselves *Camisa numero doce,* shirt number 12, as the ferocity of their support acts like a 12th man for the side, even though they were not on the pitch.

The story goes that the idea dates back to the 1925 European tour. The team was accompanied by a Boca fan called Victoriano Caffarena who helped out a lot and established a strong relationship with the players, so they named him 'Player No. 12'. When they returned to Argentina, Caffarena became as well known as the players themselves and the concept of *La Doce* was born.

La Doce is also the name of the leading Boca fan organisation, regarded by many as a criminal organisation. Like other *Barras Bravas* (Brave gangs; it sounds better in Spanish), or hooligan firms as we would call them, *La Doce* has an influence and control over football that is completely alien to Europeans. Imagine the St Pauli *fanladen* but run by a combination of Milwall's F Troop and the Krays.

In an interview with *Infosur Hoy,* the *Clarin* journalist Miguel Ángel Vicente said that the Barras Bravas began operating in Argentina with the consent of the country's soccer clubs and were used by club officials to win votes in the elections for leadership among the membership.

During the past 40 years, they have grown in size and accumulated economic power, taking control of parking lots, the people who look after parked cars and the sale of drugs within the clubs, Vicente claims. And, of course, ticket sales.

'As they gained power, the *Barras Bravas* began to challenge the very club officials who had allowed them to grow in the first place.'

'Thirty or 40 years ago, they used to fight against the fans of other clubs. Now, the fights are internal: factions from the same *Barra Brava* compete for business,' according to Vicente. This might be one of the reasons the hard-faced riot police keep ready at Argentine football matches.

Back to the party

The banners proclaim the support as the owners of the club's history. These guys are not a bit shy but the atmosphere is much more easy-going than that of St Pauli and there is no problem with taking pictures or videos like in the *Südtribüne*. At any game there are going to be a lot of Boca tourists there like me, though mostly from the rest of Argentina. I say guys but there are more women and kids there than you would expect. A lot of the kids take their father's jerseys and tie them to the huge fence to make an improvised harness from which they sit and watch the game with their hands holding onto the barrier; this gets me thinking about small boys and jumpers behind goal posts – *The Fast Show* will never die.

As the game approaches, the fans stand up and the singing begins. Argentine fans tend to have more, and slightly longer songs, than their British counterparts. 'Boca, Mi Buen Amigo' is typical and very popular before the start of the game; they sang it a lot.

Boca, mi buen amigo, esta campaña volveremos a estar contigo
Te alentaremos de corazón, esta es tu hinchada que te queire
ver campeón
No me importa lo que digan, lo que digan los demas
Yo te sigo a todas partes, cada vez te quiero mas

'Boca, my good friend, this season we will be with you again.

We will encourage you from the heart, this is your support who wants to see you champion

I don't care what they say, what others say

I follow you everywhere, I love you more and more'

The guy in front of me with his boy of around 12 years old is having a great time and filming everything. He's Argentine but clearly a Boca tourist like me.

The atmosphere is really good and not as vehement and hostile as many would expect. The absence of the away fans may have something to do with that, and Godoy Cruz are a mid-table outfit from Mendoza; that's where most Argentine wine comes from. There is no antagonism towards this team. Marcelo mentioned that this is not a great Boca side and from early on it's clear he's right. They don't really play as a team and there is little evidence of *La Garrra*. This is a side going through the motions with little passion. Godoy look a whole lot better despite being several places below Boca in the table and in the parlance of football clichés. They look like they want it a lot more.

The crowd continues to be happy and the songs keep coming. I'm thinking most British fans would be groaning a lot more than this by this time, particularly fans of bigger sides for whom the expectation, indeed the right to success, has become pathological. About ten minutes in I got a clue why. Another Boca move broke down and a guy up on my left made a very angry exclamation. This was more like an aggressive British fan demanding that the players listen to him. A big, heavy-set guy wearing an old Argentina national-side jersey turned around and had a real go at him. I couldn't get much of the rather one-sided exchange but Argentina Shirt was reminding Angry Man that they were all there because they were supporters of Boca and they had to remember that. The phrase 'concha tu madre' was used often towards the end of the tirade. You can work out the meaning of that one yourself.

Angry Man made little response. I had noticed people being a bit wary of Argentina Shirt before the game and everyone studiously tried to ignore the exchange. The old guy next to me gave one of those chuckles and almost imperceptible head shakes that indicated he'd heard all this before and had never been impressed with it. I tried a brief chat with him but his accent was a little too strong and it was noisy – it was *Boca Camisa Doce*!

Angry Man kept a little quieter for the rest of the game apart from joining in with the many Boca songs. Argentina Shirt got a little huffy towards the end of the first half and just left. I didn't get the impression that he was terribly missed.

The Goals

Boca scored against the run of play with a penalty after 34 minutes, to the relief of the fans as much as anything else. It was interesting that many of the Boca tourists were filming the reaction of the crowd rather than the penalty. The crowd's reaction was more one of relief than surging ecstasy, and there was a feeling that this game was not over. Godoy equalised ten minutes later against a wide-open Boca defence. The guy in front with his kid needed consolation. He turned to look at me with a face that said, 'How could they do that? And to us?' I shrugged and returned with a look that said, 'I feel your pain, brother.' I'd worked hard on the Spanish before the trip, but sometimes football fans don't need words.

The Second Half and the Happy Church

There were no goals in the second half. Boca enjoyed much of the possession but created few chances and the moments of South American football skill to savour came mostly from the Godoy midfield. They nearly scored the winner with a few minutes to go but a great move ended with the shot bouncing down in front of the line after it hammered the underside of the crossbar. As if in compensation for the football, my end kept on singing happily with much jumping up and down, clapping and smiling. There is a dry moat at the bottom of the *curva* where you can't see the match but people sometimes just wander down there for a chat and a break. A lot of the guys I saw down there were tough-looking older men, quite possibly *La Doce*, keeping an eye on things, but like most of the crowd they were relaxed and enjoying being there. During the game, groups of younger people would spontaneously head down to the moat, turn to the crowd and start leading a song with lots of animated jumping. This was a happy, relaxed crowd with no pressure on people to join in, no organised cheerleaders and no paranoia about being filmed or photographed.

The joyous singing transcended the mundanity of the game and the celebration of the idea of Boca through song transcended the mediocrity of this team. I'm reminded of some of the words of the American writer Karen Armstrong about the importance of ritual as a collective transcendent experience. In her *The Case for God* she writes:

'Human beings are so constituted that periodically they seek out *ekstasis*, a "stepping outside" the norm. Today people who no longer find it in a religious setting resort to other outlets: music, dance, art, sex, drugs, or sport. We make a point of seeking out these experiences that touch us deeply within and lift us momentarily beyond ourselves. At such times, we feel that we inhabit our humanity more fully than usual and experience an enhancement of being.'

Attending a game at Boca helps you understand and feel all that, and I'm glad to say that at this game there was no toxic sanctimony of *ekstasis*, to paraphrase Philip Roth. People were disappointed in the result certainly but there was no burning rage. People enjoyed the party and many were Boca tourists like me, just happy to be there.

The Politics

Complicated. Boca may not be a left-wing club as we understand that rather widely defined term but they are inextricably associated with Peronism. Rafael Di Zeo is the former chief of *La Doce* and a prominent figure in Argentina: he told the newspapers that he supported Kirchnerism during the 2011 elections.

'I am a Perón-style Peronist. I have no problem admitting that I worked to support Kirchnerism in the province of Buenos Aires during the last elections.'

Nestor Kirchner and his wife Christina are both left-Peronists as is the current President; former President of Argentina Carlos Menem and Moyana, the Independiente president, are both right-Peronists – the term Federal Peronism is also used to signify this strand of the movement. Told you it was complicated.

Seventy-one Boca fans died in a crush in River's Estadio Monumental in 1968. Boca myth suggested that the crush happened because the police were repressing the fans who were singing the Peronist March, banned by the then-fascist regime.

A leftist like Diego Maradona anxious to show his credentials will become a prominent fan of Boca, not of River. As Marcelo reminded me, River Plate started in Boca but moved to the upmarket Belgrano area once they made some money. River has the reputation of being a little posh, which accentuates the idea of Boca as the people's team. Teams can take on an identity driven by opposition to their main rivals: Rangers were just another team in Glasgow but became the protestant team in opposition to catholic Celtic; St Pauli moved to the left as SV Hamburger became more Nazi.

What is Peronism?

Based on the ideas and legacy of Juan Perón, Peronism remains a huge force in Argentine politics. Since 1946, Peronists have won ten out of the 13 presidential elections in which they have been allowed to run. The main Peronist force is the Justicialist Party. The policies of Peronist presidents have varied hugely but *The Economist* appositely described the general ideology as 'a vague blend of nationalism and labourism' in a 2015 article on 'The Persistence of Peronism'.

The Economist article also described Peronism as a brand rather than an ideology, and a brand highly linked to ethereal ideas of 'the people', a bit like Boca. This is all evidence of the power of feeling and emotion in political allegiance and power. Perón was Argentina's labour secretary after participating in the 1943 military coup and was elected president of Argentina in 1946. He developed good relations with labour leaders and introduced social programmes that benefited the working class, but much of this was actually motivated by a concern about the growth of communism. He made life better for the working class, but with the intention of helping the system survive against that which was seen as the main threat. Unions grew rapidly during his early years but when some began to genuinely pose a challenge: 'The public authorities resorted to the increasingly subordinated CGT to discipline these conflicts and displace nonconformist leaderships,' according to a paper by Maurizio Atzeni and Pablo Ghigliani, *The Labour Movement in Argentina since 1945: The Limits of Trade Union Reformism.*

Perón also had good relations with industrialists and was intent on preserving the system that served them. He was authoritarian, proclaimed himself the embodiment of nationality, tried to silence dissent by accusing opponents of being unpatriotic, and was an anti-Semite who welcomed escaping Nazis. But the creed and the cult largely survive based on the feeling that he and his wife were defenders of the working class and the poor; they were on the side of *los pobres*. What he actually said and did is irrelevant to the power of the cult, or political brand.

Some would claim that those who work to preserve capitalism through minor reforms and welfarism are not of the left at all. Like Perón, Bismarck and the economist John Maynard Keynes, they're more about sustaining the system rather than replacing it. And if they are prepared to do so with large doses of nationalism and antisemitism, they are definitely not of the left. During the Argentine Dirty War of the 1970s, the right-Peronist Argentine Anticommunist Alliance happily assassinated left-Peronists. No doubt which side they were on when the barricades went up; questions about this relative positioning have long been directed at the more 'centrist' members of the left.

Perón and Corbyn?

All this is important to politics in general and not just in Argentina. Much of Jeremy Corbyn's success in dramatically increasing Labour's membership, and share of the vote in the 2017 election, was based on feeling and emotion. Most people didn't know much about what Corbyn actually said and did, and his inadequacies as a leader didn't really matter. He was felt to be for the people that had been neglected for some time by British politics and he represented a return to 'old Labour values'. Corbyn was on the side of *los pobres*.

The admired Labour Manifesto of 2017 didn't make a lot of difference to Corbyn's electoral gains of that year, nor did the much-criticised 2019 version cause his defeat in that year's election. Most people do not read party manifestos. Corbyn failed due to the party's and the country's split over European Union membership and the effect of the concerted campaign against him run by a right-wing press terrified by the near-miss of 2017. Amongst other things, they painted him as anti-patriotic. The emotional appeal of Brexit, his own indecision on the subject and related issues around 'patriotism' helped end the Corbyn project, along with a deep hostility from his own party machine – Labour's 'right-Peronistas'?

The left should never engage in the nationalistic rhetoric common to all strands of Peronism, but does need to engage with patriotism and work to redefine this powerful emotional force in politics. Daniel Jadue's exhortation to 'get out of the institutions and get on the streets' is good advice, and in doing so the left needs to think about how it can broaden and deepen its appeal to fundamental emotions.

Conclusions

Buenos Aires is a great city in a great country and a trip to Boca Juniors should be on any football fan's bucket list. From a political viewpoint, things are complicated and can appear a little crazy, but confronting the crazy can bring some insights, and it's not an unknown factor in human history.

Perón said in 1951, 'The masses don't think, the masses feel and they have more or less intuitive and organised reactions. Who produces those reactions? Their leader.' He has a point, but beware leaders who think like that.

There is a large iron artwork depicting Eva Perón on the side of the front of the Department of Social Development in downtown Buenos Aires. Christina Kirchner got the idea for this when she was in Cuba. She said at the unveiling of the 15-tonne work:

'I saw an image of Che on the ministry building he worked in. How is it possible that a society pays tribute to a man who is not from that country and we have no tributes to a woman who not only marked the entry of women into politics and the country's most important social revolution, but who also represented the people and country with more passion than anyone in history.'

I took a photo of the mural from the huge Avenida 9 de Julio in central Buenos Aires. The avenida's statue of Don Quijote and Rocinante appeared on the left of the photo and it looked like both were recoiling in pain. I said at the time when I posted it on social media, 'There is some profound philosophical significance in this juxtaposition but right now I'm too tired to explore it further.' I'm still not sure about that significance, I'm still not sure about whether Boca is a left-wing club or not, I still don't really understand the enduring power of Peronism, but I'll definitely return to Argentina to *profundizar* a little more.

* * *

La Mano de Dios

– Vincent Raison –

It's understandable that many Boca fans think of Riquelme as more significant to Boca than Maradona. After all, he played nearly 200 games for the *Azul y Oro*, winning five Primera Divisións, three Copa Libertadores and is now vice-president of the club with whom he will always be synonymous. Maradona moved on quickly to fame and fortune in Europe, before returning a little tarnished by failed drug tests. Maradona belongs to the world, but Riquelme, to Boca Juniors. But that doesn't stop Diego Armando Maradona being Boca's most famous son.

He was famed as a footballer of rare genius, but also one who squandered that precious talent by enjoying himself with similar élan. A World Cup-winning captain, quite possibly the best footballer in history and the scorer of the 'Goal of the Century' against England in that 1986 World Cup; yet remarkably, he is renowned more for his handball. Perhaps it is because he immortalised it with his underrated quick wit by describing it as, 'A little with the head of Maradona, and a little with the hand of God.'

It was a quote of some genius, almost equal to the balance, speed and skill he showed when he danced past five England players to score Argentina's second goal. When he leapt above keeper Peter

Shilton to tap the ball into the net with his hand for the first, I felt like most England supporters: he was a cheat, pure and simple. But I soon came to appreciate his sublime talent along with something I'd paid no attention to while watching live. England, like every opponent Argentina faced, had tried to kick lumps out of Maradona whenever they got the chance. Maradona was fouled 53 times in that World Cup, a record, which of course doesn't count the times opponents got away with it, often because he still had the ball. Despite that, he managed to score five goals, register five assists and lift the World Cup. But we tend not to think of fouling as cheating. Diving is cheating. Scoring with your hand is cheating. But kicking someone? Well, it's just part of the game.

Such is the myth of British fair play, which we managed to convince ourselves and most of the world existed. It is likely that the concept of British fair play goes back to the playing fields of Eton and Rugby, which in a societal sense is as far from fair play as you can get.

Not that Terry Butcher and Terry Fenwick, England's unfortunate centre-backs that day, spent much time at the Bullingdon Club. Football has always been an accessible game to play partly because all you need is a ball and you're off. When Maradona was a kid, he often didn't even have that, and would play keepy-uppy with an orange or a bundle of rags, all the way to school. To say his beginnings were humble deflects from the poverty and violence that surrounded him growing up in the still frightening barrio of Villa Fiorito. He was the epitome of the scabby-kneed street urchin who had to be tough and cunning to survive, let alone thrive.

Of his two goals that day, it's not the 'Goal of the Century' that achieved a cultural significance beyond a ball placed in a net. Maradona inspired documentaries and fly-on-the-wall series, but it's the other goal that inspired films such as *The Hand of God*, and *Maradona, The Hand of God* and *In the Hands of God*.

In Barcelona, where he never really felt at home, there is a shop called Hand of God, run by a Marxist Boca fanatic, Sebastián, from

Buenos Aires, naturally. The shop's logo is a fist under a football. It sells its own brand of football themed clothes, but also books on St Pauli, Soviet Football and Rayo Vallecano. The Hand of God shop has three heroes, its website states: Eric Cantona – with a quote interpreted as, 'Kicking a fascist was the best thing I ever did in my career' – Diego Maradona, and Irene Gonzalez Basanta, who was the first woman to play alongside men in Spanish football, who died at the age of 19, three years after founding her own team, Irene CF in La Coruña. Three exceptional mavericks.

'We are in favour of football poetry. We like rebellious football, inclusive football, people's football. The one that is played in the streets,' says the site.

I asked Sebastián, 'Why Maradona and not Riquelme?' This was his answer:

'I'm a Boca fan and I'm in no doubt that the best player I've ever seen in a Boca shirt was Juan Román Riquelme. He gave us the most glorious times we've ever known. And we'll be eternally grateful to him for that.

'But with Diego it's something else. We gave Diego everything without expecting anything in return from the day he chose us. For preferring the blue and gold shirt, for wearing it with pride, for making us champions in 1981 and then, over the years, for going from being a player to being just another fan, one of those who Sunday after Sunday make the Bombonera beat.

'In Boca he shone in his first year, just before making the inevitable jump to millionaire European football. His comeback in 1995 was already marked by his personal problems and addiction. It wasn't what he or we would've wanted. There were no title wins. There was no glory. But despite that, we never reproached him, we never judged him, we never stopped loving him. As the song of *La Doce* says, "Win or lose, we don't give a shit."

'Because Boca cannot be understood without Maradona, and neither can Maradona without Boca.'

The Bench

– VINCENT RAISON –

FK Velež Mostar

Now we come to a remarkable club in Bosnia and Herzegovina (BiH), founded in 1922 in what was then Yugoslavia. Velež is named after a nearby mountain, which in turn was named after the Slavic god, Veles, the shapeshifter. Now they are the club of the Bosniaks – the Bosnian Muslims, but once they drew fans from across the country, from all faiths and ethnicities, just as the country itself had been a historically multi-ethnic state. But then came war. And war isn't good for nice things.

The club began life with an association with worker's rights and socialism. They wore a red star on their shirts, marking them out as anti-establishment and in opposition to local rivals, especially the already established Zrinjski Mostar.

By the time the Nazis invaded Yugoslavia, Velež had already been banned due to their involvement in an anti-government protest. When the fascist puppet government of the Independent State of Croatia was formed, many Velež players joined the Yugoslav Partisans to fight for their country. Zrinjski went on to play in a newly formed league, along with other Mostar teams. Nine Velež players were awarded the Order of the People's Hero, the Yugoslav gallantry medal, eight of them posthumously, for their service in the defeat of the fascists. The club's official history records that after the club had been banned and Belgrade was attacked:

'Nearly all members and supporters of the red team on the first day joined the battle against the invaders and their local supporters, 77 of whom laid down their lives for the freedom of their homeland.'

After the fascists' defeat, the socialist government banned Zrinjski and other Mostar teams for allowing themselves to be used as nationalist propaganda tools. Velež found themselves the only team left in the city.

Under President Tito's unique brand of socialism – opposed to western imperialism, but at arm's length from the Soviet Bloc – Mostar thrived. It became a largely Muslim city, with a substantial Croat minority and a smaller Serb community. The Neretva River divides the city and while Muslims and Croats lived together on both sides of the iconic Stari Most (Old Bridge), Croats made up the majority on the west side. But with interracial marriage accounting for 35 per cent of unions, it was truly a multicultural city.

Velež had already joined the Yugoslav First League by the time Bijeli Brijeg, their new stadium, was opened in 1958 in a western suburb of the city. With a successful youth academy providing players for the first team, Velež became a force in Yugoslav football. They were twice runners-up in the league, once on goal difference from Hajduk Split, and qualified for Europe. In the 1974/75 season they overcame a 3-1 first-leg deficit to knock out Derby County and reach the quarter-finals of the UEFA Cup. They developed a fanbase outside of their region who admired the attacking style of play dictated by their coach, Suljeman Rebac, and the home-grown nature of their success. In the 1980s they won their first major trophies, winning the Yugoslav Cup – then known as the Marshal Tito Cup – twice, and returning to European competition.

We tend to think of ultra culture as an Italian phenomenon. In fact, Hajduk Split had been taking flags, banners, flares and a bit of aggro to away matches since the 1950s. They had been inspired by Brazilian fans at the 1950 World Cup, after a group of Yugoslav sailors from Split managed to get into the Maracanã for the final. They called themselves Torcida Split 1950, from the Portuguese *torcer* – to root for – and they are the oldest football supporters' group in Europe. In response to Torcida Split, other Yugoslav teams developed fan groups. As Velež grew in popularity, so did their fan groups, The Zealots, The Eagles, Chicago and Furia emerged. By the time of the second cup final in 1986, they had become the Red Army, in keeping with the strange admiration for the fear that British hooligans provoked. The Red Army acquired a formidable reputation of their own, taking 8,000 away to Split where they proceeded to smash up the place. The following year they invaded the pitch after two penalties cost them the title on the last day. In English football parlance (that I still find ridiculous, to be honest), they were a 'respected firm'.

In the bitter war that followed the collapse of the Yugoslav state and BiH's referendum vote for independence, Serb forces attempted to subdue BiH, with a little ethnic cleansing thrown in, to render it part of Greater Serbia. In the beginning, Bosniaks and Croats fought side by side. Soon they were fighting each other, with terrible consequences for Mostar, 'That tolerant city of three faiths,' as Toby Kinder described it in his excellent paper describing the disintegration of Yugoslavia through the perspective of Velež, *Bosnia, the Bridge and the Ball*. Even the Stari Most was destroyed.

'The link between the mostly Muslim east bank and the predominantly Croat west was literally, as well as metaphorically torn to pieces,' wrote Kinder.

A consequence of the war was that even after its end in 1995, Mostar became an ethnically divided city, like Belfast or Beirut. Velež Mostar, having been a 'multi-ethnic symbol of anti-establishment pride', as Kinder put it, had become monocultural, supported only by Bosniaks. With their stadium on the Croat side of town, the local council gave it to the newly restored Croat club, Zrinjski Mostar, which meant Velež had to move to a decrepit athletics stadium in the north of the city. The various local teams played in separate leagues until 2003, by which time the Bosniak, Croat and Serb leagues had formed the Premier League of Bosnia and Herzegovina.

Although the club has struggled, suffering relegation then enjoying promotion more than once, the Red Army has grown, now as a symbol of Bosniak identity that they don't find reflected in the BiH state. They are still firmly left-wing and committed to anti-fascism.

'While the war, then, has sharpened a sense of separateness not felt in Mostar for many years, it has not changed the fundamental nature of Bosnian Islam as tolerant ... and accepting of inter-religious marriage,' said Kinder.

Most Bosniaks, along with the vast majority of Muslims across the world, oppose the fundamentalism of the Wahhabi sect, despite Saudi Arabia's support during the war. Indeed, Toby told us that Bosniaks were more likely to give up drinking for Ramadan than fast.

After coming third in the league in 2020/21, Velež returned to European competition this year, where they knocked out AEK Athens in the Europa Conference. They are firmly re-established in BiH football, winning the Bosnia and Herzegovina Football Cup in 2022, even if they can no longer represent the country's counterculture. However, in Edin Džeko, captain of Bosnia and Herzegovina, there is a Bosniak hero around whom the entire country can unite. Perhaps it helps that he has played for some of the biggest clubs in Europe – Manchester City, Roma, Inter Milan – and is therefore a source of pride rather than partisanship. But the national love for him shows that in a country of such deep wounds, football still has the power to unite what politics, ethnicity and religion too often divide.

Celtic

With Stewart Mcgill

Britain's first winners of the European Cup have among the most devoted and passionate fans anywhere, and are held in high esteem throughout the left-speaking world. That's not just because you'll find Celtic fans at all the grounds we've talked about in this book, but because of their committed support for marginalised peoples around the world and the less well off on their doorstep.

Of course, that's where Celtic came in, representing Irish immigrants in Glasgow in the late 19th century and trying to mitigate the bigotry and poverty they faced. They were competing for work in a tough working-class city, as newcomers, with a different religion, a situation repeated around the world that often leads to an abrasive welcome.

Celtic Football Club was formally constituted on 6 November 1887 at a meeting in St Mary's church hall in The Calton, Glasgow. Its stated purpose being 'to alleviate poverty in Glasgow's east end parishes'. It was Brother Walfrid who suggested the name Celtic. On 29 May 1888, Celtic played their first official match against Rangers, with some Hibernian players loaned to them, and won 5-2 in a game described as a 'friendly encounter'. Things move on.

Walfrid was originally from Sligo and was a member of the Marist Order. There was, and still is, a missionary element to this order and whilst Walfrid certainly appears to have been genuinely affected by the poverty he saw, it should also be remembered that there was a defensive element to his deeds. As the Celtic Wiki says:

'Firstly, the activities of the Presbyterians were a great concern, given that the Protestant Church was also active in feeding and attending to the poor of the East End, while simultaneously trying to "snare away" Brother Walfrid's flock. Brother Walfrid enjoyed a close and warm relationship with his Protestant cousins, but he was also fearful of tactics that he'd witnessed in his homeland, Ireland, of turning the poor against the Catholic Church.'

He was impressed by the charitable work of Hibernian in Edinburgh, the first Irish club in Scotland who had also become a very successful football club and a symbol of Irishness in the country. Hibernian did operate a Catholics-only employment policy, something that Brother Walfrid and other founders of the club like John Glass rejected immediately. John Glass is a much-neglected figure in Celtic's history who did more than anyone to turn Brother Walfrid's dream into a reality. Willie Maley, Celtic's first manager, who lasted 43 years in the job, always credited Glass as being the man to whom Celtic FC owed its existence: he established that which Walfrid founded.

Glass organised several political rallies at which Michael Davitt from the left-wing of Irish nationalism addressed crofters in the Highlands. Glass's political ideas probably guided Celtic's ecumenical approach from its very early days.

While it's hard to maintain underdog status when your trophy room is the size of Celtic's, culturally they have not forgotten where they came from. They still relate to those who face the struggles their forefathers did. Most of the UK is unaware of the massacres the English perpetrated in Ireland, or the confiscation of Irish land for the English Crown. Despite a wealth of it, history is not our strong point. Only the victims remember.

Celtic fans have shown support for the oppressed in apartheid South Africa, separatist movements in Spain, as well as refugees. You'll often see the flag of Palestine flying at Celtic Park in solidarity with a people who have had their land taken from them. When the ultra group the Green Brigade raised hundreds of them during Celtic's Champions League match against Hapoel Be'er Sheva in 2016, UEFA had kittens. Flags, of all things, were being waved at a football match. Whatever next?

UEFA decided that the flags were 'illicit banners' and fined the club around £8,600, despite Palestine being recognised by FIFA. The fans began a campaign – #matchthefineforpalestine – to make sure the club weren't out of pocket for their actions. They raised over £175,000, covering the fine and donating the rest to Medical Aid for Palestine and the Aida refugee camp, so they knew that there were people thousands of miles away who cared about their plight. The camp started Aida Celtic football club with kit and equipment sent from Glasgow to play in the Bethlehem youth league. It was a brilliant response to a petty act; an act that was just as political as the initial 'offence'.

Accusations of anti-Semitism were flimsy, with Celtic's Israeli player, Nir Bitton, given a standing ovation and Be'er Sheva players treated respectfully. UEFA had made fools of themselves, but ultimately, it raised a lot of money for good causes. Not that Bitton hasn't received anti-Semitic hate mail from Celtic fans. He has.

And the fact that it only happens after a loss to Rangers doesn't make it any more excusable. It never is. But it's a sad fact that every club has its idiots.

Bhoys fans may well wonder why they are on the bench. Shouldn't they be the first name on the team sheet? After all, the Green Brigade describes itself as 'a broad front of anti-fascist, anti-racist and anti-sectarian Celtic supporters'. It's a fair question, but most fans will already know the answer. Some of the chants and stunts between Celtic and Rangers are impossible to condone, even with the 'whataboutery' that points the finger back at Ibrox. The only person you can call a 'sad Orange bastard' without being sectarian is Donald Trump. Chanting you're a 'fat Orange bastard' at Kris Boyd is not cool; substitute 'fenian' or 'papist' and Celtic fans would rightly get annoyed at a corpulent member of the Catholic Church being so abused. Rangers fans may do much worse but that's no reason to exonerate a section of Celtic support for helping the sectarian virus survive and spread. And whilst banners proclaiming 'Know Your Place Hun Scum' may not be technically sectarian, they contribute to the cloud of sectarianism and divisiveness that still hangs over Glasgow, as divorced from any kind of Christian charity as they are from sense and decency.

Glasgow City Council published a report in 2003 that stated, 'The role of football was so significant [to their study] that it was actually felt to have replaced religion as the source and focus of sectarian attitudes and behaviours.'

Both football and religion can encourage 'othering', even if the latter is supposed to bring people together. Football needs an opponent; it needs an Us v Them. But victories can still be passionately enjoyed across the globe without perpetuating prejudice.

Entwined with all that fervour, a visit to Celtic Park is one of the most visceral, friendly and loud football days you will ever experience. The welcome is like no other. To hear *You'll Never Walk Alone* in that arena is to feel yourself lifted in brotherhood in one of the world's great amphitheatres. When Jock Stein led them to become European Champions in 1967 in Lisbon, with an entire team born within 30 miles of Celtic Park, they performed a miracle that will never be surpassed; an achievement that can never be diminished. And despite the divisiveness of some, the club still radiates decency and the fans are to be commended just for their loud support of the Palestinian cause that has been abandoned by other parts of the left; a support largely inspired by the emotional, personal and familial links that exist with the north of Ireland and other parts of the country. As the old saying goes, Celtic may not play in Ireland, but they do play for Ireland.

Celtic was born out of the need to help the poor. The club and the Green Brigade continue that tradition with its food bank drives. It is what it always was.

Bahia

In the north-eastern city of Salvador, Esporte Clube Bahia are taking a principled stand that's at odds with the climate produced by President Bolsonaro, Brazil's far-right populist leader, and his supporters. For the last five years, their campaigns against racism, their standing up for the rights of the LGBTQ community, for the land rights of indigenous people and the respectful treatment of female fans in football grounds have earned them admiration throughout Brazil and across the world.

Currently playing in Brazil's Serie B after relegation in 2021, as well as the Bahia state championship, Bahia have a proud history, mostly spent in the top flight. Indeed, aside from 46 state titles, they have twice won the *Brasileirão* title, in 1959 and in 1988, and reached the quarter-finals of the Copa Libertadores.

Salvador is one of the oldest cities in the Americas, the capital city of the state of Bahia and the centre of Afro-Brazilian culture. There is both wealth and great poverty in this port city of nearly three million. There is much beauty in its miles of beaches, but also a terrifying level of violent crime. Yet its carnival has a legitimate claim to be the biggest party in the world.

With the problems facing the region, it is all the more admirable that a football club commits itself so firmly to the rights of others. Salvador is a black-majority city, usually governed by a white, male minority. As it says on their website, 'Salvador is the city with the most blacks outside of Africa. And we're proud of it!' In 2018, during Black Consciousness Month, they wore shirts with the names of 20 historic black Brazilians, from leaders of escapéd slaves to political murder victims. They often use their shirts to make statements. In 2019, they took to the pitch with black splotches on their red, blue and white stripes in protest at the government's hopelessly weak response to the environmental disaster facing the region in the shape of tonnes of crude oil washing up on north-eastern beaches.

The club's president, Guilherme Bellintani, supports the promotion of human rights through football. Bahia joined with the United Nations Population Fund to launch #ZeroViolence Against Women, on International Women's Day in 2022. To be asked to partner with a UN group was significant recognition for the work they do and the social impact they have achieved. Again, the team wore a customised kit to mark the occasion at their magnificent Arena Fonte Nova stadium, a legacy of the 2014 World Cup.

While the European clubs we have featured focus on anti-racism and anti-fascism, Bahia stand up against some very specific Brazilian injustices, such as the predicament of the country's 2,000 indigenous tribes. One of Bolsonaro's first acts as president was to remove demarcation rights from the National Indian Foundation, which protected ancestral lands, and hand it to the government. He had always been a vocal opponent of indigenous rights and promised to open their lands to mining and agriculture interests, despite their protected status in the Brazilian constitution.

Bahia released a manifesto video featuring 12 Pataxó Indians to support the Demarcation Now movement – the campaign to protect territory for Brazil's indigenous peoples – as part of their Indigenous April campaign. They had the names of historic indigenous people put on the shirts for a game, including that of

Garrincha, the Brazilian legend, who twice lifted the World Cup, in 1958 and 1962, and was born into a Fulni-ô family, the only indigenous group in the north-eastern Brazil that has managed to keep its language alive.

While their positions are often opposed to that of the country's president, Bahia's head of communications, Nelson Barros Neto, made clear the club's political neutrality. He told us, 'Bahia doesn't call itself a "left-wing club". We carry out humanitarian campaigns, without a partisan political predilection. But, in current times, defending even basic rights has come to be seen as "communism" or something of the left.'

It is a message we've seen echoed elsewhere in this book. Left-wing can be seen as pejorative in some societies. Sadly, I have to wonder how long 'humanitarian' will remain a neutral term.

Another major Brazilian team, Vasco da Gama, also has anti-racist history. Football was more of an aristocratic game in 1920s Brazil, but Vasco had a team that was diverse in terms of race and social class and the first major team to select black players. After early success, they were asked by the league to bar a number of their black, mixed-race and working-class players that they considered 'unsuitable'. The club's written refusal, now famous, is known as the *Reposta Histórica*, the Historic Response, and eventually led to the end of racial barriers in Brazilian football. It's hard to imagine Brazil would have become such a world force in football if they had to rely on upper-class descendants of Europeans. It wasn't always such a Beautiful Game.

Racism was – and is – a big problem, structurally and institutionally, in Brazil, the last country in the Americas to abolish slavery. It's not something Bolsonaro is going to tackle. Thankfully football is important enough in Brazil to be able to potentially make a difference in areas that the powerful neglect.

Olympique de Marseille

There's a strong argument for claiming Marseille (OM) are the biggest team in France, though Paris Saint-Germain gather new fans with every child's passing birthday. PSG have finally overtaken Marseille's nine titles this season, though they are yet to match Marseille's Champions League capture of 1993. There are strong cultural differences between the clubs that fuel their intense rivalry, apart from the north/south geographic one. OM represent the working-class and diversity; PSG, power and money. While PSG have sought to subdue the ultra elements at the Parc des Princes, which have constituted both left- and right-wing groups, Marseille have no hope of doing so, even if they tried.

OM's north stand is known as Virage Nord De Peretti, named after the late founder and leader of the fan group Marseille Trop Puissant (Marseille Too Powerful). It houses not just MTP but also the Fanatics and the Dodgers supporter groups. The ultras are pretty powerful too. The five main fan groups oversee ticket sales, a unique situation in Europe. The power they wield is one reason why Marseille cannot be sold to the highest bidder. The fans are not for sale, yet they are part of the furniture. And the furniture comes with the house.

As a tribute to MTP, the club's third kit in 2010 was red, green and yellow, the colours of Africa that MTP include in many of their symbols. OM are actively trying to strengthen their bond with Africa, where they have opened two schools and the first team have toured. Commando Ultra 84, the oldest ultra group in France, and the South Winners 87 occupy the south stand, the Virage Sud Chevalier Roze. The latter are another lefty, anti-fascist mob, drawn from inner-city youth. Marseille have particular friendships with AEK Athens, who inspired MTP's existence, plus Livorno and Sampdoria.

Marseille's status as the oldest city in the country and as a Mediterranean port city means it has long been a gateway to France. Consequently, it has experienced numerous waves of immigration and is hugely multicultural, with a strong North African flavour. It's not likely to be a holiday destination for anti-immigration politicians like Marine Le Pen, which can only be a good thing. Marseille is a lively, sparky city; the most dynamic and diverse in all of France. I absolutely loved it and look forward to returning to experience the Stade Vélodrome in all its rowdy glory.

OM's passions reflect its city. The team has always had a kind of poetry, recruiting exciting players such as Jairzinho, Papin, Waddle, Ravanelli, Ribéry, Pires, Drogba and Payet. They also signed one Eric Cantona, whose childhood dream had always been to play for Marseille. Sadly, his lofty persona and penchant for speaking his mind meant he was never fully appreciated in his hometown.

One person it was unwise to be frank about was the club's former president, Bernard Tapie. The complex and controversial businessman, who owned OM between 1986 and 1994, took the club from the bottom half of Ligue 1 to the pinnacle of Europe. He oversaw the construction of one of the best teams France had ever seen, winning Ligue 1 and the Champions League in the same year. But his great success was marred by a match-fixing scandal that saw OM stripped of their national title and Tapie face an eight-month jail sentence for corruption. Big Eric didn't need a judge to make up his mind about Tapie. And once he'd expressed his opinion, his days in Marseille were numbered.

Tapie, who passed away in 2021 still proclaiming his innocence, remains a hero in Marseille, where perhaps they love a rogue. His activities have cast a shadow over that great team, however.

OM have spent 72 seasons in the top flight, more than any other team. They are regulars in Europe and usually among the best teams in France, even if they haven't won the title since 2010. However, it is their fans that really excel. It's hard to find the right words to describe them. 'Completely nuts' comes close. It's a city obsessed with football; a city with a rebel mentality. After all, when Louis XIV built Fort Saint-Jean in the Old Port, the cannons were trained towards the town, not the sea.

When things go wrong supporters don't write a pithy email. They show up in their hundreds at the training ground and set light to stuff, as they did in 2021. This year the club's president, Pablo Longoria, held a crisis meeting with fans unhappy about the treatment of certain players, the style of play and current form.

Dissatisfied after more than an hour, they demanded further meetings with the manager, Jorge Sampaoli, and the owner, Frank McCourt (the American businessman, not the writer). Because this level of support has more than one edge. They are deafening and spectacular in backing their team, but they don't turn down the volume when things go wrong.

The ultras feel it is their job to bring the madness to the stadium. It's always going to be a risky proposition. Hooliganism is once again a big problem in France, and Marseille's ultras are not going to be pushed around by anyone. There have been headlines of the wrong sort in clashes with Angers, Nice and PAOK. However, there is another side to these guys. They will also pitch up to support the poor and the homeless. To hand out stuff at food banks, away from the Press and far from the headlines.

As a one-club melting pot city, Marseille has a unique, special atmosphere that yearns to break the tedious grip that PSG have on French football. *Bon chance*.

AEK Athens

AEK Athens were founded in 1924 by refugees from Constantinople following the Greco-Turkish War (1919–1922) and the population exchange of 1923 between Greece and Turkey, another war that Britain was involved in and has subsequently forgotten. Having the roots of the club planted by displaced people has naturally seen it develop a left-wing slant and the club has maintained anti-fascist fans ever since.

There are also right-wing fans at AEK, but most fans live in neighbourhoods that are traditionally leftist. The most notorious fan group are Original 21, uncompromising leftist ultras who are not shy of a ruck but mostly give raucous, fanatical support to their team, including spectacular pyro displays and unbelievable noise. Original 21 promote the ethos of the club, one of inclusivity and diversity, as well as making a racket. They form one third of the 'triangle of brotherhood', along with Livorno and Marseille, and also maintain a strong friendship with St Pauli.

Lucas Pérez scores the only goal as Cádiz beat Barcelona at the Camp Nou for the first time.

Bebé after scoring for Rayo Vallecano against Sevilla at the Estadio de Vallecas in March 2022.

Masked St Pauli Ultras celebrate beating rivals Hamburger SV in September 2019.

Back from the brink. Bohemians Praha salute their fans in August 2005 after regaining their licence.

Liverpool players react to winning the penalty shoot-out and FA Cup at Wembley in May 2022.

Detroit City take to the field in front of the Northern Guard in May 2015.

Dulwich Hamlet line up before their FA Cup first round match against Carlisle United, November 2019.

Cosenza fans before a Serie B game against Reggina in November 2021: 'We live for you, win for us'.

Red Star's Cheikh Ndoye scores in a penalty shoot-out against Lyon in the Coupe de France Round of 16, April 2021 at the Stade Bauer.

Palestino before a friendly with the Palestine national team in the West Bank city of Nablus, in December 2016.

Boca Juniors' Sebastián Villa and Carlos Zambrano get a police escort after beating River Plate in the Copa de la Liga at the Estadio Monumental, March 2022.

Assistant manager, Samir Merzić, at the Stadion Rođeni for Velež Mostar training, March 2021.

Celtic's Callum McGregor lifts the Premiership trophy at Celtic Park, Glasgow in May 2022.

Leandro Castán of Vasco da Gama picks up an understandable red card against Bahia at Sao Januario Stadium in January 2021 in Rio de Janeiro.

Muamer Tanković of AEK Athens celebrates after scoring against Leicester City in the Europa League, October 2020 in Athens.

Hapoel Tel-Aviv fans during a Europa League match against Atlético Madrid in September 2012 in Tel Aviv.

Their natural rivals are Panathinaikos, who are said to represent Athens' high society and with whom they share the Athens derby. AEK are one of the three most successful teams in Greece, along with Panathinaikos and Olympiakos, and have a proud history in European football to go with their 30 domestic trophies. They last won the Super League in the 2017/18 season, with a dominating show of consistency that saw them lose only two matches.

The fans showed their true colours when one of their players, an Under-21 international, appeared to give a Nazi salute to the crowd after scoring. They demanded that Giorgos Katidis never play for AEK again. The Hellenic Football Federation fined him and gave him a lifetime ban from ever playing for the national team, despite his protestations of innocence. 'I am not a fascist and would not have done it if I had known what it meant,' he said on Twitter.

AEK suspended him for the rest of the season, after which he left the club.

There are a number of anti-fascist ultra groups throughout different levels of Greek football. With the rise of the far-right Golden Dawn, they are increasingly important. Thankfully Golden Dawn's vote shrank in the 2019 election, leaving them without any seats, but extremism has not gone away.

Competing with AEK in the Super League are Atromitos, who play in western Athens and are managed by former Wales coach Chris Coleman. Their ultra group, Fentagin, don't forget the Nazi persecution of their players during the occupation in World War II and provide a peaceful anti-racist presence at the relegation-threatened club. Lower down the leagues there are several left-wing ultra groups, including the Che Guevara Club at Panserraikos, a well-supported Super League 2 club in northern Greece.

Given the struggles of so many left-wing clubs though, it is heartening to see AEK are one of the biggest and best clubs in Greece. It's a country with such a complex history, for which Britain, Germany, Italy and Turkey all bear some responsibility. And it is one where anti-fascism is a significant barrier to right-wing lunacy.

Standard Liège

McGill and I did make the trip to Liège, on the train from Paris, after our visit to Red Star. We found a city that contrasted with our expectations, thinking of it as an unlovely industrial town, historically known for its socialism and opposition to Nazi occupation. But it had scrubbed up very nicely, from its magnificently photogenic railway station, designed by Santiago Calatrava, to its pedestrian central district, le Carré, filled with cool bars and lively students.

Football travel in the time of Covid had not been easy, but stadiums were once again able to admit fans by the time we made it to Belgium. Unfortunately, Standard were hit with a further ban due to crowd trouble at their match against bitter rivals Sporting Charleroi that included a pitch invasion and clashes with police and opposing fans. Consequently, we were not able to access the stadium but consoled ourselves by watching the game with Standard fans in a Liège bar, accompanied by fine Belgian beer.

Standard's Ultras Inferno 1996 are among the noisiest and most pyromaniacal in Europe; vociferous, fervent and devoted, despite a team struggling on the pitch to match former glories. They have been Belgian champions ten times, won the cup eight times and reached one European final. In 2022 they are struggling in mid-table, but you wouldn't know it from their fans, who every match generate more smoke than a new Pope.

Although recent years have seen it kick off with Charleroi on a few occasions, their traditional rivalry is with Anderlecht. Although they don't share a city – Anderlecht are from Brussels – the feud is intense and is steeped in class. Liège are seen as the workers' team while Anderlecht are perceived as representing the bourgeoisie. Many felt the ultras had gone too far in 2015 when they unfurled a huge 'Red or Dead' banner depicting their former player, Steven Defour, being decapitated, after his move to Anderlecht. It was too much for Defour, who was sent off for firing the ball into the Liège fans, and whose refusal to leave the pitch led to Anderlecht fans rioting. Belgian football is much more ferocious than you might think.

One of Standard's more famous sons is Jean-Marc Bosman, whose successful case in the European Court of Justice in 1995 forever altered the free movement of players within the European Union whose contracts had expired. Bosman's contract with Standard finished in 1990. He was prepared to move to Dunkerque, but Dunkerque were not prepared to meet the fee Standard demanded for a player they no longer wanted. Furthermore, he found his wages slashed by 70 per cent because he was no longer a first-team player at Liège. He successfully sued for restraint of trade. The injustice seems obvious now, but the impact of the Bosman ruling has been enormous for clubs and players alike. Clubs were no longer able to block a player from leaving, and players could demand higher wages due to the lack of transfer fees.

The name, Standard, sounds curiously British. It is. They were named after the Standard Athletic Club, a social club founded in 1890 by British engineers who had worked on the Eiffel Tower. They won the inaugural French championship in 1894 and still play football in local leagues, along with cricket and other sports.

Unable to take our place at the Stade Maurice Dufrasne, we found a bar showing the game, *L'Aller Simple*. McGill's local Communist Party contact, Julien, warned us off the cooking lager, Jupiler, in favour of some Trappist ale. Julien may not have been interested in Champagne, but he was a Chimay Communist, ordering their Grande Réserve, Chimay Bleue, and its nine per cent dose of Belgian happiness. The Trappists have an interesting model, a non-capitalist one you could say, so his choice was entirely consistent. They do brew beer for the upkeep of their monasteries, but any profits must go to charitable causes. Not only do they produce beer of exceptional quality, they use it to help others.

As it happened, we needed some help to enjoy the game as Standard were roundly outplayed by Cercle Brugge. They did manage to make it 1-1 in the second half, but then were robbed in the dying minutes when Moussa Sissako had a perfectly good goal disallowed by VAR. Sometimes VAR gets it wrong and this was an egregious example. Perhaps it was a good job the fans weren't allowed in the stadium, because they would have gone nuts.

Polonia Warsaw

As McGill has previously noted, symbols are not universal. It surprised us that Andy Capp had been co-opted by the left. In Poland, the Black Shirts – Polonia Warsaw – are the oldest club in Warsaw, with a fine anti-establishment and anti-fascist history, whereas in England and Italy the Blackshirts *were* the fascists. Even Polonia's name was controversial when they were founded in 1911. It's the Latin name for Poland, a country that didn't exist at that time, as it had been partitioned by the Habsburgs, Prussians and Russians. For Polonia, legend has it, the black shirt denoted their lost, carved up and occupied country. Their white shorts and red socks represented the Polish flag.

When independence was restored after World War I, Polonia became a force in Polish football, but when the Nazis occupied Poland in World War II, Poles were forbidden from practising sports, though Polonia played on illegally. Many of their players were active in the resistance against the Nazi occupation. Indeed, one of the founders, a former captain and president of the club, Tadeusz Gebethner, joined the Union of Armed Struggle and sheltered a Jewish family in his home. He was twice wounded in the Warsaw Uprising, the largest resistance movement of the war, before his capture, eventually dying of his wounds in a POW camp.

After the war, in 1946, the Black Shirts won the Polish championship for the first time. But the Stalin era was an unhappy one for them. Their black shirts were banned and they were forced to change their name to that of their new sponsors, the under-funded railway, who oversaw a decline in their fortunes, leading to relegation. Their fierce rivals, Legia Warsaw were now sponsored by the army, deepening their enmity. It was only a few years after Stalin's death that they were able to reclaim their name and identity in 1956.

After 40 years in the lower leagues, Polonia revived in the 1990s, twice winning promotion back to the top flight and, against the odds, winning the championship for a second time in 2000. The title-winning side included Emmanuel Olisadebe, the first black player to play for Poland, who became quite a legend.

The club struggled for good stewardship after their owner, Jan Raniecki, died in 2006. After a series of disastrous missteps, they were declared bankrupt in 2013 and demoted five divisions as punishment.

They have slowly been working their way back up the Polish football ladder and currently play in II Liga, the third tier. In the 2021/22 season they were promoted as Group 1 champions, after beating and overtaking Legionovia Legionowo (who were founded by the Polish Socialist Party), on the final day of the season in front of a sold out Stadion Polonii Warszawa.

They have a long-standing friendship with KS Cracovia, though that has become strained at the ultra level. Polonia's ultras are the Black Rebels, a left-wing fan group that has a good relationship with Partizan Minsk fans, who are fiercely leftist, and the Mad Rebels of the now-defunct Arsenal Kyiv, both of whom fight the tide of far-right football support in their own countries. (Arsenal Kyiv's professional team was dissolved in 2019 and they only exist in their junior teams now.) Poland is a mostly conservative country with a dominant right-wing, but the Black Rebels have been an unwavering symbol of anti-fascism for more than 20 years.

In 2020, Polonia were acquired by French-born businessman Grégoire Nilot, who took to the internet to reveal why he had decided 'to go on this crazy journey', instead of buying the more typical trappings of the wealthy. He explained that he lives in Warsaw with his wife and children, and he loves the city. He also loves football and relishes a challenge. He has set out some admirable core values he expects the club to represent, including tolerance, equality and respect; he has revived the women's team – the Black Mermaids; and he has set the club the goal of returning to the top flight by 2030.

Goals are easy to set, of course, but at least Polonia appear to have an owner who wants to give them the support they need and is mindful of what it represents.

Adana Demirspor

Adana is a major city in southern Turkey, a gateway between Europe and the Middle East, with an incredible history and rich traditions in culture and cuisine. Thankfully they also have two football teams, one of which, Adana Demirspor, were born from the working people and who are still supported by leftist fans.

There are 38 Demirspor clubs in Turkey, the name indicating that they were founded by railway workers, just like the Lokomotiv sports clubs of Eastern Europe. Adana are by far the most successful of them, but the fact they are part of such a large group causes some mickey-taking from their city rivals Adanaspor, who accuse them of being one of 38 clones and with whom they share the New Adana Stadium. Demir, however, are proud of their rail-track roots.

Adanapsor were formed by middle-class merchants and artisans who felt alienated by the working-class nature of Demirspor. Don't be fooled into thinking the Adana derby isn't ferocious though. Just ask the city police. This is Turkey we're talking about and football support is never passive. The Adana Demirspor *tifos* and *choreos* are mind-blowing and the volume intense, whatever league they find themselves in.

Happily, Demirspor find themselves in the upper reaches of the Turkish Süper Lig presently, just outside the European places after promotion in 2021. Their attack is currently spearheaded by Mario Balotelli. I hesitate to suggest Balotelli might have finally settled somewhere, as it's his first season at his tenth club. But after a torrid time in Italy, where he was repeatedly racially abused at clubs like Lazio and Hellas Verona, he is now playing and scoring regularly, though also collecting all too familiar yellow and red cards along the way. He should feel comfortable at the Blue Lightnings though, whose supporters have formed friendships with Livorno and St Pauli.

Another familiar face at Demir, to me at least, is Erhun Oztumer, who would simply be regarded as a legend at Dulwich Hamlet, where he was known as the 'Turkish Messi', before he moved to Turkey via Walsall, Bolton and Charlton. I have to confess to a little biased pride in seeing this absolute gent playing in the Süper Lig.

There is no city derby at the moment as Adanaspor are in the TFF First League. The roots of the derby though are clearly socio-economic. On rare occasions the two groups of fans do stand together, for instance at a protest against the government of Prime Minister Recep Erdoğan. It's always refreshing to see rivals able to find common ground.

People's Athletic Club Omonia 1948

Now it gets complicated. PAC Omonia 1948 are a phoenix club, formed after fans of Athletic Club Omonoia Nicosia, one of the biggest teams in Cyprus, broke away from the club's new ownership to create their own team. A rift between club and fan group, Gate 9, had developed over a number of years, with the ultras unhappy at what they saw as political interference in the club's decision-making processes. The sale of the club to American-Cypriot businessman Stavros Papastavrou in 2018, making the club a professional, for-profit organisation for the first time, proved to be the last straw.

AC Omonoia itself was forged by the schisms formed in the Greek Civil War (1943–1949). The Cypriot football authorities insisted all professional athletes denounce the Greek left and the Greek Communist Party. Leftist members of APOEL FC who refused to sign split with the club's more right-wing, nationalist members to form Omonoia and have remained opposed, ideologically and on the field of play, ever since. They still contest the Nicosia derby, or the Derby of Eternal Enemies, a contest between two entities of political, social and cultural difference.

The 1970s and 1980s were a golden era for Omonoia, winning 14 championships in 20 years to establish themselves as the dominant club on the island. They were inspired by Sotiris Kaiafas, considered the best Cypriot footballer of all time and the winner of the European Golden Boot in 1976. However, it must have felt like a decline to only win one title in the 90s. They've won four this century already, including one in 2020/21.

From the club's birth in 1948 onwards, the fans remained resolutely left-wing. Football and politics are inextricably linked in Cyprus. The team you support denotes your persuasion. A survey in 2009 found that 75 per cent of Omonoia fans voted for the Progressive Party of Working People (AKEL), as the communist party in Cyprus is known. From 1948 to 2013, most of the club's executive was drawn from prominent members of the party's hierarchy. However, despite sharing their political beliefs, fans became unhappy at the influence of the party on the club. Those who weren't members of AKEL were being excluded from membership of the club.

The club faced a financial crisis in 2013. Both the club and Gate 9 did their utmost to raise money to cover the debts that had accrued. Gate 9's support until then had been unstinting, with impressive *choreos*, *tifos* and noise, not to mention fighting with the police and rivals, especially APOEL. They had always been 'against modern football' and the way money has corrupted it, so when a change was proposed to move the club to private ownership from its membership model, they rebelled. In protest, they converted the entire north stand into a giant red flag, with the hammer and sickle, as a reminder of the club's history. Ultimately, Gate 9 members voted overwhelmingly to set up a new team that followed the principles they held dear.

They stated, 'Our values are to present a meritorious team who will respect its fans, the ultras mentality and to consist of anti-racist and anti-fascist ideas. We want to demonstrate that football clubs are not only about football, but that they are cells of democracy and active cells of the society. In conclusion, we would like to present that another way of football, not the modern one, is possible away from the money industry.'

PAC Omonia began life in a regional league and won promotion to the fourth division in their first year. They have continued to grow as a club and now play in Cyprus's second division; a remarkable rise.

Meanwhile, AC Omonoia won the championship in 2021 under the guidance of their Norwegian manager, Henning Berg, who won the Premier League with both Blackburn and Manchester United as a player. He was released in 2022 after a dismal campaign that led to the relegation play-offs.

Omonia has fan groups throughout Cyprus but also in London. In fact, Omonia Youth Club, a team in north London, was named National Grassroots Club of the Year in 2021. Their chairman, Mike Pieri, questioned fans on our behalf on a recent trip to Nicosia.

'Does AC Omonoia honour the traditions of its founders? The club was born on the back of repelling fascism. For some, the new owner, Papastavrou, turned the club from the people's club to a club like every other and those that broke away now refer to Omonoia fans merely as "customers". However, there is also the acceptance that the club needed to move on and be more modern. But did this mean selling its soul?'

It's sad to see a club of such fine traditions splitting with its fans of such strong principles. Sometimes it seems like the curse of the left. Now we may not be far away from the day when PAC Omonia will face its parent team in Cyprus's top flight. Given the passionate nature of Cypriot football, it's going to be more than awkward.

Hapoel Tel Aviv

Israel has two major sports associations, Maccabi and Hapoel. 'Hapoel' translates as 'The Worker', and Hapoel Tel Aviv's hammer-and-sickle badge reflects the club's historic ties to socialism and the working class. For 70 years the club was owned by the Histadrut, Israel's federation of trade unions. Fans continue to wave Che Guevara and Karl Marx flags at a club with a strong Palestinian following that has always been a key symbol of the Israeli left.

Originally formed in 1923, the 1933/34 season saw them win the Palestine League, winning every single match and doubling up by winning the cup. They continued to win titles after the creation of Israel, most recently in 2010. The club have competed in European competitions many times, notching up victories against Chelsea, Milan, Paris Saint-Germain and SV Hamburg along the way.

Ultras Hapoel have friendships with other anti-fascist fan groups, including those at St Pauli, Standard Liège, Omonoia Nicosia and Celtic. *Ultra Sankt Pauli* organise regular trips to Hapoel's Bloomfield Stadium in Tel Aviv.

Hapoel Tel Aviv share a city rivalry with Maccabi Tel Aviv, but the more bitter antagonism is reserved for Beitar Jerusalem, a club known for, and proud of, their far-right sympathies. They have unofficial links to the Likud party and fans infamous for chanting 'Death to Arabs'. They have another song:

'Here we are,

We're the most racist football team in the country.'

Beitar remains the only club to have never signed an Arab player. When the club signed two Chechen Muslims in 2013, fans protested with a banner declaring 'Beitar Will Be Forever Pure'. Their extremist ultra group, La Familia, set light to one of the club's offices, bringing national attention to a shame that the Israeli Football Association had tried to contain. When one of the Chechen signings, Zaur Sadayev, scored his first goal for the club, hundreds of fans walked out.

Though they are separated by more than 60km, theirs remains the fiercest rivalry in Israeli sport, one that has been characterised by violence off the field, reflecting the polar opposites of the political spectrum they inhabit. The Ultras Hapoel website describes Beitar Jerusalem simply as, 'Possibly the most repulsive club on earth. Fascist, racist fans, with management that goes along with them.'

Perhaps the club's sweetest moment came in May 2010. Hapoel had finished six points behind Maccabi Haifa in the regular season, but the title was decided by play-offs between the top six. On the final day, Maccabi Haifa only needed to beat Bnei Yehuda to win the championship, while Hapoel would have to beat Beitar at their Teddy Stadium and hope Maccabi Haifa slipped up. In the most dramatic of endings, Maccabi Haifa could only draw, while Eran Zahavi scored the winning goal in the 92nd minute for Hapoel in Jerusalem. They had won the title and the double, in the last minute, in their enemy's backyard.

The sun has indeed shone on the righteous, with Hapoel being crowned national champions 13 times to Beitar's six.

The Post-Match Verdict

– STEWART McGILL –

'The popular element " feels" but does not always know or understand; the intellectual element "knows" but does not always understand and in particular does not always feel.'

– ANTONIO GRAMSCI –

'The scorn of many conservative intellectuals comes from their belief that soccer-worship is exactly the religion people deserve. Possessed by soccer, the proles think with their feet, which is the only way they can think, and through such primitive ecstasy they fulfil their dreams. The animal instinct overtakes human reason, ignorance crushes culture, and the riff-raff get what they want.

'In contrast, many leftist intellectuals denigrate soccer because it castrates the masses and derails their revolutionary ardour. Bread and circus, circuses without the bread: hypnotised by the ball, which exercises a perverse fascination, workers' consciousness becomes atrophied and they let themselves be led about like sheep by their class enemies.'

– EDUARDO GALEANO – FOOTBALL IN SUN AND SHADOW *–*

*So does it really matter? Can football save the
world? Can the left-wing football followers'
movement help us create a fairer, more
equitable world? Can studying the very diverse
phenomenon of these football clubs help us
understand the world any better? Can that study
inform and enhance the left's ability to connect
and construct a more popular narrative in a
world largely sceptical of its vision?*

The Cult of the Hardman and the Appeal of the 'Cool'

Early in this project, we appeared on a podcast in which the
host asked us what football could do about the toxic masculinity,
xenophobia, racism and sexism associated with football and its
supporters, not wholly unfairly. The stock answer is of course that
it is society's problem: football suffers the consequences of the
socialisation system that breeds toxic male attitudes to violence,
women, people of a different race, gay people and others.

This is true but there is more to it than that and football can
play a role. A young guy who went to the same junior school as
did our children started going to West Ham a few years ago. His
social media and the attitudes displayed therein form a caricature
of those that you'd expect of a young racist West Ham thug; he also
follows England abroad and has posted a film of him and others
singing 'no surrender to the IRA' and other idiocies to a bunch of
bemused Europeans. (We acknowledge that not all West Ham
and England fans are like this, but it would be foolish to deny that
that element exists.)

Had this young guy followed a team much more local to
him, the mighty Dulwich Hamlet covered earlier, he would have
encountered a wholly different group of people with a quite different
mindset: anti-violence, anti-racist, anti-sexist and very quick to step
on any manifestations of those perversions of the human spirit.

We become like the people around us, we are pack animals, a tendency amplified in an emotionally charged collective experience like watching football. This boy would have turned out to be a different character had he gone to Dulwich rather than West Ham and encountered a very different type of older male role model. Those who do not elevate violence to a defining feature of your masculinity and despise racism, homophobia and sexism. Similarly, if he were from Hamburg, had he gone to St Pauli rather than SV Hamburger his experience would have been very different and he would have emerged a different individual.

The St Pauli phenomenon is important to understanding the value and the potential of left-wing football. People, in general, are attracted by 'cool' and young men in particular admire toughness, 'hard men' who don't back down and are prepared to fight and can handle themselves when it kicks off. This latter attraction is associated mostly with working-class young men but is by no means confined to that group: look at the rather sad little national love affair in the UK with the SAS, the general fetishisation of the military, the elevation of bullying gangsters who create misery into admired celebrities and the popularity of movies that never fail to glamorise and sanitise them.

The St Pauli brand is global 'cool', its aesthetics are attractive, striking and create a positive image for the values it represents. The fans are known to be anti-fascist and prepared to stand up for what they believe in with a righteous aggression that doesn't sink into tribal, toxic masculinity. This is an attractive image for many that contrasts with the caricature of the left as a bunch of insipid 'looney politically corrects' who knit their own yoghurt that is sold by much of the dominant media. This attitude is still best summed up by George Orwell's diatribes in *The Road to Wigan Pier* from 1936. 'Socialism draws towards it with magnetic force every fruit-juice drinker, nudist, sandal-wearer, sex-maniac, Quaker, "Nature Cure", quack, pacifist and feminist in England.' His tirade against such 'cranks' is memorably extended in other passages of the book to include 'vegetarians with wilting beards', the 'outer-suburban creeping Jesus' eager to begin his yoga exercises, and 'that dreary tribe of high-minded women and sandal-wearers and bearded fruit-juice drinkers who come flocking towards the smell of "progress" like bluebottles to a dead cat'.

This poison says more about some of Orwell's prejudices than it does socialists or socialism but it represents a sadly common viewpoint. St Pauli cannot be caricatured like this. The all-round strength of their image serves to enhance that of the values they represent. It connects with people who probably would not be reached by more thoughtful, overtly political and intellectual partisans of the same values, those that the media and the intellectual progeny of Orwell can more readily characterise as limp-wristed loonies with 'wilting beards'.

The power of the cult of 'hardness' to football fans is exemplified by the stories of One-Armed Babs of Chelsea and Tiny of Millwall, hooligan legends of the 1970s. I remember talking to some Chelsea fans in the 1970s about Babs, one of whom worked himself into a lachrymose quasi-religious ecstasy when telling of the exploits of Babs, ending with the amen of 'Babs is just so hard.' Millwall have never veered towards the almost religious but the fans will always talk about the legendary Tiny with true veneration.

The extraordinary thing about them is that they were both black: black leaders of overwhelmingly white football firms in the very racist 1970s, the toughness afforded a respect and credibility that trumped race prejudice at a time when it mattered, a lot. Maybe this strangely touching story also exhibits football's capacity to bring people together, albeit in a less than wholly positive way.

One of my old friends knew Tiny very well and used to run with that firm. He tells of calling on Tiny's house with the band of followers and the less than delighted reception that would be given by Tiny's mother, a very strict lady. 'I've told you before not to mix with those rough boys.' This caused much amusement as there weren't too many rougher than Tiny, but it was best not to show it in front of his mum.

Germany v Italy

Chelsea and Millwall's hooligan firms still tend to right-wing prejudice. Babs and Tiny left no legacy of inclusiveness, it was all about who could take who in those days. Britain's football scene remains largely unorganised and undeveloped politically.

Not so in Germany and Italy: the profound political differences between the ultra scenes and the wider political leanings of the two countries invites some speculation regarding the influence of football culture.

As Felix Tamsut says in an article in *Tortoise* in September 2021:

'In Germany, "apolitical" football simply doesn't exist. Politics is played out in its sport.'

Tamsut writes:

'Up until the end of the 1980s, right-wing hooligans had the dominant say at German stadia. Chants about sending rival fans to Auschwitz were commonplace, with some hooligan groups becoming known among the country's most notorious, racist and violent far-right organisations.

'The average German supporter, and, indeed, Germany's football clubs, knew about the far-right presence in their stands – but, in a rather similar fashion to German society's treatment of former Nazis in the first decades after the Second World War, chose to ignore the problem, instead of tackling it head on.'

(We know from the above how some fans of Hamburger SV reacted, they left and helped spark the St Pauli phenomenon.)

Two developments in the football landscape in Germany changed that. First, the *Fanprojekte* – literally fan projects, staffed by professional social workers skilled in working with young people, mostly young men. Their aim was to help football fans organise, to represent football fans and their interests, as well as provide them with a go-to place for everything from issues at home to problems with the law. Part of the *Fanprojekte's* work was focused on developing democracy and inclusion among football supporters.

The second development was the arrival of the ultra subculture in Germany. Back in the 1990s, football fans in Germany used to travel to Italy to watch games in Serie A, the top league for Italian clubs. Young fans saw the style of coordinated support in Italian stadia – the banners, flags and choreography – and decided to bring it back home with them. The first ultra groups in Germany were established in the mid-1980s, but the boom mostly took place between the mid-1990s and the early 2000s.

An important part of being a German ultra became a commitment to accessibility: the idea that people were unified by their love of the team, regardless of social status, ethnic background or religion. If you share an ultra's dedication towards their club, you're seen as worthy of sharing the terrace with them. These features helped make the voices of young, mostly left-leaning ultras louder than those of the right-wing hooligan groups that dominated before. The transformation wasn't smooth but, today, left-leaning ultras are the ones who largely have the say at Germany's stadia, with exceptions such as that of Hansa Rostock of course.

The power of the aesthetics is evident again from Tamsut's piece. These young fans bought into the style of Italian support, 'the banners, flags and choreography'. The right certainly understands the importance of appearances: a *Time* magazine article from 2019 on the rise of Ukraine's neo-Nazi Azov Batallion notes that, 'Through speeches and propaganda videos posted on YouTube and widely shared on Facebook, the Azov movement began to cultivate an online profile and *a distinctive aesthetic* [my emphasis].' Looks matter.

The German ultras may have borrowed extensively from the style of the Italians but they didn't take the politics. With a few exceptions, such as the great Cosenza and Livorno, the Italian ultras tend to be right-wing, with the far-right being very strong in big clubs such as Juventus, Inter Milan and Lazio. AC Milan and AS Roma are traditionally more left-leaning working-class clubs but their ultras have moved rightwards since the 1980s.

German and Italian regular politics reflect the differences between their ultra groups. In the 2021 Federal elections in Germany the Alternative für Deutschland, AfD saw a dip in national vote share by getting 10.3 per cent of the vote, compared to 12.6 per cent in 2017. More recent opinion polls show the party at around 12 per cent, but it struggles to move beyond its core support. At the time of writing, March 2022, the Italian far-right parties, The Northern League and the Brothers of Italy, are both polling at around 20 per cent in voting intentions. So 40 per cent of Italians support the neo-fascists.

Can all this be attributed to the influence of the respective ultra cultures? Of course not, there are numerous factors at play here, including differences in levels of guilt for the horrors inflicted in World War II, that influence the relative acceptability of extreme nationalism and racism. Relative economic performance is a factor and the Italians may feel a greater sense of powerlessness in a European Union in which Germany is seen as the major player. However, though support for the right in Italy may emerge from factors outside of the football culture, and the right-wing bias of the ultras may reflect the political trajectory of the wider society, it's legitimate to question whether that trajectory could have been different had the ultra movement projected a different set of values. Particularly given the importance of football in the country and the fact that the right-wing parties score well in the polls with younger people.

We can also wonder at how Chelsea and Millwall's respective followings would have developed had some people in the 1970s and 1980s latched on to the fact that a couple of the top boys were black. In opposing the culture of violence, had narratives of inclusivity been actively propagated as they were in Germany – as opposed to the passive submission that characterised the British 'response' to the growing racism that took over so many British football stadiums – then things could have been different here. And not just in football grounds. More people could have been prepared to argue at home and in their workplaces against racist and nativist narratives presented by some political parties and the majority of the printed media. Anti-racism and anti-fascism could have become something associated with prestigious football teams and supporter groups, not the 'limp-wristed crank' intellectual stereotypes pushed by the dominant culture and its media.

Why Are Many Football Fans Right-Wing?

Why did the Germans have to begin the *Fanprojekte?* Why does the Italian Right dominate the *Curva?* Why are so many British football hooligans still so racist?

The racist right-wing element in football crowds is generally exaggerated but it's certainly there. Historically it was wrong to ignore it and it's a mistake to do so now, the issue has to be approached with honesty. Football support reflects society and racism has been part of European culture for centuries. A basic, tribal racism that received some intellectual and scientific credibility over recent centuries as part of the attempts to legitimise slavery and empire. Both George Gosse and Enzo Traverso have written convincingly of the Nazis as no aberration in modern European history.

White working-class males form the core of a lot of football crowds. This group isn't inherently more racist than other parts of society; like many myths, this just confirms a lazy prejudice. A 2019 report by Protection Approaches on British attitudes showed that Britain's 'low-income masses', often known as the 'left behind', were not the main cause of rising racial and religious tensions.

'We were shocked by the extent to which those prejudiced views seeing minorities as a threat really carries across the full spectrum of society,' said Kate Ferguson, director of research and policy at Protection Approaches, who oversaw an online poll of 1,250 over-16s carried out on 11 January 2019. 'You expect to see people with lower incomes have more prejudiced views, but a third of the respondents who we would consider well-off held those views.'

Ms Ferguson's statement nicely reflects some middle-class prejudices – more on that later.

However, working-class males were the group hit most hard by the decline of the post-war consensus across Western economies and the beginnings of the descent into neoliberalism in the early 1980s. It was no surprise that the National Front and other groups began recruiting with some success at football grounds in the 1970s; people offering easy solutions and scapegoats are always going to find life easier when economic times are bad. And the cult of 'hardness' is strong in working-class male culture, particularly among young men. Tough guys blaming problems on immigration were always going to find an audience. Some of the racist chanting and attitudes on display in English football grounds in the 1980s were appalling and disgracefully too many of us just accepted it as part of the soundtrack to following our game. This certainly contributed to keeping football crowds overwhelmingly white, even those for clubs based in areas of high immigration. The area around the old West Ham stadium in Upton Park is heavily populated by people with ethnic origins in India, Bangladesh and Pakistan: you never saw very many in the ground.

At the end of the 1980s Western economies began a lengthy debt-fuelled recovery and real efforts were made to stamp out racism in the game. Things did improve but as we went into the 2000s it became clear that accelerating economic inequality was a concomitant of the neoliberal model and that its growth, necessary to distract attention from the inequality, was fuelled not just by debt but by the ready availability of cheap migrant labour. Among the 15 original European Union members the total number of foreigners (EU nationals and non-EU nationals) rose from 20.4 million in 1999 to 33.8 million by 2010, a 66 per cent increase. Labour from former Eastern Bloc countries, Africa and Asia, often treated poorly amidst harsh working conditions, filled vacancies. Here is not the place to debate the economic benefits of that step change in the demographics of the working population, nor who benefited from that shift. However, many working people in the host countries felt that they were not among the beneficiaries and connected their economic precarity and decline, massively exacerbated by the global financial crisis of 2008, with the mass immigration. As David Kennedy noted in 2013:

'All over Europe the extreme right – emboldened both by the willingness of the mainstream to fall in with demands for the restriction of immigration and their failure to combat the rise of extremist views have gained a hearing for their political thoughts and a foothold for their activities. The failure of European social democratic parties to curb the power of the market leaves them poorly placed to represent the victims of rising inequality and discrimination.'

The economic context of the growing threat of the right, inside and outside football, has to form part of the understanding of the phenomenon. However, culture also matters: note the showing of fascist parties in Italian polls compared to their German equivalents, note the difference in the prevailing culture of the respective ultra movements, and also note that the AfD polls well above the national average in the old DDR states like Saxony, economically deprived and where clubs like Dynamo Dresden and Chemnitz have powerful right-wing ultras.

The Importance of the Leftist Supporters Movement

The supporters covered in this book largely reflect the decent, inclusivist, anti-racist and collective values of their neighbourhoods. They play a vital role in guarding those values and in perpetuating them, often against the flow of a hostile mainstream through acting as agents of Wiliam Gerhardie's *God's Fifth Column*. Gerhardie's brilliant but largely forgotten book about the years 1890–1940 describes God's Fifth Column as those elements that wittingly or unwittingly sabotage defective human social constructs. He sees the artists as the true spokespeople for humanity rather than politicians or an intellectual establishment. Here, let's think of some of our fan movements as artists in action. Given the importance of the aesthetics and the performative element, it's not too great a leap of the imagination.

Along with standing up to the fascists through words and deeds – and I'm glad that the guys in the room next to us when we interviewed Sven were doing MMA; the fascists do it and sometimes you have to forget talking – the left-wing fan movement stands for football as focus of community celebration rather than a means of expanding market penetration.

As the Socialist Party wrote in 2010:

'Outside of the trade union movement there are very few areas of modern society where thousands of working-class people can gather under a common banner, in support of a common cause. While some may cast this aside as mere tribalism, there exists clear feelings of inter-fan solidarity, which if promoted can have a positive great impact on promoting working-class consciousness.'

By standing up to business football, and standing tall on the terraces against the violence of neoliberal individualism, leftist football fans provide a beacon and a potential focus. They show that football can promote the voices of the disenfranchised and the marginalised who have been largely abandoned by the bourgeois-dominated, traditional social democratic parties and the game can become even more beautiful by fostering cross-fan solidarity against oppression, alienation and exploitation.

The fans represent an alternative, collectivist approach to life that contrasts with the atomised life in which so many of us live, lonely behind a screen. Like St Pauli and Red Star they can stand for football as a game for everyone at a time when racists try to divide. Palestino and Celtic stand for the protection of minority community identity in the face of global standardisation. Cosenza and Rayo form the focal point of a community's radical past and identity and perpetuate those traditions. Liverpool and Everton provide examples of solidarity against the forces of facile division through their fight against Thatcher and the reaction to Hillsborough (though events since demonstrate the importance of actively protecting that solidarity).

The idea that football is just a circus designed to distract the masses can be dismissed by reference to reality. The areas of the greatest football fervour, the west of Scotland, the north-east, the north-west, have also been historically those of the greatest political and trade-union leftist militancy.

And we all need some of the hope and joy offered by the game just as a game, it's great to have clubs to follow without any sense of guilt about aligning with people who celebrate high unemployment in other working-class areas (there are 'sign on' chants directed at

Liverpool fans even now). Jack Duffin, Belfast Republican and historian, reminded me that if it hadn't have been for the illustrious history of Belfast Celtic from the late 19th century until the club was shut down by sectarian order in 1948, 'the history of the nationalist people in the north of Ireland would have been just a succession of woe'.

Football can be a joy in itself and one of the great consolations and distractions, it's even greater when enjoyed with good people and shared values. Watching football and feeling part of a unified collective is a great experience; with many clubs it's vitiated by the racism and the violence; at St Pauli, Rayo Vallecano, Cadiz *et al* you just get the shared lefty experience and a good laugh.

The Great Void: Lessons for the Left

We opened with this from Eduardo Galeano:

'An astonishing void: official history ignores soccer. Contemporary history texts fail to mention it, even in passing, in countries where soccer has been and continues to be a primordial symbol of collective identity. I play therefore I am: a style of play is a way of being that reveals the unique profile of each community and affirms its right to be different. Tell me how you play and I'll tell you who you are.'

Why the astonishing void? Galeano answers the question with the quote above. The people who write the histories whether they be from the left or the right, tend to share a degree of contempt for the working class and their game: football and its followers are seen as at best tangential to the affairs of state and the intellectual struggles of middle-class people who went to good universities, a waste of paper writing about them and the circus that keeps them distracted and at each other's throats.

This contempt for the working class was reflected by the comments of the spokesperson for Performance Approaches mentioned above: 'You expect to see people with lower incomes have more prejudiced views, but a third of the respondents who we would consider well-off held those views.'

Who would expect that? Who would expect the working class to be thick and racist? People like you, Ms Ferguson. Not everyone.

Certain sections of the left need to listen to working people rather than dismissing them as ignorant racists. The left in general could do a lot worse than look to improving football as a way of reconnecting with the people for whom it's supposedly fighting. In the UK, official 2021 BFI statistics revealed a record £5.64bn was spent on film and high-end TV production; the current Premier League TV deal is worth £5.1bn, almost the same amount. This is an incredibly rich sport so the British left should be asking questions like the following and offering solutions:

- With so much money in the game, why is it so expensive to watch? Introduce a cap on ticket prices and build more standing areas, that's how many of us like to watch the game and generate atmosphere, it's not the opera.

- Why are clubs allowed to have five or more different shirts on sale in a single season? Why are the shirts so hideously overpriced? This is exploiting developing-country labour as well as domestic consumers, merchandise should be sourced ethically and no more than two shirts allowed per season – home and away – with a cap on prices.

- Why do the same clubs dominate year in and year out? Why is money allowed to buy success? Introduce local ownership rules with fan representation in the running of clubs. Return to the system that applied for much of the game's history in which the away clubs were rewarded one third of the gate receipts. This would mean smaller clubs playing at places like Manchester United would not fall so far behind the big clubs financially and the game could be more competitive.

- Why are train and plane companies allowed to gouge prices on routes related to big games? At the time of writing a friend is trying to arrange a trip to Lyon for a West Ham UEFA Cup game: a £60 plane fare became £900 once the tie was announced. This is naked exploitation of fans' love for their clubs and should be prohibited.

As well as engaging with the mechanisms of exploitation of the working class by business football, the left should try to learn from some of the successes of the clubs we have covered above in how they project themselves.

In the late 1980s, St Pauli were a small incipient team in the middle of the German second division, watched mostly by the local lefties but gaining an international reputation for being the cool, anti-racist side to follow. Today St Pauli is a huge global leftist brand with supporters' clubs all over the planet. Irrespective of your views on the commercialisation of the St Pauli brand, its growth and that of the international network has been spectacular. SV Hamburger are historically a much bigger and more successful club than St Pauli but their international following is very limited.

Why so successful? St Pauli, and many of the other clubs we have covered, project a strong and positive image. They stand powerfully for inclusivity and equality and are wholeheartedly against fascism, racism, greed and the impact of rule by an oligarchy based on that greed. And they stand determinedly against business football, a particular hatred of the *Bukaneros* of Rayo Vallecano.

You feel good about being associated with the clubs themselves and the international networks they generate; you belong to something unequivocally worthwhile and positive and feel 'cool' in yourself about the statement your support is making.

The imagery and branding are vibrant, 'sexy' and reinforce the positivity. The St Pauli Jolly Roger conveys energy and rebellion without being menacing. The Rayo Vallecano shirt is a design classic; the rainbow away shirt of the 2015/16 season was a thing of beauty.

And the whole thing is 'fun'. Watching football and feeling part of a unified collective is a great experience. With many clubs it's ruined by the racism and the violence but not at the vast majority of the clubs we visited for this project.

The experience affords a real sense of unity and togetherness in expressing support for a range of unequivocally decent principles. This contrasts with the left's fissiparous tendencies and arguments about what Trotsky did or didn't say to Stalin in 1919. Focus on issues that people see as important and use language, imagery and behaviour that resonate and convey an inclusive energy, these are among the lessons we can and should learn.

We can't look to the game for detailed analysis of political and economic issues nor for blueprints of a future fairer society. But football at its best can connect, resonate and inspire in a way that no detailed analysis of political economy ever can, irrespective of its cogency. We end by referring you back to the two timeless quotes from the legendary Bill Shankly mentioned in the Liverpool chapter. Shankly was definitely football at its best and continues to inspire Reds from Liverpool like Jeff Goulding and political Reds like us everywhere. One is specifically about football and socialism and a definitive statement of the morality that drives the latter; the one about the bin men is an expression of universal decency, sound priorities, respect for labour and pride in the working class, principles that have always ignited the best politics.

FINAL WHISTLE.

Extra Time

– STEWART McGILL –

The No Mean City derby: United Glasgow v Napoli United

Given my love of football, the city of Napoli and people that give a damn about refugees and other vulnerable people, I was always going to like Napoli United. When I discovered they were managed by the son of Diego Maradona, the man who gave Scottish and Irish football one of their best-ever nights, Argentina 2-1 England in Mexico 1986, the sale was complete.

Before going to Cosenza in Calabria I stopped off in Napoli to meet one of the founders, Pietro. The club was formed as Afro-Napoli United in 2009 by local Neapolitans and two Senegalese immigrants. Its goal is to achieve and promote social inclusion through sport, focusing in particular on the involvement of migrants, asylum seekers and young people at risk of exclusion, residing in the Metropolitan area of Napoli. The team is now known as Napoli United and plays in the fifth tier of Italian football, *L'Eccellenza*.

My friend Sara Spiga in Napoli very kindly contacted the club and fixed up a meeting with Pietro in the north of the city. Pietro's a big, friendly guy; a proper leftist who proudly declared that, irrespective of any success, the club would never lose the principles that sparked their birth in 2009 as long as he and the other founders were involved.

Napoli is a rough-and-ready but very warm city. I've often thought of it as like Glasgow with better weather. I'd been in Napoli for a couple of days before I met Pietro and it had rained incessantly, maybe this put me even more in mind of Glasgow and I mentioned Napoli United's equivalents, United Glasgow.

United Glasgow were founded in 2011 with similar principles and aspirations to those of Napoli United. Since then the club has welcomed players from over 50 countries and makes football accessible and affordable to almost 200 players. The players represent all genders, sexual orientations, religions, ethnicities, socio-economic positions and immigration statuses.

I suggested that a game against the Uniteds of Glasgow and Napoli could be a good idea. Pietro immediately liked the idea and declared, 'If that happened I would cry.' I advised him not to cry in Glasgow. Things are changing for the better but the Mediterranean culture remains more open to displays of emotion from men. I promised to try to make this game happen.

I contacted United Glasgow on my return to Italy and their chief executive, Julie Mulcahy, called me back quickly, liked the idea and set the ball rolling. After a few rounds of discussion, with the linguistic and cultural differences being skilfully managed by Sara in Napoli, we arranged to go see Napoli United play on the island of Ischia in the middle of February, and to talk about the proposed game.

Ischia is a small island 19 miles away from Napoli in the Tyrrhenian Sea. Its population is about 20,000 but it has three football clubs – as the cab driver informed us, just saying 'the football stadium' isn't enough.

Football in the south of Italy is huge and the passion and quality run deep. Both the latter strengths were nicely demonstrated during Napoli's game against AS Barano Calico, a very tight 1-0 victory for Napoli United with passages of really fluent football punctuated with fouls and lengthy discussions about the fouls. The game's ending was genuinely tense with a controversial expulsion of a Barano player and culminated in a bit of a punch-up on the pitch at the final whistle.

I felt like breaking into a chant of 'Hello, Hello, Napoli Aggro' but wasn't sure about how it would translate, as well as being slightly unbecoming for an aspiring author who is well past middle-age.

Football doesn't always bring out the best in people but it does provide a unique international language and catalyst for the establishment of relationships. We left Napoli and Ischia good friends with Pietro, a true comrade. In the hands of people like Pietro and Julie, football can also be a force for good, bringing people together through emphasising that we are all connected, a much-needed counterforce to those that pursue their own agendas by forcing division on peoples that can and should get along.

Pietro and Julie agreed to the game going ahead and are in the process of sorting out details and funding; the UNHCR have expressed an interest in supporting the project. Our No Mean City derby is provisionally planned for late 2022 in Napoli, with the prospect of a return match in Glasgow in 2023. Hearing about the joyous reaction of the United Glasgow players to the game was very rewarding: good to know that *The Roaring Red Front* afforded something more than an excuse for a couple of old lefties to travel the globe drinking and watching football with a bunch of like-minded people, all of whom were very ready to embrace and welcome the stranger.

With special thanks to the following, without whom this book would not have been possible:

Sonny in Hamburg and everyone who spoke to us in St Pauli, especially Sven Brux and Oke Göttlich.

Samuel, Rocío and Jose in Cádiz

Frankie Taylor in Madrid

Sara Spiga in Napoli

Silverio Tucci and Roberto in Cosenza

Julien Hannotte Morais in Liège

Jeff Goulding in Liverpool

Carlos Ronaldo and Daniel Jadue in Santiago

Marcelo Antonio Guerrero, *siempre muy Boca* in Buenos Aires

Josh Donaldson in Prague

Matt Smyth in Detroit

Danny Mills, Tom, Scolly and David at Dulwich

Dan Quille

Paul Ducassou and David Bellion in Saint-Ouen

Toby Kinder

Nelson Barros Neto in Salvador

David Sztuwe

Mike Pieri

Sebastián Fischer

Lisa Martinez

Tony Collins for the foreword and the inspiration.

A very special thanks to Nick Soldinger, who helped turn our sexagenarian scribbling into something readable.

Big thanks to the following, who helped with the travelling:

Jonathan Barker; Owen Trumpeter; Nick Matthews; Paul Thomas; Rod Laird; Christopher Hicks; Valerio Bini; Christina Phillippou; Leslie Crang; Dieter Van Gucht; Charlotte Patterson; Kevin Gosling; Chloe Raison; Eric McNeil; Joe Condon; Tarun Patel; Danny Innes; Colm Ryder; Kristoffer Stien; Rhianna McGill; Danny Daly.

And, of course, our families, who had to put up with all the travelling and the moaning.

Further Reading

Kennedy, David. *Fan Culture in European Football and the Influence of Left Wing Ideology* (Routledge, 2013).

Kennedy, David. *A Contextual Analysis of Europe's Ultra Football Supporters Movement* (Routledge 2014).

Traverso, Enzo. *The Origins of Nazi Violence* (The New Press, 2003).

Mosse, George. *The Crisis of German Ideology* (Grosset & Dunlap, 1964).

Tamsut, Felix. *In Germany, Politics and Football are Inseparable* (tortoisemedia.com, September 2021).

Clubs Index